WICCAN
SPELL
A DAY

OTHER BOOKS BY SIRONA KNIGHT

The Wiccan Spell Kit
The Witch and Wizard Training Guide
The Wiccan Web (with Patricia Telesco)
Love, Sex, and Magic
Celtic Traditions

WICCAN SPELL A DAY

365 Spells, Charms, and Potions for the Whole Year

SIRONA KNIGHT

CITADEL PRESS
Kensington Publishing Corp.
www.kensingtonbooks.com

CITADEL PRESS BOOKS are published by

Kensington Publishing Corp.
850 Third Avenue
New York, NY 10022

All Kensington titles, imprints, and distributed lines are available at special quantity discounts for bulk purchases for sales promotions, premiums, fund-raising, educational, or institutional use. Special book excerpts or customized printings can also be created to fit specific needs. For details, write or phone the office of the Kensington special sales manager: Kensington Publishing Corp., 850 Third Avenue, New York, NY 10022, attn: Special Sales Department, phone 1-800-221-2647.

CITADEL PRESS and the Citadel logo are Reg. U.S. Pat. & TM Off.

First printing: August 2003

10 9 8 7 6 5 4 3 2 1

Printed in the United States of America

Library of Congress Control Number: 2003101256

ISBN 0-8065-2385-9

This book is dedicated to Michael and Skylor
for their love, laughter, and wisdom
(and for their patience)

Contents

$\mathcal{A}$CKNOWLEDGMENTS

I WOULD LIKE TO gratefully acknowledge Bruce Bender and Margaret Wolf at Citadel Press. Thanks also to Colette Russen for her expert help with the manuscript. And many heartfelt thanks to all those people who have encouraged me through the years. May the Lady and Lord bless, guide, and protect us all.

Blessed Be!

PREFACE

EACH PAGE OF THIS MAGICAL resource book provides hands-on instructions guaranteed to have you casting spells, making charms and potions, and meditating each and every day of the year. January, February, and March are filled with love spells, charms, potions, and meditations. April, May, and June focus on your health; and July, August, and September emphasize prosperity. October, November, and December offer a bevy of magic spells, potions, charms, and meditations for personal empowerment.

With strong intention and clear expectation, you can create anything you want in a very real and practical sense. A familiar saying is, "When you fail to plan, you plan to fail." In magical terms, it is your intention and expectation, your desire as well as the depth of your merging with the divine that give you focus, direction, and the power to manifest your magical goals. They are the steps for conceiving, creating, and experiencing magic every day of the year.

First you need to figure out what you want. Second, you need to formulate a plan on how to get it; and third, you need to take the actions to make it happen. This is what magic is all about. It is the merging of divine and mind in order to influence reality.

The deeper you merge when doing magic, the more powerful the results. Merging is the process of connecting to the divine no matter what your perception of it is. It is a natural feeling that you feel when you are in love, walking on the beach at sunset, or sitting next to an ancient redwood tree. Merging is the feeling you get when you are in tune and one with it all. The deepest merge you can make is with Oneness.

Oneness is everyone and everything, whatsoever it may be, whether animate or inanimate. By merging with Oneness when making magic, you reach into the source, commune with the divine, shape and gather power for attaining your magical goals.

Merging may produce sensations of relaxation, peacefulness, well-being, complete calm, spinning, dizziness, flying, whirling, or heaviness. You may feel like you are floating as you feel yourself being both everything and nothing, all at the same time.

You can enhance your merging experience by using rhythmic breathing, gazing at candlelight, dancing, and chanting, as well as listening to music, drumming, meditation, and visualization techniques. When you merge you become one with everything, diffusing like a cloud into the whole of Oneness.

When making magic, you need to integrate the ideal with the practical. This means putting your expectations into real time, and seeing how they play out—for better or worse. Try your magical goals on in your mind's eye before manifesting them. It's important to know that what you want will work for you before you go out and make it happen; otherwise you might find yourself in a situation that is far from your liking. But on the other hand, if you exercise a little focused thought, care, and wisdom, you can realize all of your dreams and truly enrich your life.

Your Magic Altar

Your altar is your magic table. The word *altar* means "high place," referring to its role as a connecting point between you and the divine. Symbolically the altar is the Goddess's sacred table, a place that is an outward expression of your personal relationship with the divine.

On a practical level, the altar serves as a sacred working surface that holds your ritual tools, focals, and other magical ingredients. As such, you can use your altar for meditation, spellcrafting, and prayer. When you approach your altar, complete with candles and incense, you are immediately filled with a feeling of magic that happens most powerfully when your spirit touches the divine.

To protect your altar surface, use an altar cloth. Traditionally the altar cloth is red or green. You can buy a new altar cloth or use a piece of fabric that you have a connection with, such as an old lace dresser scarf your grandmother gave you. You can change your altar with the changing seasons and holidays. In the spring, put fresh flowers, like daffodils and tulips, on the altar; in the summer, adorn it with roses. At Yule, decorate the surface of your altar with mistletoe, evergreen boughs, and pinecones. Each thing you add to your altar accentuates your magical experience.

You need to decide whether to have a permanent altar that is set up all the time or a temporary one set up for each occasion. If you leave it up, then situate it in a quiet spot where it won't get knocked over. If you want to put your altar away when you are not using it, then you should wrap the altar tools with the altar cloth and then place them all in a special place, such as a wooden box, for safekeeping.

If you want to make your altar less conspicuous, then set it up on a shelf in your bedroom. With opportunity and desire, you can convert your entire home and property into a large altar. At the time when you become adept at magic, you will find that every thought, every act, every living being, every object—everything becomes sacred, and life becomes your altar.

You will need to collect a few ritual tools for making magic. They are a wand, an athame, a bowl, a chalice, an incense burner, a candleholder, a robe or tunic, an object that represents the Goddess that is placed on the lefthand side of the altar, and an object that represents the God that is placed on the righthand side of the altar.

The Magic Circle

Before making magic, it's important to follow some basic steps. These are: drawing a magic circle, calling in the elements, and inviting deity into your circle.

Constructed in the shape of an egg yolk, the magic circle is symbolic of the feminine Goddess and the eternal nature of the universe. It represents the ever-beginning, never-ending cycle of birth, life, death, and rebirth.

In a practical sense, the circle is a protected sacred space that you create for doing magic in. As with any sacred space, it is a positive place where you bring in divine energy to help you attain your magical goals and build your personal patterns. It is also a place that is systematically cleansed of any unwanted, negative energy.

Once you have set up your altar with all of its tools, it is time to scribe the circle. You will need a compass, athame, wand, and bell (optional). Use the compass to find north. This is also often the directional point where your altar stands.

Begin by clearing the area of unwanted energies. Do this by facing the north. Slowly spin around in a clockwise circle with your arms stretched outward. While slowly spinning, imagine a clear cobalt-blue light washing out the area. As you spin, say:

May all evil and foulness be gone from this place.
I ask this in the Lady and Lord's name.
Be gone all evil and foulness,
Be gone, now and forevermore!

Next, ring the bell three times in front of the altar at the north in order to invite divine energy into your sacred space. Then follow these eight steps to draw a magic circle.

1. Hold your athame or wand in your power hand. Your power hand is your right hand if you are right-handed, and your left if you are left-handed. Point the tip of your athame or wand toward the north point of the space.

2. Take a few deep and complete breaths to center yourself, and then merge with the divine for a minute or two.

3. Visualize a stream of blue-white light pouring out of the tip of your athame or wand toward the north point.

4. After building a sufficient amount of light and energy, with your athame pointing outward, begin to spin slowly to the east point, visualizing the blue-white light flowing from the tip of your athame or wand into the north point and along the parameter of the circle into the east point, filling it full of light.

5. Imagine the light flowing from the east point into the south point and filling it with blue-white light.

6. Once the south point is full of light, imagine the light moving along the circle into the west point, again filling it with blue-white light.

7. Use your athame or wand to move the stream of light back along the parameter of the circle into the north point. This completes the body of your protective circle.

8. Face the altar, holding the athame with its tip upright. In your mind's eye, visualize the vibrant, light-filled circle all around you, including above and below you, and say:

> *The circle is bound*
> *With power all around*
> *In all worlds I stand*
> *Protected in all lands.*

Calling in the Elements

It is easy to call in the elemental powers to your circle. The reason for doing this is to set up a guardian at each of the elemental gates to protect your circle from unwanted energies and influences while you are doing magic. A different elemental guardian guards each of the directional gates of north, east, south, and west. They remain there until you release them. Follow these five steps to call in the elements.

1. Face north in the direction of your altar, and stretch both arms up toward the sky. Imagine that you are deep in the woods in a magical forest. Merge with the earth element and say:

> *Guardians of the north,*
> *Generous and divine powers of earth,*
> *Protect the gate of the north ward,*
> *And guard this circle and all within.*
> *Come, I welcome you!*

2. Turn and face eastward, and stretch your arms toward the sky. Imagine that you are on a beautiful hillside with a strong but refreshing wind blowing over your face and through your hair. Merge with the air element and say:

> *Guardians of the east,*
> *Generous and divine powers of air,*
> *Protect the gate of the east ward,*
> *And guard this circle and all within.*
> *Come, I welcome you!*

3. Face south and stretch your arms toward the sky. Imagine yourself lying in the sun, soaking in its radiant warmth. Merge with the fire element and say:

> *Guardians of the south,*
> *Generous and divine powers of fire,*
> *Protect the gate of the south ward,*
> *And guard this circle and all within.*
> *Come, I welcome you!*

4. Face west and stretch your arms upward. Imagine that you are sitting next to a pristine mountain lake, or if you prefer, by the ocean. Merging with the powers of water, say:

> *Guardians of the west,*
> *Generous and divine powers of water,*
> *Protect the gate of the west ward,*
> *And guard this circle and all within.*
> *Come, I welcome you!*

5. Stand in the center of your magic circle and, facing your altar, say:

Guardian spirits of earth, air, fire, and water
Grant me your power and protection tonight
Come, I welcome you!

Once you have called in the elements to stand guard at the four gates, it is time to cast your magic spells, make magic charms and potions, and meditate.

Cutting the Little Gate

If you need to leave the circle while you are making magic, simply cut an energy doorway (called the little gate) with your athame or power hand. Cut the doorway by moving your athame upward, over toward the right, and then downward to the bottom right corner. Then exit, making sure you seal the doorway with your athame. Reverse the process to get back in the circle. When possible, cut the little gate at the physical door, so you can easily come and go.

Bidding Farewell to the Elements

When you are finished making magic, bid farewell to the elements. Follow these five easy steps.

1. Begin at the north point: Merge with the powers of earth, and say:

Generous and divine powers of earth,
Please depart in peace and harmony
Many thanks for your magical presence.

2. Face east and say:

> *Generous and divine powers of air,*
> *Please depart in peace and harmony*
> *Many thanks for your magical presence.*

3. Face south and say:

> *Generous and divine powers of fire,*
> *Please depart in peace and harmony*
> *Many thanks for your magical presence.*

4. Face west and say:

> *Generous and divine powers of water,*
> *Please depart in peace and harmony*
> *Many thanks for your magical presence.*

5. Now face your altar and say:

> *Dear Goddess and God*
> *Helpful spirits and energies*
> *Many thanks for your divine presence*
> *Blessed be! Blessed be! Blessed be!*

Closing the Circle

Once you draw a magic circle, you do not usually leave it until you release it. After you bid farewell to the elements, follow these four steps to close the circle.

1. Face north with your athame or wand in your power hand, pointed toward the north point of your magic circle.

2. Slowly turn counterclockwise, and as you turn, imagine the blue-white light of the circle being sucked into the tip of your athame or wand.

3. With your athame or wand, make a cut in the energy across the boundary of where the circle has been and say:

> *The circle is now open, but unbroken.*
> *Merry meet, merry part,*
> *And merry meet again.*
> *Blessed be!*

4. Ring the bell three times in honor of the triple goddess. Your magic making is complete.

WICCAN
SPELL
A DAY

$\mathcal{J}$ANUARY

January 1 NEW YEAR'S LOVE WISH

For this spell, you will need a white candle, a bowl of cool salt water, a ball-point pen, and a candleholder.

First, turn on some soft music. Wash the candle in cool salt water and then dry it off, just as you do with all candles when using them for magic. This clears any unwanted energies from the candle. Next draw a circle of light, and call in the elements and divine powers. Use the pen to scribe your most cherished love wish for the new year on the candle. Put the candle in its holder. As you light it, say your wish out loud three times. Then say:

> *My love wish is coming true this year.*
> *So be it! So shall it be!*

As the candle burns down, meditate on the flame, all the while imagining your love wish coming true in the next year. As you meditate, imagine—see, feel, hear, taste, and smell—your love wish as if it has already come true. Be in that future "wish come true" space for a few minutes, and experience the wonderful sensations of love, pleasure, and joy. When you are done, bid farewell to the elements, thank deity, and close the circle.

January 2   JANUARY LOVE BATH

The love bath, which is used to cleanse yourself of any unwanted energies, will help you relax and get into a loving mood. It is perfect just before a night of romance with your beloved. You will need a warm bath, lavender essential oil, and a white tealight.

Fill up your bathtub (don't make the water too hot, as that will just tire you out). Put three drops of the lavender essential oil in the water. Dim the lights and turn on some favorite music. Light the candle, dedicating it to a favorite love goddess or god. Place the candle close to the tub where you can easily see the flame while you are bathing.

Immerse yourself in the bath water. As you do this, imagine any stress, tension, worry, anger, pain, or other unwanted energy flowing out of you and into the water. Then take three deep and complete breaths. As you exhale after each deep breath, feel yourself letting go and relaxing even more. Breathe in the scent of lavender as you enjoy the warm, soothing water. Look into the candle flame and visualize a night of delightful lovemaking. Say three times:

> *I am a loving and passionate person.*
> *I am worthy of giving and receiving love.*

Let your mind drift into pleasurable thoughts for at least five minutes. Then get out of the tub and drain it. As you slowly towel off, repeat the affirmation three times:

> *I am a loving and passionate person.*
> *I am worthy of giving and receiving love.*

January 3   JANUARY CANDLE LOVE MAGIC

You will need a red candle, a white candle, two candleholders, a ballpoint pen, vanilla scented oil, and a piece of rose quartz.

Turn on some soft, romantic music, draw a magic circle, and call in your favorite love goddess or god. With the ballpoint pen, write the name of the deity and your initials on the red candle. Then draw a heart around what you've written. Write the deity's name and your initials on the white candle, but encircle them with a sun symbol instead of a heart symbol. This symbolizes the linking of earthly and divine love. Next, cover both candles with a thin coating of the vanilla oil, and place them in their holders. Wipe the oil off your hands. Put the piece of rose quartz between the candles. Light the red candle. As you do, imagine its light as being a divine love that ignites the fiery passion in your very soul. Now light the white candle, and see this divine love igniting your love life even more.

Hold the rose quartz in your power hand (your right hand if you are right-handed and vice versa). Feel it warm up from the heat of your hand. Gaze deeply into the flames and say:

> *Flaming fires of divine love,*
> *Brighten my love life every day,*
> *Help me experience love and joy*
> *In many splendorous and romantic ways.*

Hold the stone in your hand while you gaze into the flames. Imagine the romantic and splendorous ways you can experience more love every day of the year. Thank deity and close the circle. Carry the rose quartz with you in your pocket or purse to encourage more love in your daily life.

January 4   LOVE MAGNET

This spell is meant to draw more love into your home.

You will need a sage smudge stick, a gold-colored coin, a red doormat, and a small magnet.

Smudge the coin, the doormat, and the magnet to clear them of any unwanted energies. Next put the doormat in front of the main entrance of your home, and hold the coin and magnet in your power hand. Merge with the power of the Goddess and say:

> *North, east, south, and west,*
> *By the Goddess, I am divinely blessed,*
> *Draw love into this home eternally,*
> *As I will, so shall it be!*

Put the coin and magnet under the doormat, and leave them there to attract love. Then recharge the coin and magnet every month or so to keep bringing love into your home.

January 5   LOVING TREE CHARM

This charm will help you connect to your natural surroundings so that you can experience and know and their divine beauty. When you link to nature, you connect with the natural cycles of life.

You will need a living tree and a chalice of water.

Go outdoors, and when you draw your magic circle, be sure to include the tree in it. Walk clockwise around the circle and sprinkle it with drops of water from the chalice. Stand next to the tree, and repeat the following blessing:

O great and mighty tree,
Bless me with your love,
Young and old, strong and free,
Reaching up for the light above,
Blessed be, so shall it be!

Next, pour any water left in the chalice on the base of the tree. Put the chalice down, and lean your body against the tree with both your palms touching the bark. Imagine the loving wisdom of the tree flowing into your palms and body. Close your eyes and breathe in the love of the tree for a few minutes. When you are done, thank the tree and close the circle.

January 6   MAGNIFYING YOUR LOVE

You will need a giant imaginary magnifying glass because today is Sherlock Holmes's birthday. What this giant magnifying glass does is help you be more aware of and focus on all the love that is happening around you. Imagine yourself as Sherlock Holmes, the great detective. See yourself becoming more aware of the details around you. Take this imaginary magnifying glass and look at all the people who love you and all the people you love. Use the glass to focus on people's subtle actions and to differentiate between what is and isn't loving to you. Examine the love relationships that you have in your life for what they are and not what you want them to be. Be a great detective like Sherlock Holmes and cut to the chase as to what's really happening in your love life and your relationships. Finally, use the magnifying glass to discover and focus on what works and what makes you feel more loved and loving.

January 7   CORIANDER SEED CHARM

According to traditional folklore, coriander contains the properties of love, sexuality, passion, healing, and longevity. Use this charm to bring more of these qualities into your life.

You will need sixty-nine coriander seeds and a red sock.

Pick up each seed and place it in the red sock. As you do this, visualize your life becoming filled with love and passion. After all the seeds are in the sock, tie up the open end of the sock so the seeds don't spill out. Hold the sock between the palms of your hands and say:

> *Demeter, Goddess of the fertile Earth,*
> *Come bless these seeds of love,*
> *So that they might grow bountiful,*
> *Reaching out to the sky above.*

After charging the seed sock with divine power, put it under your bed. You may occasionally want to take the charm out and recharge its love energy by repeating the spell as well as visualizing more love, sexuality, passion, healing, and longevity coming into your life.

January 8   BUBBLE LOVE BATH

Use the Bubble Love Bath to invigorate your spirit while soothing your body with feelings of love. Lavender is comforting and healing, while the rose has been associated with love and joy.

You will need a quarter-cup of lavender, a quarter-cup of rose petals, and bubble bath, preferably something natural and nontoxic.

Start by simmering the lavender and the rose petals in a quart of water for about fifteen minutes. Fill your tub with warm water and add the bubble bath; then add the lavender and rose water, straining the herbs out as you do. As you pour the lavender and rose water into the tub, say:

Into my bubble bath water flows
The loving power of lavender and rose.

Step into the bath and immerse yourself in the bubbles and water. Feel the comforting, loving, and joyous qualities of the lavender and rose as they combine with the bubbles. Imagine yourself being soothed and healed by feelings of love and joy.

Visualize yourself floating to a secret place in your mind's eye where everything is wondrous and fantastic. Just soak in the joy of it all for a few minutes before getting out of the tub and toweling off.

January 9   PINK LOVE CHARM

For this charm, you will need a sheet of pink paper, a pink felt-tip pen, a pinch of jasmine flowers, and a pink candle.

Draw a magic circle and call in the elements. Light the candle and dedicate it to a favorite love goddess such as Venus. On the sheet of paper, write down the positive attributes you want in your love partner, for example, "creative, a well-developed sense of humor, good-looking, intelligent, likes children, caring, respects nature, spiritual, fabulous lover!" (If you don't currently have a lover, write the qualities you would like that person to possess, whoever he or she might be.) Fold the sheet of paper in half, and then fold it in half again. Put the pinch of jasmine flowers into the paper pocket you have created. Fold the pocket in half again, and seal the charm with candle wax. Be careful not to drip wax on your skin, furniture, or the rug. Use newspaper, cardboard, or a dish to catch any dripping wax. When you are done sealing the charm, let it cool off. Then hold it in your power hand, gaze into the candle flame, and say three times:

> *I empower this love charm with passionate fire.*
> *With the abundant and creative joy of love.*

Place the charm under or near your bed, leaving it there for three months to encourage those positive attributes you wrote down about your beloved.

January 10   I WILL LOVE THEE CANDLE MAGIC

For this spell you'll need a red candle, a dish of salt water, a ballpoint pen, a candleholder, and rose-scented oil.

First, wash the candle in the salt water and dry it. Then, with the pen, write the words "I love thee" and your lover's or intended lover's initials on the candle. Inscribe your initials on top of those of your lover's. Then rub the candle with the rose oil. When you are finished, set the candle in its holder. Anoint yourself with the oil, using a drop on the insides of both wrists and one on your third eye. Then wipe the oil off of your hands. Light the candle, dedicating it to your favorite love goddess. Merge with the flame, with the fire element, and say:

> *By the loving heart of the Mother Goddess*
> *By spirit, earth, air, fire, and sea*
> *Please bring my beloved to me*

I will love thee to the depths of my soul
I will love thee by sun, moon, star, and candle light
I will love thee freely, I will love thee completely,
I will love thee with passion and compassion
I will love thee with the breath and smiles of all my life
By the loving heart of the Mother Goddess
By spirit, earth, air, fire, and sea
Please bring my mate to me,
Great Lady, I pray, so shall it be!

As you gaze at the candlelight, in your mind's eye imagine your beloved (or intended beloved) and all of the love, adventure, romance, passion, and joy you will share. Do this for at least fifteen minutes. Just let your imagination run free and have fun! Allow the candle to burn down on its own.

January 11   CARMENTALIA

Carmenta is a Roman goddess of prophecy, and is the protectress of women in childbirth. Her festival, Carmentalia, was held on January 11 and January 15, which is nine months after April, the most popular month for Roman marriages. During Carmentalia, no animal skins were allowed to be worn or used because the slaughter of animals is contrary to the birth concept.

For this spell, you will need a white candle, a piece of paper, and a pen.

Start by taking the pen and paper and writing out a short prayer of anywhere between one to four lines, asking for the blessings and protection of the goddess Carmenta. It doesn't have to be elaborate. For example,

"Goddess Carmenta, please give your blessings and protection to all women during childbirth. Thank you, blessed lady, for the protection of all the children of the world."

After you have written out your prayer, light the white candle, and speak your prayer to the Goddess. Let the candle burn all the way down. Put the prayer in a place where you will see it every day, reciting it to yourself and reaffirming the prayer and Carmenta's protection and blessing.

January 12   TURNING SPELL

Use this spell to change something bad into something good, such as making up after a fight or disagreement with someone you love.

For this spell, you'll need a white candle, a brown candle, and a black candle (all in candleholders), a plate or platter, a ballpoint pen, aluminum foil, and sea salt.

On the black candle, write "fight with [name of the person you had a fight with]." Then write the word "shift" on the brown candle. Write the name of the person you had the fight with on the white candle, and then write your initials next to the name. Inscribe a circle around the name and initials to unite them.

Cover the plate with aluminum foil; then put the candles in a row on the plate—left to right, black, brown, and white. (Leave enough room between them so they don't melt each other when you light them.) Next, working clockwise, pour a thick line of sea salt on the plate all the way around the candles. As you light the candles in order from left to right, say:

Black, brown, and white candle flame,
Into my life bring positive change,
Let a misunderstanding become understood,
So that what became bad can once again be good.

Look into the candlelight and imagine the energy shifting from negative to positive. Do this for several minutes.

After the candles burn down, throw the candle remains, foil, and salt away. Be sure to clean the plate and candleholders before using them again.

January 13   JANUARY LOVE AFFIRMATION

Love unfolds like the petals of a rose, transforming into a beauty that is boundless. Rose quartz can be used to remind you of that beauty.

For this spell, you will need a piece of rose quartz. While doing the following affirmation, hold the quartz in your receptive hand (your left hand if you are right-handed and vice versa).

Draw the natural qualities of love and beauty from the rose quartz into your body. Use deep rhythmic breathing and visualization to do this. Breathe the color of rose into your being with your inhalation, and let go of any negativity you may feel with your exhalation. Do this at least three times. Then say:

Each morning when I awaken, I feel the loving grace of the Goddess fill
me with joy and wonder. Each evening when I dream, the loving Lady
brings me dreams of beauty and peace.

Now feel the loving beauty and grace of the Goddess streaming through the rose quartz in your receptive hand into your body, mind, and spirit. When everything moves in harmony, love is what inherently follows. For a few minutes, go ahead and imagine living your daily life in complete harmony, filled with love, beauty, and peace. Allow your imagination to roam from today to tomorrow to next week, next month, next year, five years from now, ten years from now, and so on, just imagining all the hours, days, weeks, months, and years of your life being filled with love, harmony, and beauty. Keep the rose quartz somewhere you can easily see it, and repeat the affirmation at least once a day to encourage more love, beauty, and harmony in your life.

January 14   THE LOVE APPLE

Use this technique to gain greater rapport with yourself, your beloved, and the divine.

You will need a ripe red apple, a knife, and a picture of you and the person you are going to do this spell with.

Begin by peeling the apple, and cut it carefully into four individual pieces. Cut the core out of the pieces, and gently pull out the little brown apple seeds. You and your partner then take the seeds and cup them in your hands, empowering them with thoughts of love. Take the seeds and place them in front of the picture.

Take two pieces of apple each. These symbolize divine love. Feed one piece to your partner, and have your partner in turn feed a piece of apple to you. Now feed your partner the second piece. Your partner in turn feeds the last piece of apple to you. Finish by thanking the God and Goddess, both for the love apple and their continued blessings for a loving and long-lasting relationship.

January 15 DREAMING REALITY SPELL

Each of us has a dream or calling that often propels us to do what we do in life, for example our relationships and career. Use this spell to connect yourself to your calling and to transform your dream into reality.

You will need a brown candle, a white candle, paper, and a pen.

On the piece of paper, write down what you would like to ideally happen in your own life, and what you want to happen in the world while you are alive. Who would you be if you could be anybody? What is your idea of the perfect world? How would you behave? How would others behave?

Put the two candles about three inches apart, and light them, one at a time, dedicating them to a favorite goddess such as Mother Mary. Look into the candle flames. The white candle flame represents your dreams and desires, and the brown candle flame represents the "real world," where dreams become reality. Now walk around the candles until, from your view, the two flames become one flame. For a few minutes, from that vantage point, imagine your dreams blending into reality as the flames blend into one. Keep the paper on your altar or desk and refer to it often to encourage your dreams to become reality.

January 16   LASTING LOVE DANCING

Take a night off to go dancing. Tonight is the perfect time for starting a long-term love relationship that can last a lifetime. You will need two people who are looking for one another, but don't know it yet. Then on a moonlit night, perhaps while dancing, walking the dog, or at the movies, they meet. Their meeting is not chance, but fate, and the love begins.

To find true love, go out dancing tonight, either by yourself or if you are in a relationship, with your partner. Whether single, married, matched, or mated, the idea in this love spell is to create or encourage long-lasting relationships that mature through time.

As you shower and dress for your night out dancing, think about having an extraordinary evening filled with music and love. Just before you leave, look into the mirror, and say to yourself:

> *Tonight, let the divine hand*
> *Hold me softly and reveal to me*
> *My beloved, my lover, my mate.*
> *May we love each other*
> *Forever and a day.*
> *So be it! Blessed be!*

January 17   FLYING FREE LOVE MAGIC

You will need a white feather and a silver chain.

Put the silver chain around either your left wrist or ankle. Then recline comfortably, holding the white feather in your left hand. Imagine yourself shapeshifting into a swan and flying freely through the afternoon sky. Feel your wings spreading in the wind as you fly. The ground below you flows by, and you see a beautiful blue-green lake in the near distance. The banks of the lake are covered with green grass, and the water is so clear you can see your swan reflection in it. As you fly over the lake, another swan joins you in flight. The swan's eyes are exactly the same as the eyes of your beloved. You and the other swan circle the beautiful lake clockwise three times. You can feel the tremendous freedom and joy from flying through the sky with your love. Continue imagining yourself flying in swan form in your mind's eye for about fifteen minutes. Keep seeing yourself flying with your beloved, enjoying the pleasure and freedom of your adventure. Use your imagination and try to see, feel, touch, taste, and smell your adventure in the sky as a swan. When you are done, put the chain and white feather on your altar, bookshelf, or bureau to remind you of the love and pure joy you experienced while flying free. Any time you would like to fly again, just put on the chain, hold the white feather in your left hand, and repeat the visualization.

January 18   TYING THE KNOT STRING MAGIC

You will need a pink candle in a holder, a pen, neroli-scented oil, sandalwood incense, a yard-long red string, and a favorite love song.

Draw a magic circle and call in your favorite deities. Light the incense, dedicating it to deity. Write both your initials and your beloved's initials on the body of the candle. Cover the candle with a thin coating of oil and then put it in the holder. Next, anoint yourself with the oil, applying drops of oil on your forehead, throat, wrists, and the insides of your ankles. Rub the length of the red string with the scented oil. Wipe your hands, and then light the candle, dedicating it to your beloved.

Put on a favorite love song, and sit back comfortably. Hold the ends of the string in both hands. Tie six knots in the string, spacing them evenly apart. As you tie each knot, say:

> *Joined together, we will be*
> *So be it! Blessed be!*

Tie the ends of the string together. As you do this, imagine you and beloved becoming joined or marrying soon. Allow the candle to burn down completely. Tuck the knotted string under your bed until you attain the desired results.

January 19 GREAT DATE LOVE CHARM

To some ancient cultures, such as the Egyptians, Sumerians, and Taoists, the date palm symbolized the tree of life. Additionally, early Hindus believed the tree had intelligence, and was one step away from being a human being. Perform this charm before going out on a date.

You will need a red candle and three dates.

Start by lighting the red candle and saying a prayer to Aphrodite, goddess of love:

> *I summon you, great Aphrodite,*
> *Bring your power of love unto me.*

Now take the three dates between your hands while visualizing how you want your great date to go. Once your have the image firmly in your mind, breathe in deeply, and then pulse your breath three times out your nose, putting the pattern in place. Then eat the dates, savoring their loving qualities. Snuff the candle before you leave on your date, thanking the Goddess for her blessings.

January 20 BABIN DEN—THANK YOU, GRANDMOTHER

In Bulgaria, the older women, who were akin to midwives, were called *baba*, or grandmother. The custom on Babin Den, (annually celebrated on this date) was to bring flowers to your grandmother because it was thought that her wisdom was bestowed on the children she blessed.

You will need a gray or silver candle, lavender-scented oil, and a picture or object that symbolizes your grandmother.

Draw a magic circle. Next, place the picture or symbol of your grandmother in a special place where you can easily see it, for example, your altar. Rub the candle with the oil, and put it in a holder in front of the symbol of your grandmother. Wipe your hands. Light the candle, and say:

> *Thank you, grandmother for your love;*
> *thank you, grandmother for your blessing.*

Chant the name of your favorite crone goddess, such as the Celtic Kerridwen, ending the chant with "Ayea, Ayea, Ayea," to call the crone into your magic circle. Then, in your own words, thank your grandmother for all she did for you, both in this lifetime and in the many other lifetimes that you may have shared. Send her your love and blessing. Allow the candle to burn down completely. When you are finished, close the circle.

January 21 LOVE SONG AFFIRMATION

You can use this charm to empower your life with the qualities of a love song.

For this spell, you'll need a white candle and a favorite love song.

Select a song that sums up how you feel about love. Granted, things do change, and you don't always feel the same way, so just pick a song that best conveys your feelings about love at the present moment. If it's a happy song, then visualize the happiness continuing on and on. If it's a sad song, then see the Goddess helping you let go of your past hurts and replacing them with feeling of love. Light the candle, dedicating it to a favorite goddess, then put on the love song. Say this affirmation:

> *Today, I listen carefully to the loving voice of the Great Goddess. I hear the divine gift of love and hope in her every word. Like a soothing melody, her loving voice calms and sustains me each and every day. As I listen to her, I feel my spirit being filled with love.*

January 22   COMPLIMENT DAY

For this spell, you will need a small quartz crystal. Crystals are mostly made up of water molecules, much like the human body. Water is very sensitive to energy, and as such, can be imprinted. First, hold your crystal in your power hand. Imagine a clear mountain stream. Once the image of the stream is crystal clear in your mind's eye, take a deep breath, and then pulse your breath sharply out your nose. Now, imagine a more loving world where everyone is kinder and more compassionate toward one another. Once the image is clear in your mind's eye, take another deep breath, and once again, pulse your breath sharply out your nose, imprinting the crystal with the image in your mind's eye.

Put the crystal in your pocket or purse, and go out to spread love and understanding today. One way to do this is to pay someone a compliment. Sincere compliments almost always make people happy. In turn, someone you give a compliment to may spread the good will to the next person she meets, starting a compliment chain reaction that could ultimately spread around the world. Remember, an acorn is initially quite small. But after a hundred years of growing, it becomes one enormous oak tree.

January 23   APPLE PIE LOVE WISH

Apple pie signifies a wholesomeness expressed in the saying "mom, apple pie, baseball, and the girl next door."

For this spell, you will need a recipe and all the ingredients for apple pie.

Begin to prepare the pie. As you mix the pie crust dough, focus on your love wish. Imagine putting the energy of your love wish into the dough through the power in your hands and mind. As you do this, say:

Love wish come true, as easy as I love you.

As you roll out the pie crust, focus on your love wish and imagine rolling it into the dough. As you do this, say:

Love wish come true, as easy as I love you.

As you press the bottom crust into the pie pan, say,

Love wish come true, as easy as I love you.

Prepare the apple filling, once again focusing your attention on your wish. Say again:

Love wish come true, as easy as I love you.

As you add the filling to the pie, say:

Love wish come true, as easy as I love you.

Put on the top crust, and say:

Love wish come true, as easy as I love you.

Put the pie in the oven, and say:

Love wish come true, as easy as I love you.

When the pie is done, take it out of the oven and let it cool down. Invite your beloved to share a slice of apple pie with you. As you slice the pie and eat it, think to yourself:

My love wish is coming true, right now.

Then say to your beloved:

I love you.

January 24 LADY OF THE RINGS

For this spell, you will need a ring, salt water, a white candle, and three fresh bay leaves.

Begin by washing the ring in cool salt water to rid it of any unwanted energies. Next, draw a magic circle and call in your favorite love goddess. Light the white candle, dedicating it to her.

Hold the ring in your power hand. Take the bay leaves in your other hand, and crush them with your fingers. Hold the leaves up to your nose and smell their aroma. Feel your psychic senses open up and expand. Now focus your attention on the ring.

Imagine the love energies you would like in it. For example, you might want it to attract more love into your life or help you find your soulmate. Keep imparting these images into the ring. Breathe in through your mouth and visualize these images and love qualities, and then breathe the images and qualities out into the ring, pulsing your exhalation out through your nose. Do this several times to lock the program into the ring. Then put the ring on your power hand, and say:

Lady of the rings, of earth, fire, air, and sea
Please bring joy, happiness, and love to me.

Now sit quietly, gazing at the candle for several minutes. To activate the love energy of the ring, say its name, "Lady of the Rings." Wear the ring to bring the qualities of love you desire into your life. When you are done, thank the Goddess and close the circle.

January 25   ROBERT BURNS PICNIC MAGIC

Robert Burns (1759–1796) is considered one of Scotland's greatest poets because of his descriptions of country life and his satires on the political and religious hypocrisy of the day. Later in life, he collected and wrote over 368 Scottish songs including the classic "Auld Lang Syne." In earlier versions, it was said to be more of a love song.

You will need a picnic lunch, a blanket, a favorite spot in nature, a favorite piece of poetry by Robert Burns, and a willing partner.

Head out to the country with your partner. Find a nice spot, and spread out your picnic. After feasting on the food, read the poetry to your partner. Read it slowly and savor each word as if it were meal in and of itself, bringing nourishment to the spirit.

If you can, stay until the sun sets, relaxing, talking, and holding each other. Share as much as you can, building a bond that reaches into the future, sometimes forever and a day.

January 26   ROMANTIC LOVERS CHARM

You will need a red candle, a red felt-tip pen, a sheet of white paper, and three dried rosebuds.

Begin by lighting the candle and dedicating it to the Goddess. Now use the red pen to draw a heart on the paper. Trace over it three times. Then, inside the heart, write your name, a plus sign, and your lover's name. As you do this, imagine yourself and your lover experiencing a deeper and more loving relationship than you have ever experienced before. Hold the rosebuds between your hands, and say:

> *I call upon the Ancient Powers,*
> *Join our hearts with these flowers,*
> *Bringing more romance with each new day,*
> *Making love deeper in every way.*

Sprinkle the rosebuds onto the paper over the heart. Wrap the paper around the heart and flowers, folding it nine times, and carefully sealing it with wax from the candle. Place the folded and sealed paper in your bureau drawer.

January 27   LOVE'S SONATA

Today is the birthday of Wolfgang Amadeus Mozart (1756–1791), one of the greatest composers of piano music that ever blessed this earth. A great piano sonata is like a relationship; when all the pieces fit together synchronistically, it is a thing of indescribable beauty.

For this spell, you will need a piece of sheet music for a Mozart piano piece if you play, or a recording of Mozart's piano music if you don't, and a picture of your loved one.

Begin by putting the picture of your loved one on the piano next to the sheet music if you're going to play the piece, or on a shelf or stand near your stereo if you're using a recording. Focus on the picture, and as you find yourself moving into it, imagine yourself diffusing like a cloud, becoming one with everything around you, including the picture of your loved one. As you reach this diffused state of mind, say:

> *Each note of this sonata, I dedicate to you*
> *An expression of my love, that I feel each day through.*

Afterward, play the piece while expressing and visualizing the love you feel for your beloved. Feel each note become an expression of your love. When the musical piece concludes, say as a finale:

> *So be it!*

January 28　　INCUBUS LOVE CHARM

The Greeks called the dream lover an incubus. The word *incubate* means "to sit on," and to maintain conditions favorable to optimum growth. The otherworldly Incubus is symbolic of the mysterious flow of universal awareness. You can use this charm to draw your dream lover to you.

For this spell, you will need a red rose, a red candle in a holder, rose oil, rose incense and a censer, a small red cloth bag or pouch, and a towel.

Begin by rubbing the rose oil on the candle, your wrists, ankles, throat, and forehead. Wipe the oil from your hands with the towel, and light the candle and incense.

Clear your mind, take a few deep breaths, and then take the rose and hold it gently between your hands. Smell its aroma, taking a few more deep breaths as you inhale the rose's scent. Now hold the rose in front of the candle-light, illuminating it, and say:

> *Scent of rose, fill the night,*
> *Dream lover, I do invite,*
> *Scent of rose, fill the day,*
> *Dream lover, come my way,*
> *So be it! Blessed be!*

Let the candle burn down completely. Afterward, remove the flower from its stem and place it inside the red cloth bag. Put the bag inside your pillow-case to draw your dream lover to you.

January 29 PAST-LIFE ROMANCE

Oftentimes those people we are in relationships with in this present lifetime are people with whom we've had prior connections. Energy runs in soul groups that extends over many lifetimes. Because of this, patterns in our life are continuous.

For this spell, you'll need a white tealight.

Light the candle and gaze into its flame. Sit comfortably in a chair and allow your mind to regress into the past, comparing your present relation-ships to past ones. Go over each past relationship slowly, and draw the posi-tive elements from them into the present moment. This can help you move beyond the past into the present moment, allowing more energy for adven-turing into the future. By seeing our past connections, we can better under-stand our present ones.

Tonight, when you go to sleep, give yourself the suggestion to go back to a past-life romance. Repeat silently to yourself, "I will dream of a past-life romance, and I will remember my dream when I wake up." When you wake up, write down what you recall of your dream. Repeat the suggestion to yourself every night, for twenty-one nights, until you have a dream of a past-life romance.

January 30   CRYSTAL CASTLE LOVE MAGIC

The crystal castle is a personal power center that you create with your mind and with which you will do magical works. It may resemble a place you have visited in your waking life, a place you have seen in a picture, or it can be a completely original castle, made of crystal and gemstones, that only exists in your mind.

For this spell, you will need a clear quartz crystal point, a bowl of cool salt water, a bowl of cool fresh water, a soft cloth, two white candles in candle-holders, and a drum.

Begin by washing your crystal point in cool salt water. Rinse it under cool clear water for a couple of minutes. Do this with the tip pointed down to wash out any negative energies. Dry the crystal and place it on a surface with the point towards you.

Place the candles on either side of the crystal point, about four inches apart. Light them slowly, dedicating each candle to a favorite love Goddess and God.

Begin to gaze at the crystal, breathing deeply and allowing your mind to center and focus. Now begin beating slowly on the drum. With each beat, you go farther into the crystal, and begin to see and sense a beautiful crystal castle within its center. As you quicken the pace of your drumming, imagine entering the beautiful and romantic bedroom of your crystal castle. There you can express your full potential as a loving partner. Visualize your lover in the castle bedroom with you, leading you by the hand to an extraordinary bed. Each beat represents a step of your lovemaking until you and your beloved are one. When you are finished with the visualization, put the drum down and clap your hands three times to come back to the present moment.

January 31   GRAPES OF LOVE

Use this spell to ask for the blessings of the Goddess in your love life for the next twelve months.

For this spell, you will need twelve washed grapes and a pink candle. At about 11:00 P.M., light the candle. As you do this, say:

> *Goddess bless my love life this year*
> *Make it sweet, joyful, and dear.*

Hold the grapes in your hands, and empower them by saying,

> *With these grapes I'm about to eat,*
> *For the next twelve months, my love be sweet.*

Eat the twelve grapes one at a time, imagining how your love relationship will evolve over the coming year. According to Spanish folklore about the New Year, if you eat all twelve grapes before the twelfth chime of the clock on this day, then you will be extremely lucky in love over the next year. After eating the grapes, say:

> *Dear Goddess, protector from above,*
> *Blessed lady of eternal love,*
> *Make my year a loving one,*
> *Full of joy and full of fun.*

FEBRUARY

February 1   FIRE OF LOVE

Performing this spell on the eve of Bridget's Day (the day also known as Bridget's Fire), you invoke the special power of the Celtic goddess Bridget. Her name means "bright one," for she kindles the need-fire, a symbol of the loving fire in your heart and in that of your lover.

For this spell, you will need a white beeswax candle, a candleholder, and a silver needle or pin.

Begin by cupping the silver needle or pin in your hands and visualizing a love that moves beyond physical boundaries into something that is sacred to both you and your lover. Next, pierce the wick of the unlit candle with the needle or pin, place the candle in its holder, and light it. As you gaze into the candle's flame, feel your energy move into it. Within the fire, see you and your lover, reaching that place of sacred love and sacred sexuality. Let the candle burn down all the way. Afterward, take the needle or pin and fasten it to the side of your mattress. Finish by thanking the Goddess Bridget for her blessings and help.

February 2   IMBOLC PROTECTION SPELL

Perform this spell on Imbolc to protect you and your lover. One of the primary energetic properties of sweet basil is that of protection.

For this spell, you will need a pinch of sweet basil and a cup of boiling water.

Steep the pinch of basil in the boiling water for about ten minutes. Hold the cup in your hands, raise it upward as if to make a toast, and say:

> *Great Goddess, protect my lover and me in every way.*
> *So that our love may prosper forever and a day.*

Then sprinkle the basil water around your bedroom, on your bed covers and sheets, under your bed, in your hair, and everywhere you want to be protected from negative energy.

February 3   FEBRUARY MARJORAM LOVE BATH

Marjoram was one of the herbs deemed precious enough to be transported by settlers from the Old World to the New World. In both ancient Greece and Rome, couples being married were crowned with marjoram as a symbol of their everlasting union.

For this spell, you will need a quarter-cup of marjoram, a quart of water, a bathtub, and nine drops of vanilla-scented oil.

Begin by simmering the marjoram in a quart of water for twenty minutes. Next, fill the bathtub full of warm water, and add the marjoram water, straining out the herbs. Then add nine drops of vanilla-scented oil.

While bathing, imagine you and your partner expanding and deepening your love. If you are married or handfasted, imagine you and your partner renewing your vows and reaffirming your love.

February 4   ASTRAL LOVE

With this spell you will create astral love in your imagination, unhampered by physical boundaries. In this place you are often more inclined to reach for the full potential of love, unhampered by physical limitations. By seeing this full potential, you will understand that the physical limitations are sometimes self-imposed, and you'll respond by incorporating aspects of your astral love in your physical everyday life.

For this spell, you will need a small, smooth piece of clear quartz crystal, a bowl of salt water, and a bowl of cool, fresh water.

Begin by placing the piece of quartz carefully in the bowl of salt water for a few minutes to clear it of any unwanted energies. Rinse the stone with cool water for at least one minute. Dry the stone and hold it in your receiving hand as you recline comfortably.

Close your eyes and begin taking deep breaths. With each inhale, experience your body being filled with feelings of love. Sense the love spreading outward through all parts of your body, bringing a sense of wonderment and joy that spreads from your head to your toes.

Now put the stone in your power hand and fill it with the sensations of love that are resonating throughout your body. After you have filled the quartz with feelings of astral love, either keep it with you or put it in a special place so you can go back to that feeling of astral love whenever you pick up the stone.

February 5   SYMBOL LOVE MAGIC

Symbols are a mainstay of love and magic. A symbol is something that represents another thing. We use symbols to communicate on a daily basis. They are so well integrated into our world that we rarely notice how frequently we use them. Symbols can affect us on many different levels.

You will need a pink candle, a sheet of paper, and a pen.

Begin by drawing a magic circle. Next, light the candle and ask for the blessing of your favorite love goddess or god. On the paper, draw a symbol that represents love to you (a heart, a flower, yin and yang, etcetera). Now write your lover's full name and your full name around your symbol of love as if to embrace it with the letters of your names. Put the paper in front of the candle, and while staring intently into the candle's flame, say three times:

> *Two lovers guided by an unseen hand,*
> *Two lovers guided by love's command,*
> *From here to eternity,*
> *These two lovers are you and me.*

Then, fold the paper three times, and put it in a book about love (a romantic novel, for example). Allow the candle to completely burn down. Close the circle and thank deity.

February 6   TRUE LOVE

In ancient times, the priestesses of the Oracle of Delphi used bay leaves to induce a prophetic trance.

For this spell, you will need four dried bay leaves and a book of love poems.

Begin by crushing three of the four bay leaves, one at a time, between your fingers. With each leaf, focus on your true love's image if you know what he or she looks like. If you haven't yet found your true love, then close your eyes and put the crushed bay leaf up to your nose, allowing images to come forth and drift in and out of your mind. As you do this say,

> *Sweet bay with your powers of prophecy*
> *Please come show my true love to me.*

Do not crush the fourth bay leaf. In the book of love poems, select a page with a favorite passage or poem and put the remaining leaf between the pages as a reminder of your true love.

February 7 — FEBRUARY CANDLE MAGIC

For this spell, you will need a white candle, a pink candle, a red candle, candleholders, a ballpoint pen, and ylang ylang–scented oil.

Begin by drawing a magic circle. Call in the elements. Use the pen to inscribe the word *love* on each of the candles. Dress the candles by rubbing them with the oil, and then place them side-by-side in whatever order pleases you in their candle holders. Wipe your hands, and then light the middle candle. Use this candle to light the other two. As you light each of the candles, merge with the powers of fire, and say:

> *As I light this candle,*
> *I see more love coming my way*
> *Blessed be! So be it!*

Gaze into the candlelight, and merge with the fire spirit. Take a few deep breaths, and merge a little deeper with the flames. Imagine more love flowing into your life each and every day. Do this for several minutes. Take your time. When you are finished, say:

> *I see more love coming my way*
> *Each and every day.*
> *As I see it, so be it!*

Allow the candles to safely burn down. Bid farewell to the elements and close the circle. Repeat this spell as often as you like to keep bringing more love into your life.

February 8   RED UNDERWEAR LOVE MAGIC

The use of red cloth to enhance magic is widespread in traditional folklore.

For this spell, you will need a pair of red underwear, a red candle, a candleholder, and a ballpoint pen.

Begin by putting on the pair of red underwear. Next, use the pen to inscribe two hearts on the candle. Put the candle on the altar and light it. Focus on the flame, and begin to see more love in your life. As you do this, repeat the following lines nine times.

> *Love makes life magical,*
> *Magic makes everything possible.*

Continue gazing at the candle as it burns down, and imagine having an abundance of love. Know that each time you wear your special red underwear, you attract more love and magic into your life.

February 9   LOVE TALISMAN

You will need a rose-colored candle, a piece of rose quartz, and amber-scented oil.

Draw a magic circle and call in the elements. Next, light the candle, dedicating it to your favorite love goddess, such as Aphrodite. Hold the stone in your hands and put three drops of scented oil on it. Rub the oil into the stone and put it in front of the candle where you can easily see it. Anoint yourself with the oil.

Merge with the divine, with the Goddess and God, and fill your mind with a rose-colored light, the color of love. Imagine an intense flow of love and joy coming into your life, and allow those images and sensations to fill your mind.

Now, actually put your loving and joyful thought-energy into the stone. Do this by imagining a bright beam of rose light moving from your forehead and both hands into the stone. Direct all your attention, all of your mind's energy, into the stone. Imagine all your loving thought-energy being absorbed into the atomic structure of the stone. Hold the stone in your power hand, and say three times,

> *Bring me joy and love*
> *By the powers of earth, air, fire, and sea*
> *As I will, so shall it be!*

Hold the stone and imagine a bright field of rose energy surrounding the stone and shooting out ten feet in all directions from it. See and sense the love stone's field of influence a total of three times to set it in place. Then put the stone down and clap your hands three times. Allow the candles to burn down completely, and as you gaze at their light, hold your love talisman in your receiving hand. When you are finished, release the elements, thank deity, and close the circle. Carry your talisman with you to draw more love and joy into each day.

February 10   BLESSED BEES FERTILITY MAGIC

For this spell, you will need a beeswax candle, a green stone, a bowl of cool salt water, a bowl of fresh water, a sheet of paper, and a green felt-tip pen. If possible, do this spell just before a full moon.

First, clean the stone out by washing it in salt water and rinsing it in cool, clear water. Dry it. Next, light the candle, dedicating it to a goddess of fertility such as Anu or Demeter. Then use the pen to write out on the sheet of paper exactly what you expect from the spell. For example, "I, [your name], and my beloved, [name], want to conceive a strong and healthy child in the next year." Drip six drops of candle wax around your written statement, and then drip six drops of wax on top of the stone. You can use the paper to catch any drops of wax that miss the stone. Fold the stone up in the paper, folding the paper a total of six times. Then seal the paper with wax from the candle. Do this carefully to avoid spilling hot wax on yourself, your clothes, the floor, or the furniture. When you are done sealing the paper with the stone, hold it in your hands and say six times:

> *Give us your blessing, goddess of fertility,*
> *Bring us a child who is healthy and happy.*
> *Blessed bees, so shall it be!*

Afterward, bury the wax-sealed packet under the east-side roots of a fruit-bearing tree.

February 11   LINKED HEARTS LOVE CHARM

The purpose of this charm is to link you and your beloved together. It involves the use of poppets. Always remember to respect someone else's free will, and only make poppets of other people with their permission.

For this charm, you will need a red candle, vanilla incense and censer, a pen, red construction paper, Scotch tape, one-half cup of dried rosebuds and a nine-inch piece of red ribbon.

Draw a magic circle and call in the elements. Invite your favorite love goddess and god into the circle as you light the red candle.

Begin by making two poppets from the construction paper. As you do this, focus on who the two poppets represent, namely you and your beloved. To make the poppets, take two sheets of construction paper and fold them in half. On each one, with the folded end at the bottom, draw a simple outline of a person, and then write your name on one and your beloved's name on the other. Draw hearts around both names. Cut each figure out, so each one produces two outlines. Use the Scotch tape to tape the sides of the poppets closed, leaving an opening for the rosebuds to be inserted at the top. Stuff them with the dried rosebuds, which are sacred to Venus, the goddess of love. As you stuff each of the poppets, chant:

> *Beautiful roses so red,*
> *Bring my love to my bed.*
> *Love be strong in waking and my dreams,*
> *Glowing with stars and bright moonbeams.*

After stuffing and chanting over each poppet, tape their tops closed. Next, take the nine-inch piece of red ribbon and tie it firmly around the two poppets, fastening them together in a lover's embrace. As you do this, say:

> *Two as one, one as two*
> *You with me, me with you.*
> *Together again, two as one*
> *As I will, the charm is done!*

Knot the ribbon around the poppets and seal it with a few drops of wax from the candle, thanking the goddess and god you called into the circle as you do so. When you are finished, bid farewell to the elements and close the circle. Put the poppets in your bedroom where you can easily see them.

February 12   ABRAHAM LINCOLN'S COME TOGETHER POTION

Before becoming president, Abraham Lincoln gave a speech in which he said "A house divided cannot stand." Relationships and love are the same way—if you let differences and problems escalate, then you will ultimately find yourself in a state of conflict and war. The idea behind this technique is to bring your house divided back together.

For this potion, you will need a scoop of vanilla ice cream, a scoop of chocolate ice cream, milk, and a blender.

Begin by placing the scoop of vanilla in the blender, then the scoop of chocolate. Add the milk. As you turn on the blender, say,

> *White and black come together as one,*
> *Let it be so when the shake is done,*
> *Feelings of love replace feelings of hate,*
> *A love coming together is what we create.*

Finish by enjoying the milkshake, preferably with the person with whom you have been in conflict. As you sip the sweet, thick shake, imagine the two of you coming together in agreement, and feelings of love replacing all negative ones.

February 13   HAPPY LOVER-ATTRACTION SPELL

Love is the most sacred gift you can give to yourself and someone else. Desire and emotion fuel and ignite all magical adventures. Use this lover-attraction spell to bring more romance and passion into your relationship.

For this spell, you will need a photograph of your beloved, a red candle in a candleholder, and three rose petals.

Begin by setting the photograph in front of the candle. Place the rose petals in front of the photograph. Light the candle, dedicating it to your beloved. Repeat this affirmation three times:

> *Each and every day, I love my beloved and myself*
> *unconditionally.*

Next, take the rose petals and hold them in your hands. Focus on the candle flame and the image of your beloved's before it. As you do this, repeat three times:

> *Sacred petals, sacred fire,*
> *Blessed be my heart's desire.*

Let the candle burn down all the way. Afterward, tuck the rose petals in a special place.

February 14   VALENTINE'S DAY LOVE BATH

The rituals of Valentine's day are traditionally associated with the mating of birds. One custom was to kiss the first person you met of the opposite sex, and this person became your Valentine or special love for a year.

For this spell, you will need nine bay leaves (preferably fresh) and a warm bath.

Begin by tearing up or crushing four of the bay leaves into a cup of boiling water. Let them soak in the water for about fifteen minutes, then strain the leaves out, and pour the water into a warm bath.

Dim the lights, close your eyes, and relax in the bay bath for about ten minutes. Imagine your true love coming into your life. If your mind wanders, just bring your focus back to imagining your true love. Be creative and have fun!

Get out of the tub and dry off. Take the remaining bay leaves, tear them slightly, and put them in your pillowcase. As you do this say:

> *Blessed bay spirit, bring dreams of my true love to me tonight.*

As you drift to sleep, repeat to yourself:

> *Bring dreams of my true love.*

February 15   FRUITY LOVE POTION

Fruit was traditionally considered the food of the gods and goddesses, giving it an inherently divine quality.

For this potion, you will need one cup of crushed ice (or enough to fill your blender about a quarter full), a half-cup papaya nectar, half of a ripe banana, a quarter-cup peach juice, and three drops of vanilla extract.

Put all the ingredients in a blender and mix them on "high" until it's a smooth mixture. As you do this, imagine putting the power of love right into the mixture. You will have two servings, one for your love, and one for you. Slowly sip the potion together while staring into each other's eyes. With each sip, become more aware of the divine quality of your love.

February 16   A BED OF ROSES

Use a couple of roses from your Valentine's Day bouquet to help create a night of love and romance. The red rose, a symbol of love and passion, is held in great esteem by love goddesses. By scattering rose petals on your bed linens and pillows, you invite passionate love and pleasure into your bed.

For this spell, you will need rose-scented oil and two red roses.

Use the rose-scented oil to anoint your forehead, both wrists, and ankles. Take the roses and hold them in your hands, and say:

> *Beautiful roses of the lady of love*
> *On this bed of divine fragrant flowers*
> *Bring romance and passion into this night*
> *May our love shine true and bright.*

Then take the petals off the roses one at a time, and place some on your pillow and some on the bed linens. Lay back, and invite your lover into your bed. If you don't have a lover, lie back and visualize the lover of your dreams. Leave the rose petals on your bed overnight. Then collect the petals and scatter them outside under a strong and healthy tree the next day.

February 17 BRIGHT LOVE ADVENTURE

For this spell, you will need paper, a pen, a white candle, vanilla-scented oil, a small stone, and a bowl of cool salt water.

Rinse the candle and stone in the salt water to rid them of any unwanted energies. On the paper, write everything you want in a love adventure. Put the paper where you can see it. Inscribe the candle with the words "Love Adventure" and dress it with the vanilla-scented oil. As you do this, imagine the details of your love adventure. Take the stone and rub it with the oil. Wipe the oil from your hands, and light the candle, dedicating it to a favorite love goddess or god. Hold the stone in your receiving hand. As you softly gaze into the flame for a few minutes, imagine the details of your love adventure coming to life in the fire. Then say three times,

> *Love adventure so bright*
> *Coming alive in the candle's light.*

Imagine yourself entering the candle flame as if it were a doorway into your love adventure. As you enter this doorway, in your mind's eye, you can see your love adventure playing out like a movie. Continue doing this as the candle safely burns down.

February 18   LOVE THYME TEA

For this spell, you will need a ceramic teapot, three cups of boiling water, a pinch of thyme, a pinch of mint leaves, one chamomile tea bag, one green tea bag, and honey. Put all the ingredients except for the honey in the teapot. As you add each ingredient, impart loving energy into each item through your touch and thoughts. Carefully pour the boiling water into the teapot. Imagine love flowing into your life as the water flows into the teapot. Add enough honey to thoroughly sweeten the tea. As you do this, imagine how sweet your love life can be. Sip this potion together with your intended lover to encourage sweet romance and love. In hot climates, you can chill the potion or serve it over ice.

February 19   ALL MY LOVING

This affirming technique helps you to send a psychic letter to your loved one telling him or her how much you care when you aren't physically there.

For this spell, create an imaginary paper, imaginary pen, and imaginary postal service.

With your imaginary pen, begin writing a letter telling your beloved how you really feel. Express your deepest feelings of love, respect, and thankfulness in your imaginary letter. When you are done writing the letter, imagine yourself sending the letter to the person psychically through the imaginary postal service. Have fun with this. Now in your mind's eye, see the person receiving the letter. As you do this, say out loud three times:

All my loving, I send to you,
All my loving, comes shining through.

February 20 ROMANCE MIST

You will need a cup of water, six fragrant roses, a bowl, a ceramic or glass pot or saucepan, and a spray bottle.

Hold the roses in your hands, and feel their sensuous petals. Smell the roses, one by one, and drink in their heady fragrance. Now, pull the petals off of each rose one at a time and put them into the bowl. Place both of your hands into the bowl of petals and sift the petals through your fingers, feeling their softness. As you do this, think about all the romantic times you have had in the past, and the ones you would like to have in the near future. This will empower the rose petals with these romantic images and feelings. Do this for a few minutes. Then put the petals in the ceramic or glass pot with the cup of water. Simmer this mixture slowly for about fifteen minutes. Take it off the stove and let the liquid cool. Strain the water and put it in the spray bottle. Using the mist setting, spray the romance mist everywhere in your bedroom—on your bed linens, yourself, your lover, around your bed—to draw more romance into your lovemaking.

February 21 SPLENDOR IN THE GRASS

For this spell, you will need a six-inch blade of oatstraw or other edible grass. First, cut the oatstraw or grass very early in the morning. Before the clock strikes six A.M., hold the blade of grass in your mouth, face east, and say:

> *Before the next rising sun*
> [Insert name] *shall hear my call*
> *Before the next rising sun*
> [Insert name] *for me, he [or she] shall fall.*

Face west, and repeat,

> *Before the next setting sun*
> [Insert name] *shall hear my call*
> *Before the next setting sun*
> [Insert name] *for me, he [or she] shall fall.*

Then cut the blade of grass into minuscule pieces and keep in a small glass or ceramic bowl. Call and invite the one you are trying to attract to lunch today, and creatively mix the edible grass pieces with the food. As you eat lunch, he or she will fall passionately in love with you.

February 22   TO TELL THE TRUTH POTION

For this spell, you will need a pinch of dried sage, a pinch of dried cedar, a pinch of dried rose petals, and a pinch of dried rosemary.

Using a mortar and pestle or a spice grinder, grind all of the herbs together into a fine powder. As you do this, think about how you would like those people who are close to you, especially your beloved, to be more truthful with you. Think about how much easier it is when we tell the truth, especially to ourselves and those we love. Keep in mind your goal of being more truthful in your love relationships. Put the powder in a small container and sprinkle it on the floor in your place of business, in courtrooms, or at home, to draw more truth into your communications with those you love.

February 23   GARDEN OF LOVE

Gardens are magical places of nature and are sacred to the love goddesses as well as to faeries. You can use this imaginary love garden to help cultivate more romance, love, and joy, today and every day. Your love garden need not conform to the laws of nature, plus there's no need to till, plant, water, weed, or mulch this garden, as it grows magically.

For this spell, you will need a picture of a favorite garden, a picture of your beloved, a white candle in a candleholder, and your imagination.

Light the candle, dedicating it to your favorite love goddess. Next, prop the pictures up in front of you: put the picture of your beloved on the left side and the picture of the garden on the right. Next place the lit candle in its holder in front of the pictures so you can see both clearly. Gaze at your beloved's picture for a few minutes, and then gaze at the picture of the garden. As you focus your attention on the garden picture, imagine stepping into it with your beloved. Imagine being in the garden with its greenery and flowers. Imagine taking your beloved's hand and walking through your garden of love. Feel the warm sun on your face and arms, and enjoy the cool shade of the trees. Hear the birds sing nearby. Notice the plants, flowers, trees, and animals in your garden. There may be a small pond or smooth-running stream in your garden, a garden bench, or special statues or carvings. As the candle burns down, sit back or recline and continue imagining yourself and your beloved slowing wandering through your garden of love, stopping now and again to embrace and make love. Feel the loving energy, beauty, and harmony, of the garden filling you and your lover as you become one with one another and with the divine garden of love.

February 24   DREAM LOVER PILLOW

Also called a comfort pillow, this dream lover pillow can be used to help you dream about your true love.

You will need half a cup of dried lavender flowers, a quarter-cup of rose petals, an eighth of a cup of dried rosemary, six bay leaves, and a six-inch by six-inch cloth bag. (In a pinch, you can use a handkerchief or a square of cloth closed with a rubber band.) Mix the bits of herbs together with the fingers of your power hand and charge them by chanting these words of power:

> *Dream mixture, come alive!*
> *United energies now thrive*
> *Show me what I need to see*
> *Show my true love to me*
> *As I sleep, so mote it be!*

Let the mixture stand for a few minutes, and then put it into your cloth bag. After closing your dream pillow with a drawstring or stitching, tuck it inside your pillowcase. As you sleep, the movement of your head gently crushes the herbs, releasing their aroma.

February 25   PAINTING A PICTURE OF LOVE

For this spell, you will need a white tealight, a small artist's paintbrush, and your imagination.

Light the candle, dedicating it to your favorite love goddesses and gods. Then recline comfortably, holding the paintbrush in your power hand. Uncross your arms and legs, and take a few deep breaths, settling in and getting even more comfortable. As you breathe deeply, begin to imagine being filled and surrounded with warm white light, and allow the light to wash through you and relax you. Breathe the white light into your body as you relax your forehead and the muscles around your eyes. Breathe out any tension or pain. Breathe in and relax the muscles of your mouth. Breathe out any tension in your jaw. Breathe the relaxing light into your neck, shoulders, arms, hands, and fingers. Breathe out any discomfort. Breathe the soothing white light into your chest and stomach, into your upper, middle, and lower back, and breathe out any tension. Take another breath, relaxing your buttocks, pelvis, thighs, calves, ankles, heels, feet, and toes.

Now begin to imagine yourself walking down a path in the foothills on a warm summer afternoon. Nature is all around you in the form of green grasses, jewel-colored wildflowers, blackberries, mighty oaks, maples, and delicate cottonwoods. The sky is blue and the air smells of wildflowers and fruit. As you proceed down the path, a soft breeze blows and cools your skin. You can hear birds singing and the sound of running water nearby. You see a clearing straight ahead of you, and in the clearing is a large, blank canvas. In your mind's eye, take your paintbrush and begin painting a picture of love. Pretend that you can paint like a master. Paint in all the details, and then focus on the finished masterpiece. Enjoy the picture for a few minutes, and hold its image in your mind. Focus your attention on the paintbrush in your right hand, and breathe the image of the picture into the paintbrush. Imprint the paintbrush with the image, using your thoughts and breath as the carrier waves. Come back to the present moment, and feel the paintbrush in your hand. Roll it in your hand a few times. Put the paintbrush in a special place, and use it again when you want to paint more pictures of love.

February 26   BE MINE POTION

You will need two cups of low-fat milk, a teaspoon sweetened cocoa, a dash of cinnamon, three drops of vanilla, and three teaspoons of whipping cream.

In the evening, heat the milk slowly, stirring in each of the ingredients. As you do this, imagine a night filled with romantic love. Take your time, cooking the potion slowly over a low heat. Do not boil. Next, pour the heated potion into two cups. You and beloved hold the potion cups up together, and clink them together softly. Before drinking the potion, say to your lover,

> *Dearly beloved, I hope you see*
> *That you are dearly loved by me*
> *I will be yours come rain or shine*
> *Dearly beloved, please be mine.*

Sip the potion slowly, and then enjoy an evening of romantic love.

February 27   BEAUTIFUL BELL MAGIC

Bells are symbols of personal attunement. Their clear sounds reflect a resonance within the wellspring of your life, signaling great things to come. Use this spell to ring divine beauty into your daily life.

You will need a silver bell and a fancy handkerchief.

Draw a magic circle, call in the elements, and invite your favorite love goddess into your circle. Spread the handkerchief out on the ground in front of you and put the bell on top of it. Moving clockwise, take three steps slowly around the bell, pause, and then take three more steps. Pause, and take another three steps around it, pause, and then take three more. Pick the bell up, and ring it six times. After you do this, say:

> *Great goddess of love, beauty, and mystery*
> *Hear the bell as it rings out to you from me*
> *Please bless me with your beauty, blessed be!*

Ring the bell three more times, give thanks to the love goddess, and then close the circle and bid farewell to the elements. Put the bell somewhere special, and ring it every morning to encourage more loving beauty in your daily life.

February 28   SOUL MATE LOVE CHARM

Use this charm to help you discover your soulmate, the person who is your divine mate.

You will need paper, a pen, a white candle, neroli-scented oil, a bowl of salt water, and a tiny white stone.

Begin by drawing a magic circle and calling in the elements. Rinse the candle and stone in salt water to rid them of unwanted energies. Rub a thin coat of scented oil on the candle body and the stone, and then anoint yourself. Wipe your hands and light the candle, dedicating it to your favorite love goddess. Next, use the pen and paper to write down a list of the primary qualities you would like in your soulmate. Use large letters. Position the list where you can easily read it. Then take the stone in your power hand and say:

> *By the power of the goddess and god of love*
> *I pray, show my soulmate to me,*

In this flame, in this fire
Show my soulmate to me.
As I will, so shall it be!

Hold the stone and imagine magically stepping through the flame of the candle into another realm. You can see soft images before you that slowly come into focus. As they do, you see the image of your soulmate standing before you. Do this for a few minutes, making an effort to see clearly the details of your soulmate. Then fold the stone into the paper using a total of six folds, and seal the charm with candle wax. When you are done release the elements and close the circle. Snuff the candle or let it safely burn down on its own. Afterward, carry the charm with you to attract your soulmate to you.

$\mathcal{M}$ARCH

March 1   STUCK ON YOU LOVE CHARM

You will need vanilla-scented oil (you can make your own vanilla oil by putting a few drops of pure vanilla in a teaspoon of carrier oil such as apricot or extra-light olive oil), two sticks of gum, a bowl of cool salt water, a red votive candle, and a pen.

First, rinse the candle in the water to rid it of any unwanted energies. Write your beloved's initials on the candle, and then inscribe your initials over them. Rub a thin film of oil on the candle body, and anoint your ankles, wrists, throat, and forehead with the oil. Wipe the oil off your hands and light the candle, dedicating it to a favorite love goddess, such as Aphrodite. Chew the sticks of gum one at a time and put all of the chewed gum between the pictures. The pictures should face one another with the gum between them. Fold the joined pictures, and then carefully seal them with candle wax. Hold the sealed pictures in your power hand, and say,

> *Happily joined together as one*
> *Sharing love, romance, and fun*
> *Under the stars, moon, and sun*
> *Blessed be, we are One!*

Gaze into the candlelight and imagine the ways you can be closer to your beloved now and in the near future. Do this for a few minutes. Put the sealed pictures under your bed.

March 2   MARCH LOVE BATH

You will need a white tealight, lavender-scented bubble bath, and three drops of rose-scented oil.

Begin by running a warm bath. Add the bubble bath and oil. As you do this, say:

> *Lavender and rose of romance and love,*
> *Share your natural beauty with me today.*

Place the tealight where you can easily see it when you are in the bathtub. Before you get into the tub, light the candle, dedicating it to your favorite goddess of beauty, such as Venus. Get into the tub and gaze at the candlelight. Think about your best features, and imagine that they are even more attractive. See yourself as bright and shining, merge with the scents of the tub, and say,

> *May the Goddess bless me with love and beauty*
> *"Beauty bright within, shining bright without*
> *Now and forevermore. By the Lady, blessed be!*

Soak for a while, and then get out of the tub and dry off. Anoint yourself with the rose-scented oil by putting a bit on each wrist and on the inside of both your ankles. Sit or lay back and imagine feeling attractive and beautiful within and without.

March 3   CONE OF LOVE POWER

A cone of power is a cone of beneficial energy, created by you, that can be directed to a preselected destination—in this instance, your beloved.

You will need a cedar and sage smudge stick and your imagination.

For best results, perform this ritual at dusk. First smudge the area with the cedar and sage to rid your magical space of any unwanted energies. Then draw a magic circle and call in the elements. Invite your favorite love goddesses and gods into the circle.

Hold your power hand outward in front of you, and draw a circle of white light and energy of about one foot in diameter on the floor in front of you. (This circle of energy is not for standing in.) Merge with the divine, then fill your mind with a brilliant violet light. Turn to the north point, then to the east point, then to the south and west points of your magic circle, holding your power hand high in the air, building the intensity and density of the brilliant violet light. Spin around clockwise three times, and then face the circle of white light on the floor in front of you, and say:

Ayea, Ayea, Ayea!

Slowly lower your power hand, pointing to the center of the circle of white light. In your mind's eye see a shaft of white light descending from your hand that fills the circle. See it growing stronger and brighter until it becomes a powerful cone of white light. Imagine the cone picking up speed and gathering energy like a cyclone. Then draw up the cone with your power hand and say in a clear and loud voice:

I send this cone of love power to my beloved!

Release the cone by shouting:

GO!

As you release it, imagine the cone of love power going straight to your lover and showering him or her with loving energy. When you are done, clap your hands three times, and take a few minutes to regain your equilibrium. Close the magic circle, bid farewell to the elements, and thank deity.

March 4 LOVING ANGEL AFFIRMATION

You will need a picture of your beloved and a white candle.

Light the candle, dedicating it to the one you love. Place the picture by the candle where you can see it easily. As you gaze at the candle and picture, imagine becoming one with your beloved. Do this for a few minutes. Then focus all of your attention on the picture, and say:

> *You are my loving angel, my love*
> *My delight, my joy, day and night*
> *Every love song was written for you*
> *My spirit sings every moment I'm with you*
> *I long to be in your arms, wings unfolded,*
> *May we be as one. So be it, my loving angel!*

Take a few more minutes, meditating on the one you love. To affirm your love, perform this ritual with your beloved and say the words out loud to him or her.

March 5   LOVER ATTRACTION POTION

You will need a quarter-cup of apricot juice, a quarter-cup of orange juice, a half-cup of apple juice, a pinch of fresh or dried mint, and a glass.

In the morning, mix the juices together in a large glass. As you stir them together, say:

> *Apricot, orange, and apple*
> *Fruits of love and pleasure*
> *By the divine love of the Goddess and God*
> *Please bring my beloved to me*
> *So we may know that moment divine*
> *When I am yours, and you are mine.*

As you slowly sip the potion, imagine attracting a romantic and caring lover today. As you go about your day, be on the lookout for love.

March 6   LOVING YOU PLACKET

A *placket* is a magic pocket.

For this spell, you will need a red candle, a recent photo of your beloved, six pinches of dried rosebuds, two square six-inch by six-inch pieces of red paper, a stapler, tape, and a pen.

Draw a magic circle and call in the elements. Light the candle, dedicating it to your beloved. Then staple and tape the two squares of paper together along the sides and bottom edge, leaving the top open. Write the words *I Love You* on the front and back of the photo. Insert the photo into the placket and then add the rosebuds. Hold the placket in your hands, focus your mind on your beloved, and say:

Loving you delights me
Loving you excites me
Loving you empowers me
Loving you inspires me
So be it! Blessed be!

Put the placket under your mattress. Allow the candle to safely burn down. Leave the placket under your mattress for thirty nights to access its loving energy.

March 7   BE MINE TONIGHT

For this spell, you will need a bowl of cool salt water, a red candle, a pink candle, a white candle (all in holders), a pen, three small white stones, and honeysuckle-scented oil. Do this spell after dark.

Begin by rinsing the candles in the salt water to rid them of any unwanted energies. Next, draw a magic circle and call in the elements. Use the pen to write the words *Be Mine Tonight* on each of the candles and rub them with a thin coat of the honeysuckle-scented oil. Put the candles in their holders and position them in a row with white on the left, pink in the middle, and red on the right. Anoint yourself with the oil, and then rub a few drops on the stones. Put a stone in front of each of the candles. Wipe your hands, and then light the white candle, dedicating it to a favorite goddess of love. Then light the pink candle using the white candle, dedicating it to your love. Light the red candle with the pink candle, dedicating it to a favorite love god. Gaze at the candle flames for a few minutes. As you do this, imagine your beloved illuminated in their light, and then say:

> *Candles of love, lover's fire*
> *Burn strong, burn bright*
> *Beloved, be mine tonight.*
> *Candles of love, lover's desire*
> *Burn long, burn bright*
> *Beloved, be mine tonight.*

Now focus your attention on the stones, and say:

> *Sacred stones of sacred light*
> *Shine clear, shine bright*
> *Beloved, be mine tonight.*

Continue gazing at the candle flames as you imagine your beloved in your mind. When you are done, put the stones near your bed to encourage a night of romantic love and passion. Close the circle, bid farewell to the elements, and thank deity.

March 8   TRUE LOVE POTION

Inspire feelings of tenderness, fidelity, passion, and romance with this delicious brew.

You will need a ceramic teapot, four cups of hot water, two tea bags of roasted green tea, one tea bag of rosehip tea, a half-teaspoon of catnip, a half-teaspoon of pure vanilla, three teaspoons of honey, two large glasses, and ice.

First, put the water, teabags, catnip, vanilla, and honey in the teapot. Stir the ingredients with a wooden or plastic spoon. With each stir, say:

True love sweetens my life
As I stir this tea, so shall it be.

Allow the tea to steep for a few minutes, then strain it and let it cool. Serve over ice, and sip it with your lover while gazing into one another's eyes.

March 9   SEEDS OF LOVE CHARM

You can use this charm to encourage your lover to be more attentive and amorous.

You will need sixty-six sunflower seeds, a pinch of sweet basil, six dried red peppers, six pinches of dried rosebuds, a white sock, a twelve-inch piece of red ribbon, and a red felt-tip pen.

Use the red pen to draw a plus sign on the sock. Write your initials and your love's initials directly on top of the plus sign. Put the sunflower seeds in the sock and cover the seeds with the basil, peppers, and rosebuds. Knot the sock and wind the ribbon around the knotted end six times. Hold the charm in your hands, merge with the divine, and say,

Spice and seeds,
Combine your powers
And bring to me,
More love and joy
Today, tomorrow, and forevermore.
By the Goddess, blessed be!

Put the sock charm in your lover's bureau drawer to encourage a more joyful and loving relationship.

March 10   THREE LOVE WISHES

This spell can be used to tie three love wishes into your life. The triple knot is a symbol of the threefold goddess.

For this spell, you will need a white candle, a pen, a thirty-six-inch piece of red ribbon, and patchouli-scented oil.

Draw a magic circle and call in the elements. Use the pen to inscribe your three love wishes on the candle. Rub a thin coat of oil on the candle, and rub a few drops on the ribbon. Anoint yourself with the oil, and wipe your hands. Light the candle, dedicating it to a favorite love goddess or god. Take the ribbon and hold an end in each hand. Think about your three wishes. Begin to tie three knots in the ribbon, one at a time, thinking about tying those three wishes into your life. As you tie the first knot, say:

> *The first knot is for* [say your first love wish].

As you tie the second knot, say:

> *The second knot is for* [say your second love wish].

As you tie the third knot, say:

> *The third knot is for* [say your third love wish].
> *As I will, so shall it be! Blessed be!*

Take the knotted ribbon and tie it on your bedroom doorknob or door handle until your wishes come true. Allow the candle to burn down completely. Close the circle, bid farewell to the elements, and thank deity.

March 11 LOVE AND ROMANCE BATH SALTS

You will need one ounce of sea salt, one ounce of baking soda, two ounces of borax, nine drops of sandalwood-scented oil, nine drops of ylang-ylang–scented oil, nine drops of jasmine-scented oil, nine drops of rose-scented oil, an airtight container, and a warm bath.

Put the dry ingredients in a bowl and mix them thoroughly with your fingers. As you do this, chant,

> *Soap, soda, and salt of the sea*
> *Bring more love and romance to me.*

Next, add the scented oils, evenly distributing the drops of oil over the dry mixture. Stir this thoroughly with your fingers, and chant,

> *Nine times nine*
> *Lover be mine.*

Fill up your tub, tossing a handful of the salts under the running water. Swish them around until they completely dissolve. Invite your lover into your bath with you and enjoy a romantic love bath together! Store your bath salts in an airtight container. This recipe makes enough salts for four romantic love baths.

March 12 A CHARMED LIFE

You will need a small, white, beeswax candle, sandalwood incense, jasmine-scented oil, vanilla-scented oil, a small photo of you and your beloved together, and a small pouch.

Light the candle, dedicating it to your favorite love goddess. Next, light the incense with the candle flame, dedicating it to your favorite love god. Pass the pouch and photo through the incense smoke to clear them of any unwanted energies. Place the photo by the candle where you can see it clearly. Next, merge with the element of fire, with the candle flame, and say:

> *Fire sparkling like starlight*
> *Fire glowing like moonlight*
> *Fire shining like sunlight*
> *Empower our love with your light*
> *Make it strong, make it bright!*

Continue to gaze at the photo and candle flame. While you do this, imagine your love growing brighter and stronger every moment of every day. Do this until there is only about two inches of candle remaining. Next, snuff the candle out and let it cool. Then pinch off the burned wick with your fingers, and roll the candle piece between your hands until it becomes malleable. (This takes a few minutes.) Add a few drops of jasmine and vanilla oil to the soft wax, and continue to roll it in your hands. Next, flatten out the wax, and place the photo on top of it. Fold the wax over the photo, then fold it again, and then once more, for a total of three times. Put the folded wax and photo into the pouch. Hold the pouch in your hands, and say,

> *My darling, I hold you in my hands*
> *As I hold you dearly in my heart*
> *My darling, I love you*
> *May our life be ever charmed*
> *Now and forevermore.*
> *Blessed be our love.*

Carry the pouch with you for twenty-eight days. Each day, strengthen the power of the pouch by holding it in your hands and focusing on loving thoughts about yourself and your beloved. Focus on being thankful for the love you share together. Take a deep breath, and then imagine actually putting these loving thoughts into the beeswax pouch with each exhaled breath.

March 13   FORGIVE AND FORGET SPELL

Letting go of the past, especially in terms of love relationships, is essential for well-being and happiness. A symbol of the Goddess, a bowl can be used to transform your negative feelings into positive ones so you can love again.

You will need a cedar and sage smudge stick, two orange candles, clove-scented oil, paper, a pen, and a bowl.

Begin by smudging the room or area where you are casting this spell. Also smudge the bowl, paper, and pen. Next, draw a magic circle and call in the elements. Place the candles side by side about nine inches apart, and put the bowl between the candles. Light the candles, dedicating them to your favorite love goddess and god. Next, draw a large heart on the piece of paper, and tear the paper in half. As you do this, focus on the pain, hurt, and disappointment you want to let go of. Next, put the paper halves into the bowl. Hold the bowl with both your hands, and put it up to your mouth. Say all of the negative, hurtful things you want to be rid of. Be thorough. Say everything you want to let go of. Scream if you need to. When you are done, use both hands to flip the bowl over, placing it back down on the altar surface between the candles. Then say:

> *The contents of this bowl*
> *Are no longer mine.*
> *Go, negative memories,*
> *I forgive and forget the hurt*
> *Be gone all pain and sadness*
> *Broken heart now mend*
> *And love and love again,*
> *By the Goddess and God, so be it!*

Turn the bowl right-side-up, then take the paper halves and tear them up into little pieces. Throw the pieces in the garbage. Finish by smudging the area once more. Thank the goddess, close the circle, and bid farewell to the elements.

March 14   A WALK ON THE WILD SIDE

Each tree is endowed with a powerful and wise tree spirit, and each spirit is unique.

You will need a beeswax candle, cedar incense, and your beloved.

Draw a magic circle and call in the elements. Light the candle, dedicating it to the tree spirits. Then light the incense with the candle flame, also dedicating it to the tree spirits. Recline comfortably: uncross your arms and legs, and loosen any clothing that may be binding you. When you are comfortable, ask your mate to read the following guided journey out loud to you. If you prefer, tape-record the journey and play it back whenever you like. Another option is to read a few lines at a time to yourself and visualize the journey as you read along.

Gently close your eyes and begin by listening to the rhythm of your breathing. Breathe deeply, slowly, and completely. As you inhale, imagine you are breathing in pure, soothing white light. As you breathe out, imagine letting go of all the worries and tensions of the day with your exhaled breath. Breathe in white light, and breathe out any tension. As you inhale and exhale, feel your heart beating like a drum at your very center.

In your mind's eye, imagine standing in a magnificent clearing in the forest on a warm sunny day. As you look around the edge of the clearing, you see tall and powerful trees: mighty oaks, massive cedars, and stately sugar pines. You notice that each tree shimmers in the sun, surrounded by a white halo of light. Green grass covers the clearing floor, as do wildflowers of every color: yellow, pink, white, blue, purple, and red. In the near distance, you can hear the sound of the running water of a small creek, and a symphony of birdsong fills the air. The melody relaxes you even more as you linger in the wooded clearing. Carried by a soft breeze, the fresh scent of the trees, earth, and water washes over you. You are filled with the exquisite power of the forest around you, cradled in its ancient arms. The natural power surges through you, energizing you.

In your mind's eye, as you turn around in the forest clearing, you suddenly see your lover right next to you. You smile and embrace your love, delighted that you are together in this wooded wonderland. You walk together, exploring the clearing in the wild woods. As you walk along, you each bend down to pick a wildflower. As you reach a grassy spot in the clearing, you sit down together on the soft green grass, handing the flowers you have picked to one another. You kiss and hold each other as you lay back in the soft grass. Take a few minutes now just to enjoy the experience of being in the romantic forest clearing together with your love. Let your imagination run wild!

Now, take a deep breath and exhale completely. Begin moving your hands and feet, shifting your body and stretching. Then open your eyes and come back to the present moment and place.

When you are finished, close the circle and bid farewell to the elements. Snuff the candle. When it has cooled, pull the candle apart into little beeswax bits. Then go outside and scatter the bits clockwise around a favorite tree. As you do this, say:

> *Tree spirit be strong*
> *Tree spirit live long.*
> *So be it! Blessed be!*

March 15   NIGHTTIME PROTECTION CHARM

This charm helps protect children through the night.

You will need a cloverleaf, a clear crystal, three hairs from your head, three hairs from your child's head, a bowl of salt water, a bowl of clear water, and a clean white sock.

Clean the stone of any unwanted energies by washing it in the salt water and rinsing it in the clear water. Then put the cloverleaf, stone, and hairs into the sock. Hold the sock between your hands and charge the charm by saying three times:

> *Goddess and God, I pray you*
> *Empower this magic charm of white*

Protect my child through the night
Protect her [his] dreams as she [he] sleeps
By the Lady and Lord, so shall it be!

Put the charm under your child's bed. This charm is even more powerful when you charge it together with your child.

March 16 FRIENDSHIP POTION

This potion, when sipped with a friend, encourages a more empowering relationship.

You will need one cup of lemon-lime soda, a half-cup of apricot juice, a half-cup of peach juice, and two large glasses filled with ice.

Pour equal parts of the juices and soda into the glasses over the ice. Stir the potion in each glass clockwise with a spoon, and as you do, chant several times:

Friends are loyal and caring
Friends are helpful and sharing
So be it! Blessed be!

Sip with a friend.

March 17 FLOWER SCROLL CHARM

You will need a flower bush, a red ribbon, a small piece of paper, and a red pen.

Use the pen to write your dearest love wish on the paper. Next, roll the paper into a small scroll. Hold the scroll in your hands and empower it by saying:

> *By rains and winds come free*
> *Bring my dearest love wish to me*
> *By the powers of earth, air, fire, and sea*
> *By the powers of the Goddess and God*
> *Make it so! So be it! Blessed be!*

Use the ribbon to tie the scroll loosely to a flower bush. Do not fasten it too tightly. As the scroll is freed from the bush by the wind and rain, so will your love wish be made free to come to you.

March 18   VENUS AND MARS STRING MAGIC

For this spell, you will need a yard-long piece of red string, a yard-long piece of green string, a red candle, a green candle, candleholders, a ballpoint pen, neroli-scented oil, and an uplifting love song.

On each of the candles, use the pen to draw the glyph of Venus, and then the glyph of Mars right on top of it. Place the green candle to your left and the red candle to your right in their holders. Next, draw a magic circle and call in the elements. Light the green candle, dedicating it to the goddess of love. Then light the red candle with the green one, dedicating it to the god of love. Sit comfortably for a few minutes, just gazing at the candles. Breathe deeply as you sit, letting go of any worries and tensions for a few minutes. Next, take the strings and tie them together at the ends. Then slide the string in and out of your fingers, "cat's cradle" style. Use both hands to cradle the string, looping it in and out in patterns with your fingers. Slide the string length in and out while you chant:

> *Venus and Mars, together again*
> *By the power of the Goddess and God*
> *I am one with my beloved again.*

Keep working the string. Now hold the string in one hand as you put on a favorite love song. Loop the string in both hands again, and begin to work it to the rhythm of the song. Then knot the string six times. Each time you tie a knot say:

> *Our love is like a divine melody*
> *By the Lady and Lord, blessed be!*

When you are finished, close the circle, bid farewell to the elements, and thank the Goddess and God. Tie the string to your bed to empower your lovemaking.

March 19   PROPOSAL POTION

For this spell, you will need two cups of tomato juice, four dashes of celery salt, four pinches of dried basil, four pinches of dried dill, two glasses, a ceramic saucepan, and a wooden spoon. Put all the ingredients in the saucepan. Stir them clockwise with the spoon and chant:

> *Goddess and God, fill this brew*
> *With proposals of love and marriage true.*

Simmer the mixture for about ten minutes. Chill it and then strain the herbs from the potion. Serve the potion to your love to encourage a love proposal, perhaps of marriage.

March 20   LUCKY FRIENDSHIP TALISMAN

For this spell, you will need a ballpoint pen, a strawberry-scented votive candle, a bowl of cool salt water, and a piece of tumbled citrine.

Rinse the candle with cool salt water to rid it of any unwanted energies. Draw a magic circle and call in the elements. Then use the pen to write the words *Helpful Friend* on the candle. Light the candle, dedicating it to a helpful friend that you have or would like to have. Simply say:

I dedicate this candle to [person's name].

Hold the citrine in your power hand. Empower it by saying:

By the powers of earth, air, fire, and water
Great Goddess and God, bless my friendship with [person's name].
Thank you for bringing such a helpful friend to me.
By the powers of earth, air, fire, and water
Empower this stone with our lucky and joyful friendship
By the Lady and the Lord, blessed be!

Hold the stone between yourself and the candle flame so the light illuminates the stone. Gaze into the stone and start to imagine all of the ways you can help your friend and the many ways your friend can help you. Continue gazing into the stone and imagine sharing good times, having fun, and feeling happy and peaceful when spending time together. Feel the joy of your friendship. Actually think these images, thoughts, and feelings into the stone by focusing all your attention on it and directing your mental energy into the stone. Do this for a few minutes. When you are finished, bid farewell to the elements and close the circle. Give your helpful friend the citrine the next time you meet. Tell your friend that it's a lucky friendship talisman.

March 21　　　　SWEET SPRING MAGIC

The spring equinox, also called Ostara, heralds the fertility and rebirth of the earth after a long winter. Rabbits and eggs are both symbols of fertility and of spring.

For this spell, you will need a white candle, a chocolate rabbit, a glass of milk, and six small chocolate eggs.

Begin by drawing a magic circle and calling in the elements. Then light the candle, dedicating it to a fertility goddess such as Coventina (a Celtic goddess). Next, hold the chocolate eggs in your power hand and empower them by saying,

> *By the power of the Goddess*
> *By the power of earth, wind, fire, and sea*
> *I empower these chocolates with sweet spring.*
> *By the divine Lady, blessed be!*

Put the chocolate eggs aside. Next, hold the chocolate rabbit in your power hand and empower it by saying:

By the power of the Goddess
By the power of earth, wind, fire, and sea
I empower this chocolate with sweet spring.
By the divine Lady, blessed be!

Slowly eat the rabbit, beginning with the feet and ending with the ears. As you do so, gaze into the candlelight and think about the loving things you would like to create this spring, for example, a sweeter, more fruitful relationship with your mate, more understanding and loving patience with your children, more quality time with your loved ones, and so forth. Do this during the entire time it takes to eat the rabbit and drink the milk.

When you are done, close the circle, bid farewell to the elements, and thank the goddess of fertility. Give the six chocolate eggs to six different people that you care about to encourage the fruition of your loving spring creations.

March 22   AVALON ROMANCE POTION

For this spell, you will need one cup of apple juice, a chamomile tea bag, one cup of boiling water, a stick of cinnamon, a dash of vanilla, a ceramic teapot, two glasses, a half-teaspoon of lemon juice, and your beloved.

Begin by putting the tea bag, cinnamon stick, and vanilla into the ceramic pot with the boiling water. Let the tea steep for twenty minutes. Fill the two glasses with ice, and then add half of the tea and half of the juice to each glass. Put a quarter-teaspoon of lemon juice in each glass and stir clockwise thoroughly. As you stir the potion, say:

Great Lady, bring the magic of love into my life
Please give my beloved and I your blessing
So that we might know your divine power
Great Goddess, please love and guide us
By the Lady, blessed be!

Sip the potion with your beloved, and enjoy a romantic day.

March 23   DAISY LOVE WISH

For this spell, you will need a daisy.

Hold the daisy in your power hand and make an affirming love wish, for example, a new lover, a happier relationship, a more understanding partner, or more passion in your love life. Focus on your wish and say three times:

May the Goddess and God help me
May my love wish blossom like this flower
Blessed be! So be it!

Put the daisy in a vase with water, and for the following two days, affirm your love wish by gazing at the daisy and repeating:

May the Goddess and God help me
May my love wish blossom like this flower
Blessed be! So be it!

On the third day, press the flower in a book of love poems to make your love wish to come true.

March 24   LOVE MAGNET

This love magnet can be used to attract a lover.

You will need sandalwood incense, a large, three-inch diameter ring, red crocheting thread, six red beads, and a horseshoe-shaped magnet.

Draw a magic circle and call in the elements. Light the sandalwood incense, dedicating it to a favorite god and goddess of love. Pass all of the items for this spell through the incense smoke to rid them of unwanted energies. Next, tie the end of the thread securely to the large ring. Wind the thread around the opposite side of the ring three times at slightly different angles from the original tie and pull it taut, making a weblike pattern. Each time you attach the thread to the ring, wind it around the ring three times, and say:

> *Bright lover come to me*
> *So be it! Blessed be!*

Now wind the thread around the ring three times a short distance from the first tie, and repeat:

> *Bright lover come to me*
> *So be it! Blessed be!*

Your threaded design should look like an inverted V-shape. Pull the string to the left side of the ring. Then wind it about the ring a little more than halfway up the side, and repeat:

> *Bright lover come to me*
> *So be it! Blessed be!*

Adjust the thread so it looks like the lower angle of the cross arm of a five-pointed star. Then stretch the thread across to the opposite side, and wind it about the ring three times, and repeat:

Bright lover come to me
So be it! Blessed be!

Next, pull the thread back to the first tie you made, winding it around the ring three times, and repeating:

Bright lover come to me
So be it! Blessed be!

If you carefully check the angle of the thread each time you prepare to wind it at another point on the ring, you can adjust and tighten the design. Finally tie on the horseshoe magnet to the bottom. Make sure the horseshoe is pointing up. Tie the horseshoe magnet onto the ring six times. Each time you tie a knot, say:

With this magnet
I draw my bright lover to me.
So be it! Blessed be!

Knot the ends of the thread six times. Each time you make a knot, say:

Love be strong
Love be long.

Tie a red bead to each of the ends. Each time you tie a bead on, say:

Love be sensuous
Love be passionate.

Then make a loop of thread by which to hang up your love magnet. Hang it above your bedroom door to attract your beloved.

March 25   CALLING IT A DAY

You can use this spell to cancel out love spells and rid yourself of unwanted suitors. Cast it after dark.

You will need a cedar and sage smudge stick, a fireplace or wood stove, a bowl containing three cups of dried vervain, and three teaspoons of salt.

Begin by putting the bowl of vervain on the ground outside your front door. Build a fire in the fireplace or wood stove. Next, smudge your entire home, moving in a clockwise direction. Extinguish the smudge and draw a magic circle around your home. Call in the elements. With your power hand, fashion a door in the circle you've cast at your front door so you can go outside without breaking the magic circle of light. Next, exit your front door through the gate. Take a handful of the dried vervain in your power hand. Hold the vervain high above your head, facing in the opposite direction as your front door. Then loudly shout the name of the person you want to be free of and turn widdershins (counterclockwise) three times. Go back into the house, and cast the vervain into fire. Say:

> *In the past, I cast a love spell*
> *Now, the effect I do quell.*
> *May this spell be undone and* [name of person] *be gone!*
> *By the powers of earth, air, fire, and water*
> [Name of person] *shall never again return*
> *Make it so as these leaves burn!*

Repeat the process of going outside and gathering the leaves, shouting the name, turning widdershins, going inside and casting the leaves into the fire, and chanting the words of power a total of three times. Snuff out the candle when you are done. Break it into small pieces, and then throw the pieces into the garbage. Release the circle and bid farewell to the elements. When the fire has burned out and cooled, take some of the ashes and put them in the bowl. Mix the salt with the ashes and then flush them down the toilet. Rinse the vervain bowl with cool salt water to clean it.

March 26   LOVE DOWSING MAGIC

You can use these simple dowsing rods to better understand the power of your loving words and thoughts. You can also show your family how to use the rods. It just takes a little bit of patience and practice.

You will need two wire coat hangers, two plastic straws, and a pair of pliers.

Begin by untwisting the hangers and cutting them into L shapes, with the main extending arm measuring twelve inches, and the handle measuring five inches. Cut the plastic straws to fit over the handles so the extending arm swings freely. Bend the ends of the handles with the pliers to keep the straws in place. After you have assembled your rods, take one in each hand, hold the hangers waist-high with the rod arms extended straight out in front of you. Take a few deep breaths to calm your mind. Now focus on someone you really love. The arms of the rods will open outward, demonstrating the power of your positive feelings and thoughts. Next, focus on someone you don't like, someone who has hurt you in the past. The rods will swing inward, showing how your energy field contracts and diminishes with negative feelings and thoughts. You can also use the rods when you are meeting new people. Just find a quiet moment, take a few deep breaths, hold the rods, and say the person's name, and make a note of how the rods respond. If they open up, then you may want to get to know the person a little better.

March 27   LOVE BLEND POTION

You will need one cup of unfiltered apple juice, one cup of papaya nectar, six drops of pure vanilla, ice, and two glasses. Make this potion just prior to drinking it.

Pour equal amounts of the juices and vanilla into the two glasses filled with ice. Stir the potion clockwise, one glass at time, and say,

> *The fruits of love blend together*
> *Just as you and I come together*
> *I am you as you are me*
> *By the Lady, blessed be!*

After stirring and empowering the potion, drink the brew with the one you love to stimulate romance, love, and passion.

March 28   MAKING UP MAGIC

This spell can be used to make up with your beloved after an argument.

You will need a blue taper candle, lavender-scented oil, a ballpoint pen, a bowl of cool salt water, and a cup of pure water.

Clean the candle in the salt water, then draw a magic circle and call in the elements. Breathe deeply for a few minutes. As you breathe in, imagine breathing in pure white light. Fill your being with pure white light. Next, use the pen to write the words *Making Up* on the candle. Write yours and your beloved's initials on top of the words. Then rub the lavender-scented oil on the candle. Anoint yourself with the oil, rubbing a few drops on your ankles, wrists, and throat. Wipe the oil from your hands and light the candle, dedicating it to your beloved. Next, hold the cup of pure water in your hands and say:

Anger be washed away
Love brighten my day.
So be it! Blessed be!

Bring the cup to your mouth. As you drink the water, think about it washing away all of the anger and irritation you may be feeling toward the one you love. When you are done, close the circle and bid farewell to the elements. Allow the candle to burn down completely. Within the next twenty-four hours, take the initiative and do something to show your appreciation for the one you love.

March 29   LOVE APPLE SPELL

You will need an apple, an athame, two red candles, a bowl of cool salt water, vanilla-scented oil, and your beloved. I suggest taking a warm bath or shower with your partner before spinning this spell.

Wash the candles and the apple in the salt water to rid them of any unwanted energy. Rub the candles with the vanilla oil. Anoint your beloved and have him or her anoint you. Wipe the oil from your hands, and light one of the red candles, dedicating it to your beloved. After you do this, give your love a passionate kiss. Then have your mate light the second candle with the first candle flame. Again, enjoy a passionate kiss. Now focus all of your awareness on the flames of the two candles for a few moments, and say:

Candle burning, candle bright
Show the way to sweet delight
Candle burning, candle bright
Your lustful fire heats the night.

Then have your beloved repeat:

> *Candle burning, candle bright*
> *Show the way to sweet delight*
> *Candle burning, candle bright*
> *Your lustful fire heats the night.*

Next, cut the apple into four sections. Holding a piece in your hands, say:

> *This, a gift so divine*
> *Gives its love for all time*
> *This, with nectar so sweet*
> *Venus and Mars once again meet.*
> *So be it! Blessed be!*

Feed the apple piece to your beloved. Next, have your beloved take an apple piece. Empower it by repeating:

> *This, a gift so divine*
> *Gives its love for all time*
> *This, with nectar so sweet*
> *Venus and Mars once again meet.*
> *So be it! Blessed be!*

As you eat the apple pieces, imagine a night of romantic and passionate lovemaking with each other. Repeat the process with the remaining two apple pieces. Let the candles burn down as you enjoy a night of sensuous, sweet love.

March 30   LOVE POWER TEA

This is used to strengthen your love.

For this potion, you will need a ceramic or glass pot, two cups of boiling water, two rosehip tea bags, a dash of cinnamon, a pinch of lavender flowers, two teaspoons of honey, a wooden spoon, and two cups.

Put the ingredients in the pot and pour the boiling water over them. Stir well. As you stir the potion clockwise, say:

> *I love my beloved*
> *My beloved loves me.*
> *So be it! Blessed be!*

Then cover the mixture and let it steep for five minutes. Pour the potion into the cups and sip it with your beloved. As you do, say to your love,

> *I love your eyes*
> *When you look at me*
> *I love your touch*
> *When you touch me*
> *I love your smile*
> *When you smile at me*
> *I love your spirit*
> *When you uplift me*
> *I love who you are*
> *Just the way you are*
> *To me you are a shining star.*

March 31 BEACH BLANKET LOVE AFFIRMATION

You can use this spell to affirm your love.

You will need a bowl of cool salt water, a gold candle, a picture of the beach, sandalwood-scented oil, beach music, and a beach towel.

Clean the candle of any unwanted energies by washing it in the cool salt water. Next, dress it with the sandalwood oil. Anoint yourself with the oil. Then draw a magic circle and call in the elements. Light the candle, dedicating it to your favorite love goddess. Gaze at the candle flame for a few minutes while you think about your deepest desires, especially the ones that make you feel all warm inside. Now phrase your desire in a positive way. Tune into how you feel inside when you say your affirming phrase. If it makes you feel warm all over, like laying on your beach blanket on a warm sandy beach, then you are right on track. For example, your love affirmation might be:

I want my relationship with my beloved to expand with boundless love and joy.

When you find the affirming phrase that makes you feel all warm inside, then you are plugging into your power source. Now rethink, rephrase, and re-feel your affirmation until it feels absolutely blissful. Then take your beach towel and snuggle into it. Imagine being on the beach, lying peacefully on your beach towel in the soft, warm sand, feeling completely safe and relaxed. As you snuggle deeper into your towel, imagine your love affirmation getting stronger and brighter. Be there, feel it, and keep feeling it, until you feel warm all over inside. If you can feel it, you can make it so. Allow the candle to completely burn down. Snuggle into your beach towel for at least five minutes every day for twenty-eight days to reaffirm your love.

 PRIL

April 1   APRIL FOOL'S HEALING CRYSTAL

In Celtic Mythology, Gwydion is a wizard and god of kindness and healing who is associated with April Fool's Day and the Milky Way. Tap into Gywdion's healing power this evening by going outside after dark and gazing at the night sky.

You will need a clear quartz-crystal point.

Go outdoors, stand comfortably, and place your crystal down next to your feet. For a few minutes, close your eyes and imagine your entire body being filled with the bright white light of the stars. In your mind's eye, slowly scan your body and check for any places where you feel pain and discomfort. You may want to flex and stretch your body to locate these places. Next, pick up the crystal in your power hand. Now breathe in deeply, imagine lots of healing white starlight in your mind's eye, and then pulse your breath sharply out through your nose. As you do this, imagine the white starlight filling up the crystal and your entire body. Each time, directly after you pulse the white starlight into the crystal and your body, say:

> *Divine healing starlight*
> *Make me healthy tonight.*

Do this at least three times, focusing on starlight pouring into and filling the parts of your body that are painful. Visualize yourself being completely filled with healing starlight energy. Continue to gaze at the stars, and breathe in their energy, their bright white light. Again, breathe in and pulse your breath sharply out through your nose while imagining that you are sending this healing image into your being and into the crystal in your hand. Still holding the stone, say:

> *With every breath of divine starlight*
> *I am completely healed tonight.*
> *So be it! Blessed be!*

The stone may become warm or hot as you do this. Breathe in and out in a rhythmic pattern for a minute or two. Breathe in to the count of three, hold your breath for three counts, and then exhale for three counts. As you do this, imagine the white starlight filling yourself and the crystal. After you are done, carry the crystal on your person. Repeat the process every night to strengthen the healing starlight energy in the stone and in yourself. Whenever you need to recharge yourself with healing starlight energy, just hold the crystal and pulse your breath, imagining the bright white light filling and healing your being.

April 2   SPIRIT GUIDE SPELL

This technique is great for finding the answer to a personal question. It taps directly into the power of your spirit guides, which are energies that generally help you in life.

You will need a silver candle in a candleholder and a cup filled with fruit juice.

Begin by lighting the silver candle. As you gaze intently into the flame, say:

> *Spirit guides, I call to you tonight,*
> *I seek the wisdom of your light.*

Take the cup of fruit juice in both your hands, hold it up toward the candle, and say:

> *I,* [your name], *seek the answer to* [state your question
>   or concern].
> *Please share your wisdom with me now!*

Now slowly drink the juice. As you do this, imagine the answers you seek flowing into your being. See and sense the power and wisdom of your spirit guides empowering you.

April 3   RIBBON HEALTH BELT

For this spell, you will need a belt and three twelve-inch lengths of ribbon—one green, one gold, and one white.

Begin by tying the green ribbon on one end of the belt. As you do this, say:

> *Green is for health.*

Next, tie the gold ribbon onto the middle of the belt. As you do this, say:

> *Gold is for wealth.*

Then, tie the white ribbon on the other end of the belt As you do this, say:

White is for spirit.

When you are finished tying on the ribbons, put the belt around your waist while saying:

> *Divine belt of power,*
> *Embrace and empower me,*
> *Fill me with health,*
> *Fill me with energy.*
> *By the Lady, blessed be!*

April 4   BEAUTIFUL BODY SPELL

This spell draws on the sacred power of the mistletoe which can be found on oak, apple, pine, elm, spruce, and poplar trees.

You will need a white candle, a candleholder, a ballpoint pen, and a sprig of mistletoe.

Begin by using the pen to inscribe the words *beauty*, *health*, and *wellness* on the body of the candle. Next, use the pen to write your initials to cover the inscribed words. Do this three times. Place the candle in the holder and light it. Hold the sprig of mistletoe in your power hand. Gaze into the candle flame, merge with the powers of fire, and say three times:

> *By the ancient power of mistletoe,*
> *Let the divine Goddess within me flow,*
> *Beauty, health, and wellness too,*

These are the energies I ask of you
Blessed be! So shall it be!

Tuck the sprig (or tape it) into the corner of the mirror you regularly use. Each time you use the mirror, the mistletoe will remind you of your desire for beauty, health, and wellness.

April 5 — MAKING A HEALING CRYSTAL

In Irish mythology, the goddess Creide placed Art, son of King Conn, in a crystal chamber. In this chamber the healing rays of the sun and moon converged into one. After a month he had acquired a new strength and energy. This story alludes to the healing power of crystals, the same power you will be accessing with your healing crystal.

You will need a cedar and sage smudge stick and a piece of tumbled clear quartz.

Start by lighting the smudge stick and holding your crystal in the smoke until it feels clear of any unwanted energies that may be stored in it. Be sure to completely extinguish the smudge stick when you are done clearing the crystal. Next, take the crystal and cup it between your hands while thinking of everything that you associate with healing, such as feeling healthy and energized, freedom from pain, being flexible and agile, and a warm, glowing feeling that makes you feel good all over.

After you get your healing images firmly in your mind, take a deep breath, hold it, and imagine those healing images and thoughts. Pulse your breath sharply out through your nose, and as you exhale, imagine sending the healing energy into the crystal. You can do this by imagining the energy moving into the crystal from your third eye (forehead between your brows), or you can imagine the energy moving into the crystal through your hands. Repeat the pulsed-breath process three times. When you are done, keep the crystal in a special place where you can take it out anytime you need some healing energy. You can either hold it in your hand to energize your whole body with healing energy or place the healing stone on the part of your body that isn't feeling well. Recharge it with healing energy from time to time by using the same technique of pulsing your breath and sending healing thoughts into the crystal.

April 6   GETTING OVER GRIEF

You will find times in your life when it seems impossible to let go of painful feelings of grief. This is especially true when you have lost someone close to you. This magical technique is intended to help you through these times by releasing the grief and replacing it with loving and nurturing thoughts.

For this spell, you will need a pink candle and a candleholder, an eighteen-inch piece of black ribbon or string, and a pair of scissors.

Begin by inscribing a heart on the side of the candle, and then placing it in the holder and lighting it. Stretch the black ribbon or string out in front of the candle, and imagine all of thoughts of grief moving into and becoming the ribbon or string. Take the scissors and cut the ribbon in half. Then take the halves and burn them in the candle flame while saying:

Sacred fire, cleanse my grief with your flame,
Warm my heart and soothe my soul once again.
By the divine love of the Goddess and God, so be it!

After you have burned the ribbon, gaze into the candle and say a short prayer to the divine, asking Goddess and God to help you let go of your grief and feel the joy of life warming your heart and soul once again.

April 7   HEALING SPELL

You will need a green candle, an athame, a fireproof pan or cauldron large enough to safely burn a sheet of paper, a cup of water, a bowl of salt, two sheets of paper, a pen, and an envelope.

If your athame is not dulled, make sure the blade will not damage the surface you are working on by placing a cutting board underneath your work. Next, draw a magic circle around the area your are working in. Light the candle, dedicating it to a goddess or god of healing. Then use the pen to draw a picture of yourself, and clearly outline the area in your body that you want to be healed. Your picture need not be work of art. Next, write all the specifics of the problem next to the problem area. Highlight the area by circling it three times. If there is more than one problem, do a separate healing pentacle for each one. Now take a deep breath, merge deeply with oneness, and use your athame to excise the problem or illness, carefully using the tip of your athame to cut and scrape the problem area on the paper. Then burn the paper in the pan or cauldron. Set the ashes aside for now.

Next, take the other sheet of paper, and draw another picture of yourself, this time without the problem, making the drawing a little larger and brighter. All around and across your image, write down the qualities of good health that you desire. Focus all your attention on the drawing. Merge with oneness, and chant three times:

> *On this magical eve, I am healed*
> *Blessed be! So be it!*

Merge with your drawing in front of you. Become one with it. Imagine the healing already being complete. Move your imagination into the future a few minutes and allow yourself to feel a magical sense of well-being and splendid health. Now move your awareness back to the present moment and say:

> *Blessed be! So be it!*

Fold the drawing into a small square. Carefully seal it with candle wax. Put the sealed paper into the envelope. Draw three symbols of the Goddess on the outside of the envelope. (Examples of such symbols are a star, a circle, or a spiral.) Put the envelope somewhere it won't be disturbed.

Next, pour the cup of water into the bowl of salt. Mix it together and pour the bowl of salt water over the ashes in the pan or cauldron. Use your athame to stir the ashes counterclockwise three times, being careful not to spill any of the mixture. Take the pan or cauldron outside and set it down. Dig a small hole with your athame. Pour the contents of the pan or cauldron into the hole. Cover it and put three rocks on top. Leave the area looking as undisturbed as possible. Finally, go back indoors, and clap your hands three times. Thank deity and release the circle. Wash all of your tools with salt water, rinse them in clear water, and dry them. Allow the candle to burn down safely on its own.

April 8   BUDDHA'S BE HAPPY SPELL

Buddha believed that anger was a major waste of energy, and that a person's anger only created more pain and suffering in life. The purpose of this work is to help you move past your anger, turning this wasted energy into something that is creative and productive.

You will need a red balloon and a sage and cedar smudge stick.

Begin by thinking about what you are angry about or the person you are angry with. Once you have those thoughts in your mind, then begin blowing up the balloon. With each breath, imagine your angry thoughts and feelings moving from you into the balloon. After you have filled it full of all of your thoughts and feelings of anger, tie the balloon off, and leave it in a closet. You don't need it anymore. Light the smudge stick and breathe in the smoke. Allow the smoke to flow over your body. (Note: If you don't like smudge smoke, use sage and cedar oil in an oil diffuser or in a pan of boiling water.) Feel the smudge smoke clearing out any residual anger that might be left over. Breathe into the smoke any residual anger. When you are done, you will feel brighter, cleansed of your anger, and ready to start a new day.

In a few days, the balloon in the closet will deflate. When it does, just toss it in the garbage, tossing your anger away too.

April 9   TRI-COLOR BLESSING OF HEALTH

Blue is traditionally the color that breaks up and washes away negativity. Green is the color that symbolizes healing, fertility, and new growth. Gold is the color of the sun. It encourages the new healing and growth.

For this blessing you will need a bright blue candle, a green candle, a gold candle, and sandalwood-scented oil.

Begin by rubbing each of the candles with oil. Anoint yourself with the oil, rubbing drops on the insides of your ankles, your wrists, your throat, and the back of your head. Wipe the oil from your hands and light the blue candle, dedicating it to a favorite healing goddess or god or divine energy of your choosing. Focus on the candle and imagine the color blue in your mind. Imagine the color blue washing away and disolving all the negativity, illness, and pain within your body, mind, and soul. Breathe the color blue into your body. Ask the Goddess and God to help you cleanse your body, mind, and soul of any negativity, illness, or pain. Pay particular attention to areas you know to be problems. You know your body better than anyone else. You know what's right and wrong with you. Use this knowledge and allow the blue light to wash out any problem areas.

Now light the green candle with the blue one, dedicating it to the same healing deity or divine energy. Imagine the color green flowing into your body, mind, and soul. See and sense yourself as a vital person, filled with healing energy. Imagine that you are completely healthy, happy, and feeling better than ever before. You know what makes you feel healthy and what doesn't. Imagine eating healthy, healing foods and drinking plenty of fresh water, juices, and delicious herbal teas. Imagine the green healing light of the candle completely filling you. Breathe in the color green into your body, mind, and soul.

Next, light the gold candle with the green one, again dedicating it to the healing deity or divine energy. Imagine the power of the sun and its warming golden light filling your body, mind, and soul. Breathe in the color gold, and breathe out the color gold. Fill yourself with golden healing energy. See and sense the power of the sun inside and outside of yourself. Continue to focus on the candles as you feel yourself completely revitalized with healing energy. Allow them to safely burn down.

April 10   HEALING CANDLES SPELL

You will need a ballpoint pen, jasmine incense (or jasmine oil in a diffuser if you are sensitive to incense smoke), a candle to represent yourself (select your own color), a blue candle, and a white candle.

Begin by lighting the incense, dedicating it to deity or divine energy. Next, inscribe your full name and birth date on the candle that represents you. Light the candle, merge with the powers of fire, and say:

This candle represents me and who and what I am.

Next, inscribe the blue candle with your full name and birth date. This candle symbolizes the illness, pain, or negativity being cleared out of your body. Light the blue candle with the candle that represents you, merge with the powers of fire, and say:

This candle represents my body being cleansed of all illness.

Then inscribe your name and birth date on the white candle. This candle symbolizes divine power. Light the white candle with the candle that represents you, merge with the powers of fire, and say:

This candle represents my divine spirit and its healthy, bright nature.

Now gaze at all three candles for several minutes while chanting:

Healing candles of three
Let your healing powers flow into me,
So be it! Blessed be!

Allow the incense and candles to safely burn down.

April 11 GETTING RID OF NIGHTMARES

The word *nightmare* derives from the Old Norse word *mara*, referring to a spirit that sat on the chests of sleeping people. By learning this easy-to-do lucid dreaming technique, you can permanently halt unpleasant nightmares.

You will need some lavender oil and a sprig of rosemary.

Begin by applying three drops of lavender oil to the top of your head, on the insides of both wrists, and on the bottoms of your feet. As you do this, say:

Unwanted nightmares,
I bid you farewell,
Now and forevermore!

Next, cover the rosemary sprig with nine drops of lavender oil and put it under your bed to induce sound, protected sleep. After you get into bed, stare intently at your hands for at least fifteen minutes. Focus all your attention on your hands, concentrate fully on them, and get to know their every nuance. Now close your eyes, and take a few deep breaths, still seeing the image of your hands in your mind. Chant the following:

My hands help me
My hands wake me

From bad dreams.
Blessed be!

Look intently at your hands again. Close your eyes and repeat the chant:

My hands help me
My hands wake me
From bad dreams.
Blessed be!

As you drift to sleep, cross your hands over your chest or stomach. In your mind's eye, imagine your hands protecting you. Keep imagining them until you fall asleep. If you find yourself having a bad dream, all you have to do is imagine your hands, and you will immediately wake up.

April 12   THE WELL OF HEALTH

The ancient Celts revered the healing effects of wells. Springing up from deep below the ground, they were considered to be supernatural in origin, and the Celtic people tossed coins into them as offerings to the resident spirits.

You will need three silver coins, two green candles in holders, three chamomile tea bags, three teaspoons of baking soda, a warm bath, and your favorite scented oil.

Place the three coins in a row on the edge of the tub so that they touch one another. Next, put the candles on each end of the row of coins. The candleholders need to touch the coins (this connects their energies). Now put the tea bags and baking soda in the bath. Step into the water and get comfortable. Light the candles; merge with the candle flames, the powers of fire, and as you focus of the flames and coins, say:

Divine spirit, I ask for your blessings,
So that your sacred waters will heal my body,
In exchange, please accept my offering,
So that your blessings will always be part of me.

Now put the coins into the tub one at a time. As the candles burn down, sit or lay back in the well of health, noticing how warm and silky the water feels as it flows over your skin. Allow the soft water of the healing bath to absorb all of your pain, hurt, and illness. Imagine yourself releasing your emotional, physical, and spiritual pain into the healing bath. Keep doing this until you feel a sense of relief. Finish by briskly toweling yourself off and applying your favorite scented oil to refresh your body, mind, and spirit.

April 13 FREE FROM STRESS MAGIC

Today is Thomas Jefferson's birthday. This spell can help you free yourself from the things that enslave you. Often these are the things that stress you out.

You will need a red candle, a blue candle, and a white candle.

The red candle represents your stress, the blue one symbolizes getting rid of your stress, and the white candle signifies a divine state of bliss.

Begin by lighting the red candle. As you do, imagine all of your worries and stress being burned away in the candle flame. Say:

I am now free from stress,
And any feelings of excess,
I am now free from worry
And no longer feel hurried.

Imagine your stress and worry burning away in the candle flame. Do this for a few minutes and then light the blue candle. Gaze at the candle and imagine any residue worry and stress being neutralized in its flame. Imagine being completely free of worry and stress. As you continue gazing at the blue candle, say,

> *I am completely free from stress,*
> *And any feelings of excess,*
> *I am completely free from worry*
> *And no longer feel hurried.*

Light the white candle and say,

> *I am free of stress*
> *and filled with bliss.*
> *Blessed Be!*

Continue gazing at the candles. Take several deep breaths. As they burn down, imagine your worries and stress melting down with them.

April 14   PURPLE PLACKET FOR HEALING YOUR SPIRIT

The color purple has long been associated with your spiritual or higher self. Illness and disease often begin on that spiritual level before they manifest on the physical level. This is why it's important to regularly cleanse and heal your spirit.

You will need a purple candle, a purple felt-tip pen, three bay leaves, a recent picture of yourself, two 7 by 7-inch square pieces of purple paper, and tape.

Begin by lighting the candle and dedicating it to the divine being or energy you associate with healing. Next, tape the two squares of paper together on three sides, leaving one side open, and use the purple felt-tip pen to write the word *Heal* on both sides of the placket, on both sides of the picture, and on both sides of each of the bay leaves. When the ink is dry, insert the picture and the leaves into the placket, and hold it in your hands. Charge it by saying three times:

> *Energies with the power to renew,*
> *Hear me now as I call to you.*
> *Heal my body, mind, and soul,*
> *Let your blessings make me whole.*

Finish by taping the open side of the placket so that it is completely closed. Place it in the front of the candle, and visualize healing power moving into and filling the placket. Keep it in a conspicuous place where you can regularly use it to heal your body, mind, and soul.

April 15   HERB HEALING POTION

For this potion, you will need a jar with a lid, two cups of olive oil, a teaspoon of lemon juice, a pinch of thyme, a pinch of rosemary, a pinch of sage, and a clove of finely minced garlic.

Begin by placing all of the ingredients except the oil in a sterile jar. Next pour the oil into the jar. Secure the lid and refrigerate the mixture for nine days. Once a day, starting today, shake the jar vigorously, and chant:

> *Each and every up-and-down motion,*
> *Strengthens the power of this healing potion.*

Visualize the healing properties of the herbs blending with the olive oil as you shake it. Imagine healing energy from your hands charging the potion with even more healing energy.

On the ninth day, use your potion for healing. Leave it out at room temperature until it liquifies, and then use the herb healing potion on salads, fresh and steamed vegetables, potatoes, and toasted bread. (Note: You must refrigerate your herb oil potions. Herb oils stored at room temperature will go bad and can cause botulism. All herb oil potions should be used within two weeks.)

April 16   SHINING BRIGHTLY SPELL

For this spell, you will need a white beeswax candle and a round crystal wineglass filled with sparkling cider, juice, or white wine.

Light the candle, dedicating it to a favorite god, goddess, or to the divine energy of your choice. Slowly dip the index finger of your power hand into the liquid in the glass. Move your finger clockwise along the rim of the glass to create a high-pitched tone. As you do this, gaze into the candle flame. In your mind, imagine your light shining as brightly as the candle's. After doing this for a few minutes, lift the glass up with your power hand and say:

> *Blessed flames of bright light*
> *May my light shine both day and night.*

Finish by slowly drinking the liquid, feeling the rejuvenating and illuminating qualities of the elixir move throughout your body. You can feel your light shining within and without as you allow the candle to safely burn down.

April 17   IMPROVING YOUR MEMORY

For this spell, you will need three pinches of rosemary, three pinches of rose petals, three dashes of lemon juice, three pinches of mint, three crushed bay leaves, and a cup of boiling water.

Begin by putting all the ingredients except the water into a cup. Carefully pour the boiling water over the herbs and lemon juice, and let the brew steep for a several minutes. As it steeps, stir it in a clockwise motion and focus all your attention on the potion. Say:

> *Sacred herbs empower this potion,*
> *Granting it the ability*
> *To give clarity of mind,*
> *And improved memory.*

After the potion has cooled, you can anoint your body with it, add some to your bathwater, or sprinkle it around your study area or desk. As you do this, imagine your memory becoming sharper and stronger.

April 18   HEALING CRYSTAL CIRCLE

Often energies that you encounter throughout your working day have a tendency to embed themselves in your energy field, and can sometimes be the cause of health problems. This spell will help you clear yourself of any unwanted energies. Perform it at the end of your workday at a time when you are ready to relax.

You will need your favorite crystal or gemstone.

Begin by sitting back in your favorite chair with your favorite stone cupped in your power hand. Close your eyes and imagine a clear stream of water. When the image is firmly in your mind, pulse your breath sharply out your nose, and imagine sending the image into the stone with your exhaled breath. Do this three times. Next, imagine something healing, and once again send the image into the stone by pulsing your breath out your nose. Do this three times. Now imagine that you are in a circle of healing stones. Your entire being is being bathed in a healing light that moves both inward and outward. Move through the various experiences of your day by first bringing them into focus, thinking about them for a moment or two, and then releasing them into the healing light. This healing light neutralizes these images and sends them out into the universe like fireflies that seem to float ever upward. After you have released the negative energy of your day, once again imagine yourself being bathed in the healing light. Finish by breathing deeply three times and closing the circle until the next time you need to be bathed in the healing light.

April 19   FIRED-UP MAGIC

This technique is good to use when you have been sick but are beginning to improve. It will fire you up and help you feel better faster.

You will need a blue candle in a candleholder, sandalwood oil, a ballpoint pen, and a pinch of dried sage.

Begin by using the pen to write your full name on the candle. Dress the candle with sandalwood oil, sprinkle it with dried sage, and place the candle in its holder. Next, anoint yourself with the oil, putting three drops on the top of your head, a drop on your third eye, and three drops on the insides of each wrist and ankle. Wipe the oil from your hands, light the candle, and say:

Powers of earth, wind, fire, and water,
Bring your healing energy to me,
Peace, health, love, and laughter,
By this divine light, so shall it be!

As you stare into the flame of the candle, feel the fire energizing all the aspects of your being. The element of fire can both cleanse things as well as spark life. Allow the bright candle flame to fire you up and get you ready for the day.

April 20   GREEN GODDESS HEALING SOUP

This soup, like an elixir of life, can help heal the sick and strengthen the immune system.

You will need three chopped cloves of garlic, three chopped stalks of celery, three chopped green onions, three cups of vegetable broth, three chopped carrots, three pinches of basil, three squirts of Bragg's,* and 1 table-spoon of olive oil.

Heat the oil in a large ceramic pot over medium heat. Add the chopped garlic, celery, onions, carrots, and basil. Sauté them until golden brown, and then add the vegetable broth and Braggs. Bring the mixture to a boil, then lower the heat. Stir the mixture in a clockwise direction as it simmers and chant or sing:

---

*This is a brand name for a flavoring mixture of amino acids. It is sold at many groceries and health food stores and is good in soup and stir-fries.

Healing soup, gift from the Green Goddess,
Let your healing powers be strong and true.

Cook the mixture for about an hour or until the vegetables are soft. Ladle the healing soup into a mug and slowly eat it. While enjoying it, visualize the soup's healing powers entering your body with every spoonful you eat. From your mouth, throat, and stomach, the healing nourishment moves outward to every cell, revitalizing your entire body.

April 21   BANISHING STONE

This spell will help you get rid of illnesses and unhealthy habits by putting them into a stone and banishing them from your life.

You will need a stone, a bowl of water, and three tablespoons of sea salt.

Begin by holding the stone in your power hand. See your health problems in your mind's eye. Visualize these problems moving from your being into the stone in your hand. As you do this, say:

Banishing stone,
Fill yourself with my problems,
So that I may be well again,
So be it! Blessed be!

Stirring counterclockwise, mix the three tablespoons of salt into the bowl of water; then add the banishing stone. Again working counterclockwise, swish the stone around three times. Leave the stone in the bowl of water for a few minutes; then take the stone outside, and safely throw it as far as you can away from yourself.

April 22   EARTH DAY GARDEN

The health of the earth depends on each of our contributions to the whole of nature. By planting an Earth Day Garden, you heal both the earth and yourself.

You will need a circle of earth (this can be anything from some soil in a pot to a circle of land out in your garden) and a collection of seeds and plants.

Begin by tilling the soil and adding any compost or fertilizer you might have. Next, bless the soil by getting down on the ground, placing your hands in the dirt, and saying,

> *Mother of creation*
> *Grant me your blessings*
> *So that my garden will thrive,*
> *Creating joy and love while it's alive.*

Plant your seeds or transplant your plants into your Earth Day Garden. Finish by watering your garden thoroughly. Visualize your garden becoming florescent with life. Each day visit your garden, and as you tend it, say a blessing for its continued good health and well-being as well as the continued good health and well-being of the earth, our mother.

April 23   EXPERIENCING YOUR INNER CHILD

The movie *Citizen Kane* revolves around a rich man's last words—"rosebud"— which turns out to be the name of a sled from his childhood. Your inner child is something you carry with you throughout your life, and this is a technique for getting in touch with it.

You will need a white candle and a happy childhood memory.

Begin by lighting the candle and focusing your attention on its flame. Play out in your mind the events of your happy childhood memory. Recall exactly what it was like to be a child at that time: See, feel, hear, smell, and taste the experience. Just let yourself flow with the experience, because after all it is a part of you. Your mind is like a computer that stores every experience; it's just a matter of going back and accessing the information. Take a few minutes and make an effort to remember what it was like to see things for the first time. This is what being a child is about, seeing the possibilities and boundlessness of things rather than the limitations. Take a few minutes and just look around your world, at those people you love, at the work you do, with the eyes of a child, as if you were seeing these things for the first time.

April 24   HEALING ROSE SPHERE

Rose is the color of love and of the heart chakra. Love is the most powerful energy that you will encounter in life. It has the power both to enlighten and to heal.

You will need a small rose-quartz sphere, a bowl of clean, cool water, and a little love.

Take three deep, complete breaths to center yourself. Now rinse the sphere in the water for at least a minute. Dry it; hold it in your receiving hand. Sit or recline comfortably, and hold the stone up and gaze at it. Focus all your awareness on the crystal, and imagine the rose sphere first as a rose-colored stone for a few moments. Look at its details, its coloration and shape. Continue to focus on the sphere. Now begin to imagine it as a magical rose-colored sphere that contains powerful, healing and nourishing light. Imagine the rose sphere as pure rose-colored healing light for a few minutes. Next, take a deep breath and imagine breathing in the powerful rose-colored healing light from the sphere into your body. Breathe in the healing light all the way down into your feet. Imagine the light flowing upward into your ankles. Breathe in and imagine filling your calves, knees, thighs, hips, pelvis, and buttocks, with the healing light. Feel the healing rose-colored light flow upward through your lower, middle, and upper back. Imagine the healing light flowing through your stomach and chest, over and through your shoulders, arms, elbows, wrists, hands, and out your fingertips. Imagine it filling your neck, throat, face, and head, flowing all the way through the top of your head. Now take another deep breath, and imagine the loving, healing light radiating throughout your entire body, indeed, your entire being. Know that you are one with the loving, healing light. You are love. Love is you. You are one. As you continue to breathe the light into your being, know that you are blessed with eternal and divine love. You are filled with loving, healing light, and you feel energized and revitalized. When you are done energizing yourself, be sure to put the rose sphere somewhere you can use it whenever you need to revitalize yourself with the healing light.

April 25   BLESSINGS FOR GOOD HEALTH POTION

Sometimes it is important to ask the divine for its blessings—particularly when it comes to good health. This spell does that—plus it tastes good!

You will need a half-cup of orange juice, a half-cup of papaya juice, one ripe banana, one ripe mango, and four ice cubes.

Put each of the ingredients into a blender. As you add each ingredient, empower it with the blessings of the divine by saying,

> *Oh great and mighty ones,*
> *Guardians of earth, air, fire, and water*
> *Give this potion your blessings for good health,*
> *Ayea! Blessed be!*

Now blend all the ingredients until the potion is thick and smooth, and pour it into a glass. Before drinking the potion, toast your good health, the good health of your loved ones, and the good health of the planet Earth. As you slowly sip the potion, think of all the blessings in your life such as the people who love you, your talents, and some of your favorite moments. Feel the blessings of good health and happiness flowing through you with each sip you take. Imagine these blessings nourishing each and every part of your body, mind, and soul.

April 26   ADDICTION SPELL

There may come a time in your life when you find yourself addicted to something, be it junk food, television, cigarettes, or alcohol. This spell will help you minimize and break these addictions.

You will need a white taper candle, a ballpoint pen, a sage and cedar smudge stick, and a garbage can.

Begin by using the pen and writing your addiction on the candle. For example, you might write "coffee" or "cigarettes." Then draw an X through the word. Light the smudge stick and pass the candle through the smoke for a few minutes. As you do this, say:

Smoke of cedar, cleanse me of this addiction,
Let my strength burn bright and never dim,
I no longer need [name of addiction]
I know I am healthy and bright,
Today, tomorrow, the next day, and every day
Blessed be! So be it!

When you are done smudging the candle, break it into small pieces. As you do this, imagine breaking your addiction once and for all. With each piece you break off, say:

I am no longer addicted to [name of addiction] *right now.*

Throw all the pieces in the garbage, imagining throwing away your addiction once and for all. Repeat this spell as often as you need to.

April 27   TREE POWER MAGIC

The people who created the Findhorn Garden in northern Scotland did so by consulting the spirit of each plant to find the best way to care for it. The idea of this spell is to become one with the spirit of the trees and the earth and to discover our sacred and empowering connection.

You will need a tree with which you can sit down and do this meditation, plus your imagination.

Begin by putting both of your palms on the trunk of the tree, and imagine its basic spirit. Imagine its roots growing deep within the ground, and then see its trunk and limbs, its leaves, and the tree in its entirety. As you do this, repeat over and over:

I am the tree,
The tree is me,
And together,
We live forever,
As one.

Visualize yourself connecting with the essence and spirit of the tree you are touching as well as all trees—beings who have existed considerably longer than humans on the Earth. Your roots are your ancestors, your trunk is your life's foundation, and your branches are your many aspects. Your leaves are like your thoughts, which act as receptors of light, turning it into renewed growth toward the divine source.

April 28   RED, WHITE, AND BLUE BEAUTY SPELL

You will need a ballpoint pen, a red candle, a white candle, a blue candle, a red flower (such as a rose), a white flower (such as a daisy), and a blue flower (such as a bachelor's button), a bowl of cool salt water, and a small mirror.

Rinse the candles in the salt water and dry them. Place the mirror face up in front of the candles, and put the flowers on top of its reflective surface. Next, use the pen to inscribe your full name on each of the candles, and then write the word *beautiful* on top of your name. Light the red candle first, and as you do, say:

Powers of fire, powers of red
Bring out my beauty, from toe to head.

Next, light the white candle with the red one and say:

> *Powers of fire, powers of white*
> *Bring out my beauty, day and night.*

Then light the blue candle with the white one and say:

> *Powers of fire, powers of blue*
> *Bring out my beauty with all I say and do.*

Hold the mirror with the flowers on it so you can see your reflection. As you do this, say three times:

> *Mirrored flowers of red, white, and blue*
> *Reflect my beauty in all I say and do.*

When you are done, allow the candles to safely burn down. Keep the flowers fresh in a vase of water for three days. When the blossoms are spent, put them under your favorite flower bush to encourage your inner and outer beauty to flourish and blossom.

April 29 LONG-LIFE POTION

The secrets to long life have been sought by many down though the ages. This potion is intended to help you enjoy a healthy and long life.

You will need two cups of unfiltered apple juice, a quarter-cup of cranberry juice, three teaspoons of honey, and one cinnamon stick.

Heat the apple juice, cranberry juice, honey, and cinnamon stick in a ceramic or glass pot over low heat. Warm the potion very slowly, for at least an hour. Stir the brew often, always in a clockwise motion. Each time you do, chant over and over:

Apple, berry, honey, and spice
Help me live a long, happy life.

This recipe makes two servings. You can drink the potion by yourself or share it with a friend. Pour the potion into a mug, and as you slowly sip the spicy brew, imagine yourself living a long and healthy life. Move your mind into the future. Actually imagine yourself growing older and older. Imagine yourself as an elderly, bright person, filled with energy, joy, and curiosity. Know that your mind is sharp and your body agile. Imagine the many people—young, middle-aged, and elderly—all around you. Know that you are well loved in this long life you are now living.

April 30   HEADACHE COLOR CHARM

For this charm, you will need strips of colored paper or cloth in red, orange, yellow, green, blue, indigo, and purple, and a white envelope to hold the strips in. (You can paint the colors onto white strips of paper if you like.)

Begin by closing your eyes and taking three deep breaths. Focus in on your headache pain—its intensity and location. Now imagine this pain as a red circle on your forehead (or wherever the headache pain is most intense). Open your eyes, and focus on the red strip of paper for a moment. Close your eyes again, and imagine the redness of your headache. Open your eyes, and look at the orange strip of paper. Close your eyes, and imagine the redness of your headache turning into orange. Take a deep breath and imagine breathing the color orange into your the area of your headache. Now open your eyes, and look at the yellow strip of paper. Close your eyes, and imagine the orangeness of your headache becoming yellow. Breathe the color yellow into your headache area. Next, open your eyes, and look at the green strip of paper. Close your eyes, and breathe the color yellow into your headache area. Once again, open your eyes, and this time look at the blue strip of paper. Breathe the color blue into your headache area. Open your eyes, and focus on the indigo strip of paper. Close your eyes, and breathe the color indigo into your headache area. Then open your eyes, and look at the purple strip of paper. Close your eyes, and breathe the color purple into your headache area. Finally, open your eyes, and focus on the white envelope. Close your eyes, and breathe the color white into the headache area for several minutes. Take several deep and complete breaths, and then open your eyes. Your headache pain will most likely be gone.

Keep your headache charm envelope handy, in a desk drawer or in your purse, so you can use it whenever you need to. Also, as you get more adept at this healing method, you can simply imagine the colors in your mind's eye without referring to the colored strips of paper or cloth.

$\mathscr{M}$AY

May 1   MAY DAY HEALING STONE

You will need a piece of aventurine and some morning dew. Begin by getting up in the morning and taking your piece of aventurine outside. Aventurine is a healing stone that is noted for its abilities to strengthen eyesight, increase perception, and calm emotions. Cover the stone with the dewdrops that cover the grass and low-growing flowers. The dew gathered on May Day morning has powerful healing properties. As you cover the aventurine with dewdrops, say three times:

> *Healing morning dew of grass and flowers*
> *Flow into this stone and fill it with your power*
> *Blessed be! As I will, so shall it be!*

Carry the stone with you in your pocket, in a medicine bag, or in your purse to continuously access its healing energies. Recharge the stone by regularly taking it out in the morning, covering it with dew, and repeating the spell.

May 2   A HANDFUL OF FORGIVENESS

As you grow older it is best to let go of past anger and grievances, which have a tendency to weigh you down, and which eventually can impinge upon your health. It's best not to hang onto these grievances, and to forgive certain people in your life.

You will need a white beeswax candle, a sheet of paper, and a pen.

Begin by writing down the names of five people that you have a grievance with and want to forgive. Light the candle, dedicating it to a favorite goddess or god. Set the sheet of paper in front of the candle so you can easily read the names. Now go down the list while saying the following forgiveness blessing:

> [Name of person]
> *I forgive you as I hope you will forgive me,*
> *So that we might forever live in harmony,*
> *As I will, so may it be.*

Say the blessing for each person on your list. Fold the piece of paper three times, and seal it with candle wax. Dig a small hole outdoors, and bury the paper. If any of the anger persists, perform the spell over again as many times as it takes for you to forgive the person. With some people you might find it takes a few times, but in the end it's worth it, because you're not carrying around all that negative baggage anymore.

May 3   MAY HEALING WISHES

For this spell, you will need three green candles, a sheet of paper, and a ballpoint pen. First, imagine that a fire genie has just appeared, and you have been granted three wishes for better health. Write down the wishes on the piece of paper. Place the paper in front of the candles, and refer to it as needed. Each of the three candles represents a wish, so inscribe each one with a healing wish—one wish per candle. Light the first candle, focusing your attention on the flame. Imagine your first wish coming true and say:

> *Fire genie of the light*
> *Whose power burns bright*
> *Let my healing wish become reality.*
> [State your first healing wish.]
> *One, two, three, I am healthy.*
> *So be it! Blessed be!*

Imagine the magical genie granting your healing wish. Move your mind into the future and focus all your attention on seeing and sensing your wish coming true. Light the second candle, and focus your attention on the flame, seeing your second healing wish coming true. Say:

> *Fire genie of the light,*
> *Whose power burns bright,*
> *Let my healing wish become reality.*
> [State your second healing wish.]
> *One, two, three, I am healthy.*
> *So be it! Blessed be!*

Once again, imagine the genie granting your wish. With all of your being, imagine your healing wish coming true. Next, light the third candle, and focus your attention on the flame. Imagine your third healing wish coming true. Say:

> *Fire genie of the light,*
> *Whose power burns bright,*
> *Let my healing wish become reality.*

[State your third healing wish.]
One, two, three, I am healthy.
So be it! Blessed be!

Once again, imagine the genie granting your wish. Move your mind into the future, and visualize your wish coming true. Allow the candles to safely burn down on their own. As they do so, make a few notes on the paper as to some of the steps you can take right now to move your healing wishes along in the right direction. Each step you take may seem small, and the process can be frustratingly slow, but as long as you progress in a positive direction you are moving toward a more healthy you. Tape the paper to your refrigerator and refer to it every morning and evening, imagining the healing taking place within you. Continue doing this until your healing wishes come true.

May 4 MAY BAY-LEAF HEALING BATH

Bay has a soothing quality to it, particularly when it is added to warm water. In this spell, each bay leaf represents a healing quality that you want to bring into your life.

You will need three bay leaves, a tub of warm water, and your May Day Healing Stone (see May 1).

Begin by placing the bay leaves one at a time into the tub of warm water. As you submerge each leaf in the water, imagine its healing qualities flowing into the bath. Next, with your Healing Stone in your power hand, step into the warm water, and get comfortable in the tub. Close your eyes and imagine that you are at the seashore. In front of you is an easel, on which is a blank canvas and paints. Imagine picking up the paints and painting a portrait of yourself. Paint the picture of yourself exactly how you would like to be—vibrant and healthy. As you do this, feel the healing waters in the tub all around you. Take several deep breaths, and imagine breathing in the healing power of the bathwater. When you are done, towel off, and put the stone in a safe place to use again.

May 5   BLESSING YOUR FOOD

This technique was first taught to me by my dear friend Marcel Vogel, who always believed that food should be blessed before you eat it so that it would be filled with divine energy. This blessing will give your food more vitality. Obviously, the health benefits of wholesome food far outweigh those of junk food, so keep in mind this blessing can only enhance what is already there.

Perform this blessing over food you are about to eat.

Begin by placing your hands, palms down, over the food. Imagine a bright, white light moving from your hands into your food. This light is one of health, vitality, divinity. It is the white light of Goddess and God. Move the energy into the food, energizing and blessing it. Finish by giving your thanks for the food by saying:

> *Dear Goddess and God,*
> *Bless this food you have provided me,*
> *Thank you for your divine gift*
> *In the name of the Lady and the Lord*
> *Blessed be!*

Now eat your food, feeling its vitality filling your body with each bite. Imagine each bite helping you feel stronger and healthier.

May 6   FLOWER PRAYER

Flowers are one of the wonders of creation that can be enjoyed by everyone, young and old. They can provide the highlight for a great painting, photograph, or beautiful room. Their fragrance can delight the senses in ways that perfumes can only attempt to replicate.

You will need some flowers; these flowers can be in a garden, a pot, or they can be cut flowers.

Begin by sitting in front of the flowers. Notice their color, shape, texture, and fragrance. Next, imagine yourself going a step beyond, and move into the essence of the flowers. As you do this, recite the following prayer:

> *Blessed Mother of Creation,*
> *Whose light shines like the sun,*
> *I pray for a gentler, kinder, sweeter life,*
> *Where we all learn to live as One,*
> *In communion with the flowers and the trees,*
> *By the Lady, forever may it be!"*

May 7   MAY DANCE MAGIC

Shamans often use music and dance to facilitate healing and journeying. Music and dancing can create an altered state of consciousness, a state that is very conducive to magic.

You will need a favorite up-tempo song and an area in which to dance in. Begin by turning on the music. Dance in time to the music in a clockwise circle. Feel yourself being energized by the music. As you dance, begin chanting:

> *I am healthy and bright,*
> *Filled with a magical light.*

Chant and dance around the circle several times. When you feel strong and energized, step into the center of the circle you have been dancing around and shout:

> *Ayea, Ayea, Ayea!*

Imagine all the chanting, music, and dancing energy filling you completely with healing energy. For a few minutes, allow the music move you to a place where you merge with the divine, giving you a feeling of elation and pure bliss.

May 8   ROSEMARY-HONEY HEALING TEA

Rosemary traditionally has been used as a healing remedy for colds, indigestion, or fatigue. This tea is particularly useful at times when you are feeling depleted or depressed.

You will need three tablespoons of fresh rosemary, a strainer, honey, two cups, and boiling water.

Begin steeping the rosemary in a cup of boiling water for fifteen minutes. Next, strain the rosemary out by pouring the liquid through a strainer into another cup. Add honey to sweeten the tea. Allow it to cool a bit, then hold the cup of tea in your hands and empower it by saying:

May the essence of honey and rosemary
Impart their healing powers into me
So that I might feel strong and healthy
With the blessings of nature, so shall it be!

Now sip the tea slowly, imagining the healing powers moving into your body.

May 9 GOOD-HEALTH AFFIRMATION

Studies by Dr. Larry Dossey show that people who think they are unhealthy are seven times more likely to get sick and die than people who think they are healthy. This shows how powerful your mind is, and how crucial it is to believe in your own good health.

You will need a white candle and holder, a ballpoint pen, and rose oil.

Begin by inscribing the candle with your full name. Inscribe the words *good health* on top of your name. Next rub the rose oil on the candle and place it in its holder. Anoint yourself with the rose oil, and then wipe the oil from your hands. As you light the candle, say:

Each and every day, I am strong and healthy in every way.

Merge with the candle flame and continue repeating aloud:

Each and every day, I am strong and healthy in every way.

Imagine yourself as being in excellent health, feeling strong and happy. Imagine vitality and vibrancy filling and radiating from your entire being.

May 10 ORGANIC HEALING POTION

Because of the extensive use of pesticides and chemicals in food, it is a good idea to cleanse the toxins from your system at regular intervals. This organic healing potion is the perfect way to do this.

You will need one stalk of organic celery, two organic carrots, three peeled organic potatoes, four cups of spring water, and a sprig of fresh organic thyme.

Begin by chopping the celery, carrots, and potatoes and putting them in a ceramic pot with the spring water and the thyme. Let the mixture cook on the stove for twenty to thirty minutes. While it's cooking, occasionally go over and give the potion your blessings by saying:

> *Mother Goddess, bless this food*
> *With your divine healing power.*

Let the potion cool, then puree it in a blender. Sip it while feeling its healing vitality filling you.

May 11 BROWN GROUNDING SPELL

The color brown signifies grounding. This technique brings you back into balance and grounds you.

You will need a brown candle, some seeds, and a flowerpot filled with fresh, clean earth.

Begin by lighting the candle, dedicating it to a favorite divine presence by saying:

Loving and divine one,
I light this candle for you.

Cup some earth in your hands and become one with it by saying:

Elemental powers of earth,
I am one with you
I am balanced and grounded
So be it! Blessed be!

Take a moment to notice the way the soil feels in your hands; its tactile properties, its energy, and scent. Put the earth back in the pot, plant the seeds in the soil, and grow something wonderful.

May 12   GOOD HEALTH BINDING

When you bind yourself to something, you connect your energy to it.

You will need a green candle, a three-foot piece of green string, and three nine-inch-long sticks.

Begin by lighting the candle and dedicating it to a favorite healing Goddess or God. Take the three sticks and begin tying them into a bundle with the green string. As you do this, say:

These three sticks represent myself,
The green string is good health,
I bind my body, mind, and soul with this healing energy,
As I will, so shall it be! Blessed be!

Once you have wrapped all of the string down the length of the bundle of sticks, tie a knot so that the binding is taut. After the candle has burned all the way down, take a little of the warm wax and rub it into the bundle of sticks. Place the bundle somewhere safe as a physical reminder of your metaphysical binding to the forces of good health.

May 13 BALANCING YOUR FIRST CHAKRA

Your chakras are energetic systems within your being that need to be regularly balanced for you to stay healthy. Your first root (or chakra) symbolizes survival and matters of trust; it is represented in your body by the bones, the base of the spine, and the digestive system. Many lower-back problems stem from the first chakra.

You will need a red candle and an onyx or hematite stone.

Begin by lighting the candle. Invoke a divine being of your choice by saying:

> *Oh! Giver of life!*
> *Let your healing powers*
> *Envelope my being.*

Place the stone on the base of your spine. Become one with the stone; imagine its healing properties moving into your root chakra. Visualize the color red in that spot. Breathe the color red into and out of your chakra. Now say:

> *Give me strength,*
> *Give me healing,*
> *Wipe the slate clean,*
> *So I can live my dream.*

Imagine becoming strong and filled with vigor. Feel the healing energy becoming present in your lower back and then moving outward in spirals. Visualize your first chakra in complete balance.

May 14   BREAD BLESSING

Bread has long been thought to have the power to sustain life. I have used the "bread cure" with my pet companions, and they now demand their daily bread, as they equate it with being strong and healthy (plus they like the tasty treat!).

You will need three cups of flour, one cup of milk, one teaspoon of olive oil, three teaspoons of sugar, a package of dry active yeast, and a bowl.

Blend all the ingredients together into the bowl, blessing each as you add it by saying:

> *Dear Lady, bless this flour,*
> *Dear Lady, bless this milk,*
> *Dear Lady, bless this olive oil,*
> *Dear Lady, bless this sugar,*
> *Dear Lady, bless this yeast.*

Mix all the ingredients with a spoon until they form a ball that you can work with your hands. Add more flour if its too wet, and add milk if it is too dry. Knead the ball until it resembles clay. As you knead it, say:

> *Dear Lady, bless this bread.*

Next, put the dough into a baking dish and put it in a warm place to rise. Once the dough has risen to two or three times its size, put it in an oven preheated to 350°F. Bake it for forty-five to fifty minutes. Before you eat the bread, say:

> *Wheat from the earth,*
> *Milk from the Mother,*
> *Together with the living power of yeast,*
> *They bring to me this healthy feast.*
> *By earth, air, fire, and water, blessed be!*

The most important thing to remember when making bread is that the yeast is a living entity. As such, it must be fed and given an environment that is conducive to its well-being. It feeds on sugar and it likes an environment that is warm (around 80°F.).

May 15   HEALING HANDS

Your body has an energy field around it that is directly connected to your physical body. This technique uses your hands to balance that field and help soothe parts of your body that hurt, such as your stomach or knee.

You will need your May Day Healing Stone (see May 1).

Begin by taking your piece of aventurine in your hand, lying down, and getting comfortable. Breath in deeply, and slowly exhale, feeling all the tension in your body being released. Next, put the piece of aventurine on the area of your body that you want to heal. Feel the energy of the stone begin to interact with the energy of your body. Focus on that area; place your power hand on top of the stone, and begin slowly soothing it by moving your hand and the stone in clockwise circles while chanting:

Healing hand,
Healing stone
I feel your energy,
Heal my body.

Move the tips of your fingers lightly along the contours of your skin in the area of your body where you are working. Imagine healing energy shooting out from your fingertips, charging the area with healing energy. Feel the energy soothing the place you want healed. Finish by taking three deep breaths, and as you exhale the last one, imagine the healing energy that emanates from your hands moving outward, balancing the energy field around your entire body.

May 16   MAGICAL HOUSE CLEANING

Brooms (or *besoms*) can be used for astral traveling as well as for sweeping away unwanted energy and dirt in the house. (Refer to my book *The Witch and Wizard Training Guide* for complete instructions on making your own besom.)

You will need a cedar and sage smudge stick, a fireproof bowl, and a broom (a traditional straw one is the best).

Begin by lighting the smudge stick and blowing on it so the smoke fills the space. Use the bowl to catch any hot ashes. As you do this, say:

All evil and foulness be banished,
By the will of Oneness,
So be it! Ayea!

Repeat the procedure in the other rooms in your home you want to cleanse until the whole house is cleaned. Take the broom and move through your home, making sweeping motions. This sweeps any remaining unwanted energy out. Say:

> *With this broom*
> *I sweep all unwanted energy*
> *From this room.*

Imagine a white light filling your home and radiating from every room. Say:

> *Dear God and Goddess, bless my home*
> *Fill it with divine love and light*
> *With happiness and joy*
> *Now and forevermore*
> *So be it! Blessed be!*

May 17 BALANCING YOUR SECOND CHAKRA

Located at the womb or genitals, the second chakra has to do with sexuality, emotions, and creativity. When you balance this chakra, you begin to perceive the connection between sex and creation. Your second chakra has to do with a creative drive that is the essence of success and failure. Although they appear separate, they are merely different polarities of the same thing, of Oneness. All the diverse aspects of the universe integrate together to form the weave of Oneness, which by all definitions is the all-knowing, all-being divine.

You will need an orange candle, sensuous music, and a stone such as red jasper, bloodstone, fluorite, or cat's eye.

Begin by lighting the candle and dedicating it to the divine energy of sensuality and creation. Put on some music that lends itself to the mood. Hold the stone in your power hand, place it on your second chakra, and say:

> *You are the force that runs between flower and seed,*
> *You are the energy that fulfills my every need,*
> *I am you and you are me, and we are all together,*
> *We are part of that divine that lives forever;*
> *Ayea! We are one! Ayea! Ayea! Ayea!*

As you stare into the flame of the candle, imagine all of your sexual and creative forces coming into together into a strong and powerful current, like a river. You can move this energy toward any creative projects you might have, such as sewing a dress, writing a poem, or starting a new business.

May 18　　　　SUNSHINE HEALING POTION

The sun gives its energy to every growing thing, particularly the vegetables and fruits that flourish in the spring and summer months. This potion uses the sun's healing vitality. When you drink the potion made from these ingredients, it will fill you with the sun's healing energy.

You will need a banana, a mango, a pear, a cup of spring water, and one teaspoon of vanilla extract.

Begin by peeling the banana, mango, and pear, and then seeding the mango and pear. Put all the ingredients in a blender. As you blend everything together, say:

Thank you, bright sun for these gifts,
That you grew with your nurturing rays,
I now make this sunshine healing potion,
So that I may feel the healing warmth of your ways.

Pour the mixture into a glass. You can strain out some of the pulp to make it less thick, but remember that the pulp is a natural source of fiber and is healthy for you. Before you drink the potion, make a toast to the sun, saying:

Oh great sun,
Thank you for this potion,
Which I am about to drink.

Sip the potion slowly, imagining its healing sunshine power filling your body and bringing you good health.

May 19   HEALING PRAYER FOR THE EARTH

The earth is being assaulted by the destruction of our public and private forests, the pollution of our air, global warming, and the decimation of our streams, rivers, and oceans. The only way we are going to overcome this assault is by making our own space more in tune with nature. We can all make a dramatic difference with our own gardens. The transformation can be dazzling and delicious!

You will need a large, living tree and a lot of magic.

Begin by walking clockwise around the tree three times. Stop and place both palms on the tree's trunk; tune into the tree by breathing in deeply.

Imagine moving your awareness into the trunk, limbs, and leaves of the trees for a few moments; then breathe out. Do this several times until you have a feeling for the tree's essence. Now say:

> *Dear God and Goddess, Great Father and Mother,*
> *You who are the givers and creators of all life,*
> *I send to you all the love in my heart and soul*
> *I pray you grant me the strength of this tree*
> *Please God and Goddess, grant me its wisdom and beauty*
> *By the Lord and Lady, blessed be!*

Feel your energy merge with that of the tree. At the moment that this happens, say "thank you" to the God and Goddess and to the tree. As you do, imagine a kinder and more loving world, one where the earth is vibrant and pollution is no longer a threat. Each of us can help change the future for the better. Your intention and what you do with it is the key.

May 20   BALANCING YOUR THIRD CHAKRA

The third chakra is located in the upper part of your stomach (your solar plexus), just under your rib cage. It is the source of your power and your will to move forward and achieve great things; however, it can also trap you in a loop where you are constantly trying to control and manipulate the people around you, driving you and them crazy. Your third chakra has to do with eating disorders, ulcers, and digestive problems. By balancing your third chakra, you lessen your chances of having problems in this area.

You will need a yellow candle and a stone such as gold calcite, carnelian, or gold citrine.

Put the candle in a place where you can sit comfortably in front of it. Light the candle and dedicate it to the divine. Using your power hand, place the stone on your third chakra. Merge with the candle flame and say:

> *You who are sacred and divine,*
> *I seek the power that is mine,*
> *Give to me my birthright,*
> *So that I might shine bright,*
> *Ayea! Ayea! Ayea!*

Become aware of the stone on your third chakra. Feel its pulsating energy flow into you, empowering and soothing your stomach. Do this for several minutes to fill the area with healing energy.

May 21   CREATING A HEALING CIRCLE

For this spell, you will need a bowl of earth, sandalwood incense, a white candle, a cup of water, and a clear quartz crystal (preferably a crystal point).

Set all of the items on your altar or another steady surface. Light the candle and incense, dedicating them to your favorite healing deities. Take the crystal in your power hand; use it as an athame to draw your magic circle in a clockwise motion. After setting the crystal back on the table, pick up the bowl of earth. Hold it upward at the north point of the magic circle and say:

> *Goddess of the North*
> *Let your healing powers*

Come into this circle.
By the Lady, blessed be!

Put the earth back on the table; hold the incense in your power hand at the east point of the circle and say:

Goddess of the East
Let your healing powers
Come into this circle.
By the Lady, blessed be!

Put the incense back on the table; carefully pick up the lit candle. Hold it at the south point of the circle and say:

Goddess of the South
Let your healing powers
Come into this circle.
By the Lady, blessed be!

Put the candle back on the table; pick up the cup of water. Hold the cup at the west point of the circle, and say:

Goddess of the West
Let your healing powers
Come into this circle.
By the Lady, blessed be!

Your healing circle is now energized and ready. Sit or recline in it for about thirty minutes. As you do, merge with each of the elements of earth, air, fire, and water, and ask them what you can do to heal yourself completely.

Make a note of the impressions you receive, and use any helpful information to facilitate your healing. When you are done, close the circle.

May 22   SACRED CIRCLE HEALING

To use a sacred circle for healing, you create a magical space set up for that specific intention. You ask the divine to be part of your healing circle.

Begin by casting a sacred circle as outlined on May 21. Once the circle is cast, think of a health problem you have that you want to heal. Chant over and over again the name of a deity or divine energy with which you connect spiritually. As you do this, imagine bright, royal-blue light washing away the unwanted illness. Do this for five minutes. Next, imagine bright, kelly-green light filling you completely, growing new and healthy patterns in your body. Do this for five minutes. Then, imagine bright, golden light filling your body, recharging it with sunshine. Continue chanting the name of the divine energy over and over again until the energy in the circle rises to a level of intensity that fills you full of light and love. At this point, throw your hands upward to the sky and shout with jubilation:

Ayea, Ayea, Ayea!

With the last *Ayea,* leave your arms up in the air, reaching out and connecting with the divine. Allow the divine energy to fill you completely. Finish your sacred circle healing by saying:

Dear Goddess and God, I pray you,
Let your healing light flow through me,
By the Lord and Lady, blessed be!

When you are finished soaking up the divine healing energies of the sacred healing circle, close it.

May 23   TEMPLE OF HEALTH

The Temple of Health is a place you invoke within yourself where the healing energies of the divine converge into a vortex. When you go there in your mind's eye, you become a conduit, transmitting the healing energy into an ailing part of your body or to someone else who is in discomfort.

You will need an imaginary golden chariot and an imaginary offering to the divine.

Begin by sitting back in a comfortable chair. Breathe deeply several times to relax and center yourself. Close your eyes and imagine yourself getting into a golden chariot drawn by three white mares. The chariot takes you to a place where you are surrounded by a lavender light that starts at a point above you and spirals down, forming a cone around you. The cone of light transforms into a beautiful healing temple. Within the temple is an altar. You move toward it, and with reverence, place your imaginary offering on it. The divine accepts your offering, and the healing light surrounding you begins moving into your being. Suddenly whatever you touch or direct your mind toward is filled with healing light. Imagine directing this energy into the area in your body that needs healing, or send this healing energy to someone else. Thank the divine for the healing light. Step back into your chariot and return to the present moment. Open your eyes, and take a couple of deep breaths as you stretch your arms and body. Remember that you can return to the Temple of Health whenever you like.

May 24   BALANCING YOUR FOURTH CHAKRA

Your fourth chakra (the heart chakra) can be a problem area for many of us as it deals with such aspects as feelings of love, empathy, and compassion. It is where you feel your emotions. It is represented in the body by the heart and lungs. When you use this technique, concentrate your energy in those areas.

You will need a green candle and a piece of rose quartz.

Begin by holding the stone in your power hand. Imagine the stone being completely cleared of all unwanted energy as you breathe in, and then pulse your breath out your nose. After clearing the stone, charge it by imagining something or someone you associate with love, and use your breath to pulse the image into the stone.

Light the candle, dedicating it to a favorite healing goddess or god. Put the rose quartz in your power hand, and hold it on your heart chakra, right over your heart. Feel the stone energizing the entire area and filling it with a bright rose-colored light. Breathe the color rose into the area, and breathe out any unwanted energies. Starting at your fourth chakra, the rose colored light moves outward throughout your body, until you feel yourself floating on a cloud of ecstatic happiness and pure joy. Once you feel yourself filled with feelings of love and joy, say:

> *Spirit of Love,*
> *I feel your blessings,*
> *Fill me with compassion and empathy,*
> *For myself and others around me.*

Now, imagine that loving and healing energy continuing to fill your heart and lungs. As the candle burns down, go through all the people in your life, and let go of any ill feelings you have toward them. Forgive them by simply saying:

I forgive [name of person].

Replace your negative feelings with feelings of empathy and compassion. Then bless and send love to the people in your life that are important to you. Continue to do this for several minutes.

May 25   CONNECTING WITH YOUR FAMILY

Science purports that the webs that spiders weave are actually held together by an electromagnetic force. This force is akin to the power that binds the universe together. Energies are either attracted to or repelled by one another.

You will need a white candle, a green candle, a purple or lavender candle, and a spider's web.

Begin by finding a spider's web and spending some time examining and becoming aware of the many ways it interconnects. Each strand is a link in the whole web. When something touches any part of the web, the spider is immediately aware of it. This represents your connection with yourself, your family, and the divine.

Light each candle in succession: The white candle represents yourself as a spirit free of color and conditioning; the green candle represents your family and friends that provide an environment that is conducive to growth; and the lavender candle represents the divine spirit that is always present in many forms. The divine spirit is the electromagnetic glue that connects everything together.

Imagine the flames of the three candles becoming one, burning like a giant sun whose flaming webs connect you with your family and the whole of the divine. What was once separated becomes one, and at that point say:

From infinity,
Came Oneness,
And from the One,
Came the many,
And now we are part,
Of the eternal family.
Ayea! So be it!

May 26   IT'S A WONDERFUL LIFE

In the Frank Capra movie *It's a Wonderful Life*, George Bailey, played by actor Jimmy Stewart, encounters a number of woes in his life and receives divine intervention, which comes in the form of an angel named Clarence.

You will need one red candle, one purple candle, one white candle, a ballpoint pen, and lavender oil. In this technique, the red candle represents your old self, the purple candle symbolizes the divine, and the white candle is your new self.

Begin by writing *old self* on the red candle; on the purple candle, write your name or a symbol for the divine; and on the white candle, write *new self*. Apply lavender oil to all of the candles, and then anoint yourself with the oil. Wipe the oil from your hands. Light the red candle and say:

Blessed be,
The self I used to be.

Next, light the purple candle and say:

> *Blessed be,*
> *Mother of eternity.*

Light the white candle and say:

> *Blessed be,*
> *The self that is now me.*

As the three candles burn, merge with the power of the flame, and say:

> *It's a wonderful life with each new day,*
> *I love myself and the world around me in every way,*
> *Ayea!*

May 27   LONG-DISTANCE HEALING

Space and distance do not pose a problem in this type of healing, as it is done with psychic energy. Healing energy moves beyond the time/space continuum. This means you can effectively do a healing for someone anywhere on the planet.

You will need a photograph of the person to be healed.

Create a healing circle as outlined on May 21. Place the photograph on the surface in front of you. Feel yourself become one with the person. This connects you with the person before you start the healing. Next, select a set of three divine energies. Make an effort to use deities who match the person receiving the healing. Start chanting the names of the divine beings you have selected in series of three. Using Anu, Odin, and Isis as an example, the sequence would go as follows:

Anu, Anu, Anu,
Odin, Odin, Odin,
Isis, Isis, Isis,
Anu, Anu, Anu,
Odin, Odin, Odin,
Isis, Isis, Isis,
Anu, Anu, Anu,
Odin, Odin, Odin,
Isis, Isis, Isis,
Ayea, Ayea, Ayea.

When chanting, start out slowly and begin building both in volume and cadence. When you say "Ayea" three times at the end, bring the healing energy together, and as you say the last "Ayea," throw your arms up to the sky, and imagine the healing energy that you have built up moving outward from the healing circle and directly to the person who needs the healing.

May 28   HOLLYHOCK CHARM

The word *hollyhock* means "holy mallow." Hollyhocks taste like mild green onions and were originally cultivated in Europe for their nutritional and medicinal value. They are particularly known to be helpful for ailments of the stomach.

You will need a blue candle, a clean, pesticide-free white hollyhock blossom, and a green cloth pouch.

Begin by lighting the blue candle, dedicating it to a favorite healing goddess. Say:

All negativity and ill energy,
Be cleaned from all parts of my body,
So be it! Blessed be!

Next, pull three petals from the hollyhock blossom with your power hand, hold them up, and say:

I am one with the healing power of this flower.

Now eat the petals slowly and imagine the healing power flowing into your body. Put the hollyhock blossom into the pouch and say:

With this hollyhock blossom as a sign
May this healing charm be divine,
So be it! Blessed be!

Tie or sew the pouch up so the hollyhock remains inside. Now empower your healing charm by saying:

Oh great and mighty ones that be
Guardians of earth, air, fire, and sea
May your divine healing power fill this charm
And keep us healthy and free from harm
So be it! Blessed be!

Place the charm just outside your front door to keep those inside your home healthy and free from harm.

May 29   PROTECTION TALISMAN

One of the basic ways to stay healthy is to prevent illness in the first place. This technique involves making a talisman that will help ward away disease.

You will need a green candle, a red candle, and a clear quartz crystal.

Begin by holding the crystal in your power hand. Imagine the running water of a clear mountain stream. Once the image is in your mind's eye, then take a deep breath and pulse your breath out through your nose, imagining sending the clear mountain stream into the crystal. Now light the green candle, dedicating it to the Goddess, and the red candle, dedicating it to the God. Put the crystal between and in front of the two candles so that they all form a triangle. Now gaze intently into the crystal, becoming aware of all of its aspects. Imagine healing light moving into the crystal and becoming part of the latticework of the stone. The stronger your imagination is, the more powerful the talisman will be. Once you feel the image has become fixed in the crystal, say:

> *Oh great and mighty ones,*
> *Guardians of well-being and health*
> *Please fill this talisman with your divine power,*
> *So that it wards away disease and prevents illness*
> *So be it! Blessed be!*

Allow both candles to safely burn down. Put the crystal in a small pouch or medicine bag, and carry it in your pocket or purse or wear it around your neck.

May 30   BALANCING YOUR FIFTH CHAKRA

The fifth or throat chakra influences communication, self-expression, and problem-solving. The physical problems that can arise from an imbalance in this chakra include problems in the mouth and throat, and stiffness in the neck and shoulder areas. When using this technique, concentrate your energy on these areas.

You will need a blue candle and a piece of sodalite or lapis lazuli.

Begin by lighting the candle and dedicating it to your favorite deity. Hold the stone in your power hand and put it on your fifth chakra. Breathe deeply a few times. As you do this, imagine a bright, royal-blue light moving in and out through your throat chakra with each breath. Imagine all the negativity dissolving from your being. As a result, you will feel vibrant and healthy. Feel the stone pulsating with a healing energy that awakens your creative expression. Your creative spirit soars freely. Up above everything, you gain a perspective that you have needed, but haven't explored before. Now say:

> *Muse, be with me,*
> *From here to eternity.*

You will begin to feel a balance in your throat area. Experience a warm, glowing feeling that begins in your throat, and within moments, moves outward throughout your entire being.

May 31   GOOD HEALTH BLESSING

Unfiltered apple juice is a natural healing potion, and is particularly helpful in getting rid of kidney stones and toxins in your body. Cinnamon was once used by Hebrew priests to anoint their places of worship. Medicinally it was used as a tonic to boost the immune system.

You will need a green candle, a glass of organic unfiltered apple juice, and a pinch of cinnamon.

Begin by lighting the candle and dedicating it to a goddess or god of good health by saying:

Dear Goddess of good health,
This candle I dedicate to you.

Now set the glass of apple juice in front of the candle. As you sprinkle the cinnamon into the juice, say:

Dear Goddess of good health,
I ask for your blessings.

Drink the apple juice, savoring each sip as a gift from the Goddess of good health. After all the juice is gone from your glass, hold it up high and say:

Dear Goddess of good health,
Thank you for your blessings,
On this lovely spring day in May
Ayea!

$\mathcal{J}$UNE

June 1   BALANCING YOUR SIXTH CHAKRA

The sixth chakra, located in your forehead just above your eyebrows, is referred to as your third eye because it houses your psychic abilities, which include telepathy, divination, and clairvoyance. Balancing this chakra enables you to better see the subtle nature of your life, and to distinguish between healthy and unhealthy patterns.

You will need a purple candle and a piece of amethyst or moonstone that has been cleared of any unwanted energy.

Begin by lighting the candle and dedicating it to the divine. Place the stone on your third eye, and begin breathing slowly and rhythmically while staring deeply into the flame of the candle. Sense your psychic awareness growing with each breath. Become aware of every part of your physical body and see how it connects with your spiritual being. Feel them become one and say:

> *I am One with my total being,*
> *Continually expanding my understanding,*
> *Of myself,*
> *And the world around me.*

Place the stone in front of the candle, and let the candle burn all the way down. Afterward, use the stone as a reminder of your psychic ability, placing it on your third eye anytime you want to balance it.

June 2   HANDS-ON HEALING

You can do anything you want to if you put your mind to it. When you use hands-on healing, your hands act as a conduit for divine energy. This technique uses the sixth chakra (the third eye) to visualize the healing. You psychically see the diseased tissue, illness, or discomfort being healed and revitalized.

First tap your third eye (your forehead between your eyebrows) with the index finger of your power hand nine times in three series of three. Then hold your hands about a quarter to a half inch above the problem area, and move them slowly back and forth. Take a deep breath, and as you exhale, feel the energy in this area being activated. Breathe in again, and visualize blue light moving into the problem area and clearing out its unhealthy patterns. If the area is inflamed, then in your mind's eye see the area being cooled off and washed clean by the blue light. Next, lay your hands directly on the skin of the problem area. Sometimes this may not be possible if there is pain when the area is touched. In this case, keep your hands just above the area. Say:

> *The healing light flows through my hands,*
> *Into this place that needs to be healed,*
> *Making it well again.*

Focus all of your attention on the problem area and visualize an immense flow of healing energy in the form of bright blue light moving from your hands into the area. Often your hands will really heat up, and you actually can feel or see the energy moving out of your hands. While laying your healing heads on the area, chant:

Hands help me, hands heal me.

After the last time you do the chant, say:

Ayea!

Keep your hands on or above the area, and feel the healing energy flowing into and through it. Imagine the area feeling better and better. Do this for at least fifteen minutes. You can repeat this technique as often as needed.

June 3   SENDING FLOWER FAERIES

You will need a pot of flowers, or better yet, use the flowers growing in your garden or yard.

Select someone or some situation that you would like to send healing and loving flower faery energy to. Then, sit or stand comfortably, and focus all of your attention on the flowers in front of you. Look at them in a new way. See every nuance of the petals and stems. Take a deep and complete breath, and smell their fragrance. Feel the texture of the flowers with your fingers. Softly brush your face with their velvety petals. Commune with the flowers and listen to any messages of nature they may convey to you. Imagine the flower faeries, the divine spirits that inhabit the flowers and help keep them healthy. These faery spirits may be small winged beings; tiny white, pink, gold, lavender, blue, or green spheres or dots of light; or they may look like gigantic divine beings that seem to flow from the flowers themselves. You may actually see the faeries, or you may sense them in another way. Just keep focusing on the faeries for a few minutes.

Now imagine the person or situation you want to send the divine flower faery energy to. Once you get that image in your mind's eye, ask the flower faeries to fly to that person or situation. Ask them to fill that person or situation with all of their divine healing energy. Take a deep and complete breath, and as you exhale, actually imagine them all flying to and filling the person or situation with divine healing light and love. Keep using your breath to move more and more healing flower faeries to the person or situation. Do this for at least five minutes. You may feel light-headed or a bit dizzy. This is a natural response when working with the faery energy. Just keep focusing on the flower faeries and sending them to the person or situation. (Note: Do this technique just before calling or seeing someone you are having problems with, for example your boss or a friend, to set a more positive healing atmosphere for communication.)

June 4   POTION FOR RELIEVING STRESS

Lavender contains a substance called linalool, which has been shown to slow nerve impulses. Because of this lavender eases tension and even helps muscle spasms. This is great potion to drink when you finish work, just before going to bed, or anytime to relieve stress. Relieving stress is a key component in staying healthy longer.

You will need a teaspoon of lavender herbs and a cup of boiling water.

Put the lavender herbs in the cup of boiling water. As you do this, say:

> *Water of life and fragrant lavender so sweet*
> *Empower this potion with your healing power.*
> *As I will, so shall it be!*

Let the potion steep for fifteen minutes. Strain out the herbs, and sip the mixture slowly. As you sip the potion, imagine all the stress being washed from your body by the fragrant, healing lavender water.

June 5   HEALING THE EARTH

For this spell, you will need a stone, a feather, a tealight, and a cup of water.

Begin by gathering together the items needed, and then take everything outdoors—somewhere you won't be disturbed and where you won't disturb others, such as your backyard, garden, high-rise rooftop, or your apartment balcony. Perform this magical work as close to dawn as possible. First, face north and hold the stone in your hands. Feel its shape and texture. Smell the stone, and brush it softly against your face. Merge with the stone, with the earth element. Imagine becoming one with the land, the trees, plants, and stones. Do this for a minute or so, and then say:

> *Healing powers of the north*
> *I ask that you now come forth*
> *Earth grow, wind blow*
> *Fire warm, water flow*
> *Natural rhythms that be*

Help us heal our planet
So shall it be!

Next, pick up the feather. Face east, and brush the feather over your face. Wave it in the air to and fro, as if it were a bird. Take a deep breath in and out, and feel the air in your lungs. Merge with the air element, with the air you breathe, with the breeze and wind. Do this for a minute or so, and then say:

> *Healing powers of the east*
> *I ask that you now come forth*
> *Earth grow, wind blow*
> *Fire warm, water flow*
> *Natural rhythms that be*
> *Help us heal our planet*
> *So shall it be!*

Pick up the tealight. Face south, and light the candle. Set it down where it can burn safely. Make certain it is safe! Then merge with the fire element, focusing your attention on the candle flame. Do this for a minute or so, and then say,

> *Healing powers of the south*
> *I ask that you now come forth*
> *Earth grow, wind blow*
> *Fire warm, water flow*
> *Natural rhythms that be*
> *Help us heal our planet*
> *So shall it be!*

Next, pick up the cup of water, and face west. Take three sips. Feel the water flowing into your mouth, down your throat, and into your body. Dip your fingers in the water, and feel its cool wetness. Smell the water. Merge with the water element for a minute or so, and then say:

> *Healing powers of the west*
> *I ask that you now come forth*
> *Earth grow, wind blow*
> *Fire warm, water flow*
> *Natural rhythms that be*
> *Help us heal our planet*
> *So shall it be!*

Now face north once again, and say,

> *By the divine powers of the universe*
> *Blessed be! So be it!*

June 6   SWEET AND SOUR FOOT BATH

Apple cider vinegar contains more than thirty nutrients, a dozen minerals, and essential acids and enzymes. It has been used in preventative medicine for sore throats and colds, as a digestive aid, as an arthritis tonic, and as a skin enhancer. Aloe vera gel is also a potent healing substance.

You will need a foot bath or basin of warm water, a soft towel, a half-cup of apple cider vinegar, vanilla extract, and a half-cup of aloe vera gel.

Add the vinegar to the foot bath. Soak your feet for about 15 minutes, chanting over and over:

Heal my feet, heal my soul.

Remove your feet from the foot bath, and dry them with the towel. Add three drops of vanilla to the aloe vera gel, and apply one half of the sweet-smelling mixture to each foot, slowly rubbing it in. As you do so, chant:

Every minute, every hour
I am filled with healing power.

Your feet will feel refreshed, more flexible, and ready to take a relaxing walk.

June 7 BALANCING YOUR SEVENTH CHAKRA

Located at the top of your head and referred to as your crown chakra, your seventh chakra is your connection to your spiritual self and your overall connection to the divine. This is also the area where your soul enters and leaves your physical body. By balancing this chakra, you can positively influence your entire being—physical, mental, and spiritual.

You will need a white candle and a piece of clear or rutilated quartz that has been cleared of any unwanted energy.

Begin by lighting the candle and dedicating it to the goddess or god of your choice by saying:

Oh great and divine one,
Let your light flow through me
So be it! Blessed be!

Next, hold the crystal in your power hand and place it on the top of your head. Take a deep breath in and out, and imagine lots of white light moving in and out of your seventh chakra. Feel the power of the divine energy pulsating through your chakra and then into your entire body. Feel your immortal spirit as it meets your mortal self, and see how the two interact and affect the whole of who you are. Feel the energy of the stone circulating throughout your being and say,

> *I feel your divine healing power,*
> *Pulsating throughout my being in harmony.*

Continue to breathe the white light in and out of the top of your head, and imagine your seventh chakra completely balanced and in harmony with the universe.

June 8   FRIENDSHIP CHARM

Sharing, caring, and friendship are vital parts of a healthy living experience. This charm can be used to bring more of those qualities into your daily life.

You will need a yellow candle, a yellow rose, a yellow pouch, and a photo of a good friend.

Begin by lighting the candle, dedicating it to your friend in the photo. Next, place the photo and rose together by the candle where you can easily see them. Focus on the candle flame first, merging with the powers of fire for a minute or so. Now focus on the photo of your friend. Think about the happy times you have shared and how much you care about each other. Do this for a couple of minutes. Then change your focus to the yellow rose, merging with the beauty of the flower for a couple of minutes. Take the rose in your power hand and touch it. Breathe in its fragrance. Hold the rose up in front of you, and say:

By the power of this flower
More sharing and caring fill each hour
As I will, so shall it be!

Now place the rose on top of the photo. Fold the photo around the rose, and put the folded photo and rose into the pouch. Hold the pouch between your palms, and charge it with energy by saying:

Charm of friendship, charm of sharing
I charge you with compassion and caring
As I will, so shall it be!

Carry the pouch when you are with your friend to strengthen your friendship.

June 9   POSITIVE, HEALTHY YOU AFFIRMATION

You can heal many of your problems by applying positive mental images and affirmations. Your perception directly correlates to your state of well-being. By using positive affirmation, you can actually move toward what you say and picture in your mind's eye. Use your imagination to reach out to a more positive and healthy image of yourself. By doing so, you lay the groundwork for bringing that healthy you into physical reality.

You will need a white candle, a small card, and a pen.

Begin by lighting the candle, dedicating it to a goddess of healing such as Bridget (Celtic) or Meditrina (Roman). Sit quietly and gaze at the flame for a few moments. Take a deep breath and exhale, just letting go of any stress you may be feeling. Next, close your eyes and imagine a more positive, healthy you. See yourself as fit and happy, enjoying your life to the fullest in splendid health. Now open your eyes, and gaze at the candlelight again. Merge with the element of fire as you study the flame. Become one with the flame. Then imagine the healing light of the Goddess entering your body, helping you to become that image of a more positive, healthy you. Keep breathing the healthy, positive image into your being. Now open your eyes, and say:

Each and every day, the divine light of the Goddess flows through me and helps me become more positive and healthy. Her healing light flows through every cell of my body, healing my mind, body, and spirit.

Close your eyes again, and imagine that positive, healthy you in your mind. Breathe the image into your being for a minute or so. Repeat this affirmation at least nine times a day for best results. (Note: You can write the Healthy You Affirmation on a small card such as a business card, and carry it with you. Refer to it and say the affirmation at least nine times a day.)

June 10   HEALING WATER

The innate intelligence of each cell in your body knows where to find sustenance. The main information carrier in your body is liquid crystal. The weave of your crystallike fluid threads is highly sensitive to light, tone, and vibration as well as any change in physical, emotional, and spiritual being. Quartz crystal vibrates at the same basic rate as water. Because they vibrate at the same rate, when the crystal is charged, or programmed, with healing images and energy and then placed in water, the healing energy actually charges the water.

You will need a clear quartz crystal and a glass bottle filled with spring water.

This technique was taught to me many years ago by Marcel Vogel at his laboratory in San Jose, California. First, clear the crystal. Do this by holding the crystal between your palms and imagining a single dot of white light on a black background, like a single bright white star in the night sky. Get the image firmly set in your mind. Next, take a deep breath, and pulse your breath through your nose. As you do this, imagine setting the image of the single bright star into the crystal through your breath and intention. Do this three times.

To program the crystal, think of an image that means *healing* to you. It might simply be the color green. It could be the image of the Goddess or God. It may be an image of your child or beloved, or perhaps an image in nature: the forest, the ocean, a beautiful garden, or a waterfall. Whatever the image, keep it simple. Focus all of your attention on it for a few moments. Now take another deep breath, and pulse this healing image into the crystal. Do this three times to charge the crystal with healing energy. After you have programmed the crystal, carefully put it into the bottle of water. Gently swirl the crystal around the bottle in a clockwise motion a few times, and then hold the bottle upward in your hands, and say:

> *With this divine healing crystal water*
> *Happiness and good health flow into me*
> *So be it! So shall it be!*

Now pour yourself a glass of water from the bottle. As you sip it, imagine its healing energy flowing into your body.

June 11   LUCKY BAMBOO HARMONY CHARM

You will need a Lucky Bamboo plant (Dracaena sanderiana), which is a trop-
ical plant available in plant shops, nurseries, and many stores. Lucky Bamboo
isn't actually bamboo, but part of the agave family of plants. It resembles
bamboo and is used in Feng Shui (the ancient Chinese method of balancing
the energies of rooms and spaces in tune with nature).

Begin by holding your Lucky Bamboo plant on your lap. Study the plant
from all different angles, and feel its texture. Smell it. Get in touch with the
essence of the plant. Now, still holding it in your lap, say:

> *Living charm of luck and harmony*
> *Bring fortune and joy to me.*

Put the plant on the east side of your living room to promote harmony
and good health. After one year, plant your Lucky Bamboo plant outdoors in
a large pot with rich soil. Put it in the east section of your yard or home, and
watch its transformation into a shrub known as the ribbon plant with its
glossy, green-and-white striped leaves. You can give Lucky Bamboo plants to
your family and friends to bring them harmony and good health, too.

June 12   JUNE DREAM MAGIC

Cast this spell at night just before going to bed to help find answers to
pressing personal questions.

You will need a white candle, a cauldron or large pan, and a cup of your
favorite fruit juice.

Draw a magic circle of white light around your bedroom. Then, light the candle, dedicating it to your favorite goddess. Hold the cup of juice in your hands and say:

> *Blessed be this divine cup of wisdom.*

Carefully place the cup of juice inside the cauldron or pan. Hold both of your hands over the cup, palms down, and say:

> *Dear Goddess, fill this cup,*
> *With the wisdom I desire!*
> *Clear my insight.*
> *Blessed Lady of wisdom*
> *I,* [state your name], *seek the answer to this question.*
> [State your question.]
> *Dear Goddess, I pray you*
> *Share your wisdom with me tonight!*

As you slowly drink the juice, imagine the answers you seek flowing into you. Know that the wisdom of the Goddess is filling you with the answers that you seek. Now say:

> *Knowledge and wisdom abound,*
> *Reasons and answers resound,*
> *Within and without,*
> *Circle front and center,*
> *Goddess dream with me tonight.*

Snuff out the candle, and get into bed. As you drift to sleep, silently repeat to yourself:

> *The answers are in my dreams.*
> *I will remember when I wake up.*

In the morning, write down what you recall about your dreams and thank the Goddess for her wisdom and help. Close the magic circle. Repeat this spell until you receive helpful answers. These answers may not necessarily come from your dreams, but may also come to you in your waking state as well. The spell triggers the divine knowledge within.

June 13   HEALING ROSE BATH SALTS

The natural healing qualities of the rose oil in these fragrant bath salts soothes your heart and spirit.

You will need one cup of sea salt, 1 cup of Epsom salts, a half-cup of baking soda, eighteen drops of rose essential oil, a large Ziploc bag, a glass jar, and a warm bath.

Put all the ingredients, except the rose oil, into the Ziploc bag. Zip the bag closed. Mix the ingredients in the bag together, gently kneading them with your fingers. As you do this, chant:

> *Soothe my heart, soothe my spirit.*
> *Blessed be! So be it!*

Continue doing this for a few minutes until the salts are completely blended. Now open the bag, and add the drops of rose oil. Close the top. Gently knead the oil into the mixture. As you do so, again chant:

> *Soothe my heart, soothe my spirit.*
> *Blessed be! So be it!*

When the salts are completely blended, store them in the glass jar. Then draw a warm bath, and pour a half-cup of the healing bath salts into the water. Swish the salts around to dissolve them. Step into the tub, and soak for at least five minutes. As you soak, softly chant:

> *Soothe my heart, soothe my spirit.*
> *Blessed be! So be it!*

For best results, use up the healing bath salts within the month.

June 14   FREEDOM CHARM

In the United States, June 14 is Flag Day, a day we honor the red, white, and blue colors of our flag and the empowering freedom it stands for. You, too, can honor your country and your freedom by making and using this simple charm.

You will need a blue sock, a red candle, a white stone, three pinches of thyme, three bay leaves, a smudge stick, a cup of water, and a bowl of clean soil.

Begin by lighting the candle. Dedicate it to your country. Light the smudge stick and smudge the sock, stone, herbs, cup of water, and bowl of earth. Next, put the stone and herbs into the sock. Knot the sock securely. Hold the knotted sock charm in your receiving hand, and use your power hand to consecrate the charm. First, sprinkle it with the earth from the bowl, and say:

> *With the powers of earth, I do consecrate this freedom charm*
> *Let courage, union, prosperity, and joy follow*
> *As I will, so be it. Blessed be!*

Next, smudge the charm with the smudge smoke, and say:

With the powers of air, I do consecrate this freedom charm
Let courage, union, prosperity, and joy follow
As I will, so be it. Blessed be!

Pass the charm swiftly and carefully through the candle flame, and say:

With the powers of fire, I do consecrate this freedom charm
Let courage, union, prosperity, and joy follow
As I will, so be it. Blessed be!

Lastly, sprinkle the water from the cup on the charm, and say:

With the powers of water, I do consecrate this freedom charm
Let courage, union, prosperity, and joy follow
As I will, so be it. Blessed be!

Put the charm in your top bureau or desk drawer. Take it out now and again to remind you to honor and cherish your divine Goddess- and God-given freedom.

June 15   BLESSED BEES MASK

You will need a natural skin cleaner or soap, three teaspoons of honey, a soft washcloth, a soft towel, and a natural skin moisturizer.

Begin by washing your face and neck with the soap. Dry off, and apply the honey to your face and neck in a thin, even layer. As you apply the honey with your fingers, softly chant:

Blessed honey of the bees, bless me with natural beauty.

Recline for about fifteen minutes, listening to soft music if you like. Next, rinse your face and neck with warm water, using the soft washcloth. Pat your skin dry with the towel, and then apply the moisturizer.

June 16   CLIMBING TO THE STARS MEDITATION

Do this meditation at dusk, in a safe place outdoors, if possible. Or you can do this on your balcony, or even in front of a picture window. The important thing is to be in a position so you can see the first star of the night.

Stars have divine aspects. In the Celtic tradition, Cassiopea's Chair is considered the Court of Danu (the mother of the Celtic gods). The Northern Crown is called Caer Arianrhod, or the Castle of Danu's Daughter, and the Milky Way is called Caer Gwydion, or the Castle of Danu's Son. By star-walking, you shift your awareness, and access the divine healing powers of the stars. By moving your awareness through the stargates (energetic portals used by the Lakota Sioux, Egyptians, and Mayans) to a specific star, you can bring back that star energy to help heal yourself.

You will need a piece of turquoise.

Begin by asking a healing goddess or god for divine assistance during your starwalking. Take a few deep breaths to center yourself, and hold the stone in your power hand. Now focus on the night sky and watch for the first star. Once you see it, move your awareness up toward the star. Move higher and higher, ever higher into the night sky. Imagine walking toward the star as it comes closer and closer. As you move higher and higher, you feel lighter and brighter. You see an energy gate before you, and you walk effortlessly through it. As you do, you experience a soft popping sensation. As you glide through the stargate, there is a being of pure white light waiting for you. This is your star guide, a magical being who will answer one pressing question. Ask this being your question now. Then, listen for the thought-form reply.

Your star guide beckons to you and you move closer to the first star of the night. As you move closer and closer, you realize that this star, that every star, is alive with energy. Continue to focus on the star energy, and allow yourself to become one with the star. You and the star are both made of the stars. By starwalking through the sky to the first star of the night, you reconnect with your own stellar heritage and cosmic roots. Your stellar self becomes a source of energy. As you become one with the star, your intuition grows stronger, as do your healing abilities and creative powers. Do this for several minutes.

When you are done starwalking, come back to the present moment by slowly opening your eyes and sliding back into your physical body. Thank your star guide, and then write down your experience. Tonight as you fall asleep, hold the piece of turquoise in your receiving hand, and imagine yourself climbing into the heavens and tapping into the divine healing energy of the stars.

June 17   STOMACH-SOOTHING DILL TEA

Beyond its use as a spice in flavoring foods, dill also can be used to soothe your stomach and reduce indigestion. It is part of the carrot family.

You will need two teaspoons of dill seeds, two cups of water, and a ceramic or glass pot.

On low heat, simmer the dill seeds in the water for about twenty minutes. Let the mixture stand and cool, and then strain out the seeds. Hold the cup of tea between your hands, and charge it with healing energy by saying three times:

> *Blessed be, this healing tea*
> *By the Lady, blessed be!*

Sip the mixture slowly, drinking as much as you need to soothe your stomach. Before each sip of tea, say:

> *Blessed be, this healing tea.*

June 18   SMUDGE YOUR WAY TO HEALTH

Smudge sticks can be used to clear yourself and your home of unwanted energy.

You will need a few sprigs of fresh sage and lavender, colored cotton string, and scissors.

Begin by trimming the sprigs into nine-inch lengths. Bunch the branches together. Wind the string about 1 inch from one end and make a knot. Next, wind the string all the way down from the tips to the stems (top to bottom), winding the string around the outside of the branches in a crisscross pattern as you go. As you do this, chant:

> *Blessed be the Goddess*
> *Blessed be the God*
> *Blessed be the healing powers*
> *Of these divine herbs.*

Now wind the string around the stems, and tie a knot. Say:

I am tying good health into my life.

Tie another knot around the base of the stems and say:

I am tying joy into my life.

Tie a third knot around the stems, and say:

I am tying harmony into my life.

Use the scissors to cut any extra string at the base of the stick. Then set the smudge stick out in the sun to dry. Once it dries, light the stick with a candle flame. Gently blow on the stick to get it smoking. Be sure to use a fire-proof dish or pan to catch any hot ashes. Smudge yourself and your home with the purifying smoke to feel fresh and free from any negative energies. (Note: This may trigger your smoke detectors, so open the windows and turn on fans when you smudge to keep this from happening.) Use your smudge anytime you need to clear the space around or within you. Be sure to completely extinguish your smudge stick when you are finished. The easiest way to do this is to dip the burning tip in water.

June 19   GARDEN OF THE MIND MEDITATION

The garden of the mind is a magical place of healing that grows in your imagination. In this garden, there is no need to water, weed, or mulch. You need to be somewhere you won't be disturbed for about fifteen minutes. This technique can be used during work breaks to refresh and revitalize your energy.

You will need a photograph or painting of a beautiful garden.

Begin by putting the picture of the beautiful garden where you can easily see it. Sit or recline and take several deep and complete breaths, letting go of any stress or worries you may be feeling. Now focus all your attention on the picture, and imagine stepping into it, like Alice stepping through the looking glass. Enter the garden. Close your eyes, and visualize the garden in the picture in your mind. Open your eyes, and look at the picture again. Now close your eyes, and once again, imagine the garden picture. Next, go a step further, and in your mind begin to make the garden in the picture your very own garden. Personalize it with your imagination. Add flowers, trees, shrubs, and other plants you want in it. Place stones, trellises, benches, fountains, sun dials, and gazebos in it if you like. Invite the birds, animals, and insects you want into it. Give your garden otherworldly qualities such as helpful flower and water faeries. Rearrange and cultivate the garden in your mind in any way you desire. Imagine it orderly or untamed, sunny or partially shady. Fill it with a pond, stream, or waterfall. Now imagine yourself standing in the middle of this extraordinarily beautiful garden. Take a deep breath and breathe the magical beauty of the garden into your body. Take another deep breath, and breathe in the harmony and peacefulness of the garden. Take another deep breath, and breathe in the divine healing energy of the magical garden. Now breathe normally and keep focusing on being in the middle of your beautiful garden of the mind. Do this for at least five minutes. Become one with the healing energy of the garden. When you are done, slowly open your eyes. Then, clap your hands three times to bring you back to the present moment. Remember, you can return to the magical garden in your mind anytime you desire.

June 20   BLOOMING MAGIC

The flower is the symbol of florescence. Midsummer's Eve is the time when plants and flowers in nature come into bloom. It is the most vital point of growth and being. Like the flowers, you also have times of florescence, when your ideas, relationships, and inner self bloom with vibrant energy. For example, you experience cycles where you go from times where you are very productive, to periods where you just want to sit back and reflect upon things in your life. This ritual celebrates the fact that there is a time to dig and prepare the ground, a time to plant seeds and cultivate your dreams, and a time to harvest your full potential and tap into your personal florescence.

You will need some living flowers in a flower pot or in a garden. Perform this spell on Midsummer's Eve (the eve of the Summer Solstice).

Begin by getting in a comfortable position in front of the flowers. Touch the flowers softly with all ten of your fingertips. Feel the softness of the blooms. Take a few deep breaths and imagine breathing in their beauty and energy. Become one with the flowers and imagine your energy meshing completely with theirs. Feel yourself being revitalized and blooming just like the beautiful flowers in front of you. Take a few minutes to do this. Now, while still touching the flowers, say:

> *I am the flowers,*
> *The flowers are me,*
> *We are one.*
> *I am the flower blooms,*
> *The flowers blooms are me,*
> *We are one.*
> *I am the color of the flowers,*

The color of the flowers is me,
We are one.
I am the fragrance of the flowers,
The fragrance of the flowers is me,
We are one.
I am the flowers,
The flowers are me,
We are one.

Take a few more minutes, imagining that you are one with the beautiful blooms and are coming into your personal florescence.

June 21   SUMMER SOLSTICE HEALING CHARM

You will need a plate, three pinches of allspice, three teaspoons of barley, three pinches of chamomile, a photograph of yourself, a green candle, and a small green pouch. Begin by lighting the candle, dedicating it to a goddess or god of healing. Gaze at the candle and imagine yourself as being healthy, joyful, and creative each and every day. Now put the plate in front of the candle, and put the photograph on the plate, face up. Sprinkle a circle of all-spice clockwise around your picture and say:

Natural healing energy fills and surrounds me.

Sprinkle a circle of barley clockwise around the allspice circle and repeat:

Natural healing energy fills and surrounds me.

Sprinkle a circle of chamomile clockwise around the barley circle and repeat:

Natural healing energy fills and surrounds me.

Place your hands palms-down over the photograph, and charge the photograph and herbs by saying:

I charge this solstice charm
With the natural healing energy of these herbs.

Fold the photograph three times; put the folded photograph and the herbs into the small pouch. Hold the pouch in your hands, and empower it by saying:

Sacred solstice charm,
Heal and protect me
From all illness and harm
As I will, so be it!

Set the pouch in front of the candle as it burns down safely. Carry it in your pocket or purse to promote personal healing and protect you from illness and harm.

June 22   COPPER RUNE CHARM

In the Kalevala, an ancient collection of Nordic magic healing charms, the words for "to cast a spell" are interchanged with "to sing." This demonstrates the ancient union of magic and song. Sound is magical. It can be used to add power and energy to charms.

You will need a twelve-inch-long piece of thin copper wire and a smudge stick. (You can purchase copper wire at most hardware or craft stores.)

First, smudge the copper wire to remove any unwanted energies. Then hold it in your hands for a few minutes until it is warm. Next, fold it in half to a 6-inch length. Then fold it in half again into a 3-inch length. Shape the folded wire into the Sowilo Rune [ᛋ]. This rune, also called the "S" rune, is the same whether upright or reverse, and is called the noninvertible rune. The Sowilo rune strengthens you using its powerful solar energy. It motivates and stirs your healing energies. While you are shaping the wire, sing a simple song to power the rune. For example, to the tune of "Twinkle, Twinkle, Little Star," sing:

> *Sun Rune, Sun Rune, oh so bright*
> *Fill me with your healing light.*

Keep singing the simple tune over and over again, as you run your fingers down the length of the charm from top to bottom. Carry the rune charm with you, and hold it whenever you feel depleted and need to recharge your energy. For more in-depth information about making rune charms, refer to my book *The Little Giant Encyclopedia of Runes*.

June 23   CLEAN SWEEP MAGIC

For this spell, you will need three eighteen-inch cedar branches, three nine-inch sage branches, three eighteen-inch oak branches, an ordinary broomstick, and green twine. You will need to go out to the country, or if you're lucky, your backyard, to find your branches. Respect any NO TRESPASSING signs you encounter, and be sure to ask and thank the trees from which you remove the branches. You can grow the sage in your garden or purchase it at a store.

Begin by assembling the sage branches around the larger cedar and pine branches, making the stem ends even. Bind all the cut ends together with the green twine, and bind the bundles to your broomstick. Wind the string around and around to secure it. Knot the string nine times. Each time you knot the string, say:

> *I tie the healing energy of the Goddess and God into*
> *this healing broom.*

Now use the broom to sweep out negativity and sweep in healing energy. Go through each room in your home and gently sweep the floor, starting at your front door, moving clockwise, and ending at your front door. You are not so much physically cleaning your home as you are cleansing it with energy. With each sweeping motion, imagine your home being cleansed by a bright, cobalt-blue light. Then, imagine the healing energy of the Goddess and God filling your home. As you sweep, chant over and over:

> *Sweep out evil, sweep out ill,*
> *Sweep in healing, by the Lady's will.*

Use your healing broom anytime you want to sweep negativity out of your home and healing energy into it.

June 24 HEALING SANDS MEDITATION

A comfortable healing space in your mind's eye can positively influence the healing process. It serves as a special place of balance, far removed from the denial and slow death of ordinary reality. It's a place in your imagination, a place of transformation.

You will need three handfuls of clean sand in a bowl, and a white candle.

This meditation is best done at dusk. Begin by dimming the lights and lighting the candle. Place the bowl of sand where you can easily reach it with your power hand. Sit back or recline, and gaze at the candlelight. Take a few deep breaths to relax, and shift your body around a little to get even more comfortable. Now put your hand in the bowl of sand, and run your fingers slowly through it. Close your eyes, and continue slowly running your fingers through the sand in the bowl. As you do this, imagine being at the seashore, at a favorite beach, or perhaps a place you have created just for this meditation. Imagine the water, the sand under your feet, the smell of salt in the air, and the moist, salt-licked breeze that caresses your face. Be there completely in your mind. Continue to sift the sand slowly with your fingers as you imagine this beautiful beach. Now visualize yourself sitting down on the soft sandy beach, and sifting the sand with your fingers. Each time you do this, it's as if the burdens and pain of the past pour out of you and into the sand.

Continue letting go of all the sadness, grief, and pain of the past as you sift the sand with your fingers. Do this for at least five minutes. Now imagine lying back on the warm sandy beach, relaxing even more, and feeling restored and uplifted. Do this for at least five minutes. When you are done, open your eyes, and clap your hands three times. Take the bowl of sand outside, face west, and dig a small hole. Pour the sand into the hole, and place a rock on top of it. Go back inside and allow the candle to burn down safely on its own. As it does, gaze at the candlelight, and think about the steps you can take today and tomorrow to make your life happier and healthier.

June 25   FOOT MASSAGE MAGIC

Your feet have thousands of nerve endings that correspond to the many muscles, glands, and organs in your body. When you massage your feet, your entire body benefits from your healing hands.

You will need relaxing music, a soft towel, three tablespoons of sea salt, warm water, a large pan or foot bath, and a natural moisturizer.

Begin by turning on the music. Next fill the pan or footbath with warm water and add the sea salt. Gently swish the salt around in the water until it dissolves. Now soak your feet for about twenty minutes. As you soak them, imagine all the pain and discomfort flowing out of your feet. Say three times:

> *All discomfort and pain*
> *Dissolve into these healing waters.*

Then take your feet out of the bath and dry them with a soft towel. Sit comfortably and extend your left leg. Bend your right leg so you can easily massage your right foot. Apply the moisturizing cream to your hands, and then to your right foot, rubbing from your ankles to your toes. Use your fingers, and then your knuckles to massage your sole. As you massage your foot, chant:

> *All discomfort now go,*
> *Healing energy now flow.*

Do this for several minutes. Next, use your thumbs to massage small circles on your sole and heel area. Chant:

> *Healing circles 'round they go*
> *Divine healing energy now flow.*

Finish your foot by gently pushing each toe outward, and then pulling each toe outward. When you are done with your right foot, repeat the procedure on your left foot.

June 26   PRAYER FOR HEALTH

You will need a small tumbled quartz crystal. You can use your Healing Stone (see May 21) if you like. The divine power of prayer can be used to promote healing and continued good health. Starting this morning, each and every morning, hold your crystal in your power hand and say this prayer for health:

> *Dear Lord and Lady*
> *God and Goddess of creation*
> *I ask that your divine healing light*
> *Restore and fill me*
> *I ask that your divine healing spirit*
> *Restore and fill me*
> *I ask that your divine love and grace*
> *Restore and fill me*
> *I ask this in the Lord and Lady's names*
> *Blessed be the God and Goddess!*

June 27   JUNE HEALING AFFIRMATION

You will need two duplicate photographs of a happy event and a pen.

First, write this affirmation on the back of each of the photographs:

> *Today and every day, I feel healthy, loving, creative,*
> *and joyful. So be it!*

Carry one of the photographs with you, and put the other one in your home where you will see it on a daily basis (like on the refrigerator). To uplift yourself, you need to let go of any negative emotions you may be feeling, replacing them with positive thoughts and feelings. This uplifting affirmation can help you do just that. To ward off sadness and depression, positive affirmation helps you to alter your perspective and look on the bright side. I also suggest that you play a lot of uplifting and joyful music, with happy lyrics and bright melodies. Watch screwball comedies and romantic movies that make you laugh. Take an elevator or the stairs to the rooftop of a high rise, or better yet, walk up to the top of a knoll, canyon, hill, or mountain to get above it all for a while. When you look down on things, they don't seem so looming and depressing. While doing each of these kinds of uplifting activities, be sure to read the affirmation on the photograph at least three times. Also, look at the photograph and remember the happy memories it evokes. When at home, read the affirmation on the refrigerator photograph at least three times a day. Do this for at least twenty-one days to uplift your spirits and let go of any sadness and depression you may be experiencing.

June 28 WILLOW HEALING WAND

You will need an eighteen-inch willow branch, blue and gold embroidery thread, and lavender water. Begin by winding the thread around the branch from the base to the tip. Cover the branch with the thread like a second skin. Now hold the covered branch in your hands. Bless it by sprinkling lavender water on it and saying:

> *Powers of water and sea*
> *Bless this healing wand*
> *With your divine energy.*

Now hold the wand in your hands, and close your eyes. Imagine the divine healing powers of the wand flowing into your hands and throughout your body. Use your imagination to direct the divine energy to different parts of your body that are most in need of healing.

June 29   BEAUTY MASK SPELL

This beauty mask is designed even for sensitive skin.

You will need a cucumber, dry milk powder, three drops of lavender essential oil, a half-teaspoon of olive oil, a food processor, lavender water, and your favorite moisturizer.

First, peel and dice the cucumber and put it in the food processor. Add the milk powder and the lavender and olive oil. Say three times:

> *Healing potion of beauty, grant your powers to me.*

Turn on the processor, and blend the ingredients to form a paste. Apply the paste to your face and neck. As you do this, chant:

> *Mask of beauty, grant your powers to me.*

Recline for about fifteen to twenty minutes to gain the most benefit from the mask. You can set a timer if you like. All the while you are reclining, keep your eyes closed and imagine your skin becoming softer and more supple. Imagine feeling more and more beautiful and attractive. When it is time to remove the mask, use a soft washcloth and warm water. Next, apply the lavender water over your face and neck to tone the skin. Last, apply your favorite skin moisturizer.

June 30   FRONT DOOR PROTECTION CHARM

You will need a six-inch by six-inch piece of green cloth, a twelve-inch length of gold ribbon, six small cloves of garlic, three dimes or other silver-colored coins, and three bay leaves. Begin by putting the cloves, coins, and leaves into the middle of the cloth. Gather the ends of the cloth together, and then secure the contents of the charm with the golden ribbon, winding it around the charm six times and knotting the ends of the ribbon three times. Next, hold the charm between your palms and charge it by saying:

> *Charm of protection, charm of healing*
> *I charge you with divine and loving power*
> *Bring happiness, abundance, and joy to my home.*
> *By the Lady, Blessed be! So be it!*

Now carry the charm into all the rooms of your home. Start at the front door, and go clockwise through the house, winding up again at the front door. Take your time. As you do this, chant:

> *Happiness, abundance, and joy enter my home each and*
> *every day of the year.*

As you chant, imagine your home filled with loving people and pet companions, with happiness, abundance, and joy. Imagine all of these wonderful things coming into your home through your front door each and every day of the year. When you are done, tie the charm on the inside of your front door to bring more happiness, abundance, and joy into your home.

$\mathcal{J}$ULY

July 1   MONEY JAR

You will need a silver candle, a small magnet, water, a dollar bill, and a glass jar with a lid.

Light the candle, dedicating it to a god or goddess of prosperity, for example, Dagda (Celtic) or Demeter (Greek). Fill the jar halfway with water. Hold the magnet in your power hand for a minute or two until it warms up. As you do this, imagine drawing more money, prosperity, and wealth into your life each and every day. Carefully drop the magnet into the jar of water. Add water to fill the jar, and then screw the lid on tight. Hold the jar in your hands and chant for a minute or two:

> *Blessed money jar*
> *Bring prosperity*
> *From near and far.*

Allow the candle to burn down on its own. Put the jar in a sunny window for eight days. Each day, hold the jar in your hands and repeat the chant for a minute or two. On the eighth day, open the jar and sprinkle several drops of water on the dollar bill. Set it aside to dry. Then sprinkle the water around your home, starting at the front door, and moving clockwise through the rooms of your home. Sprinkle the water outside your front and back doors.

Finally, rub the remaining water all over your hands. Next, sit or recline comfortably and imagine drawing all the riches you desire into your life in the next days, weeks, months, and years. Let your imagination go and really enjoy the feeling of having plenty of money, of being prosperous and successful. Remove the magnet from the water, and put it on your refrigerator. On a sheet of paper, write:

I am drawing riches into my life each and every day.

Use the magnet to fasten the paper to the refrigerator. Read the affirmation at least four times a day to bring more money and wealth into your life. Write the same affirmation on the dollar bill, and keep (don't spend it!) the dollar in your wallet or purse.

July 2   FLOWERING PROSPERITY

Within each flower exists the blossoming power of Goddess and God. You can use this power to help your finances and business ventures blossom as well.

You will need a pot of petunias.

Begin by setting the pot of petunias in front of you so you can easily see and touch them. Focus your awareness on the petunias. See them from all angles. Touch the blossoms and smell them. Merge with the energy of the flowers and say three times:

> *Blooming flowers of beauty*
> *Bring me continued prosperity*
> *So be it! Blessed be!*

Then put the pot of petunias outside in a warm, sunny location, and water them regularly. Pull off any spent blooms to encourage new growth and more prosperity. As the petunias continue to bloom and thrive, so will your bank account.

July 3   MUSICAL WISH SPELL

You will need a white candle, a bowl of cool salt water, a ballpoint pen, a small card, vanilla-scented oil, and a favorite song that you like to listen to again and again.

Turn on a favorite song, and sing or hum along with the music. Now think about how much money you would like this year. Decide on a specific amount. Now use the pen to write that amount in large numbers on the card. Set the card in front of you where you can easily read it. Next, wash the candle in cool salt water, and dry it. Use the pen to also inscribe your money wish, the amount on the card, on the candle body. Then apply the vanilla oil to the candle. Anoint yourself with the vanilla oil, and wipe the oil from your hands. Turn the song on again (if you have a repeat function on your player, use it). Light the candle, dedicating it to a god or goddess of wealth such as Lugh (Celtic) or Fortuna (Roman). Sit or recline comfortably, and gaze at the candlelight. Take a deep breath, and as you exhale, let go of all the tensions you may be feeling. Take another deep breath, and imagine breathing in a bright, green light. Breathe out any tension, and then breathe in the bright, green light again. Do this at least eight times. Turn the song on again if necessary. Get up and dance around and sing along with the tune, all the while imagining having the amount of money you wished for. See and sense your money wish coming true in the near future. Step into that future for a few minutes, and really enjoy having the prosperity you desire and deserve. Feel the happy and pleasant sensations and a sense of joy and success. Continue doing this for at least five minutes. Allow the candle to burn down completely. Put the card in your wallet, purse, checkbook, or bankbook, and leave it there until you have received the amount of money you wished for. Also, play the song you used for this spell frequently, and your newfound money will be music to your ears.

July 4   INDEPENDENCE COIN CHARM

In honor of Independence Day in the United States, this coin charm can be used to help you attain financial independence.

You will need a red candle, a white candle, a blue candle, a smudge stick, and a silver dollar.

Dedicate each of the candles to a goddess of prosperity such as Anu (Celtic), Lakshmi (Hindu), or Freya (Norse). Write the words *Financial Independence* on each of them, and light them in order: red, white, and blue, dedicating them to freedom and independence. Light the smudge with the white candle flame, and smudge the silver dollar. Hold the coin in your power hand, and charge it by saying three times:

> *By the divine power of the Goddess and God, I charge*
> *this silver coin with freedom and financial independence.*

Allow the candles to burn down safely, and completely extinguish the smudge stick. Carry the Independence Coin Charm with you in your pocket, wallet, or purse. Be sure to recharge it once a day by holding it in your power hand and repeating:

> *By the divine power of the Goddess and God, I charge this silver coin with freedom and financial independence.*

July 5   PENTACLE PROSPERITY

You will need a wand, amber incense, paper, and a green gel pen.

Draw a magic circle and call in the elements. Light the incense, dedicating it to a favorite goddess or god of prosperity. Then draw a large pentacle on the sheet of paper with the green gel pen. Inside the head, arms, and legs of the pentacle, draw a large dollar sign. Then gaze at the pentacle, and imagine a bright green light totally engulfing it. Now imagine the pentacle expanding. As you do this also imagine your prosperity expanding. Imagine having all the money you need. Point your wand at the pentacle, starting at the head, and moving clockwise around it. As you do this, chant:

> *Magic pentacle of prosperity*
> *Money and riches bring to me*
> *By the Lady, blessed be!*

Put the pentacle on your altar, and recharge it once a day by pointing your wand at the head, arms, and legs in a clockwise pattern and repeating:

> *Magic pentacle of prosperity*
> *Money and riches bring to me*
> *By the Lady, blessed be!*

July 6 WELCOMING WEALTH SPELL

This spell welcomes prosperity and wealth to your home.

You will need a green doormat with the word *Welcome* on it, sandalwood incense, eight pinches of fenugreek, and a silver-colored coin.

Begin by lighting the incense, dedicating it to a goddess and god of wealth. Then pass the doormat and coin through the incense smoke. Put the doormat in front of the door you use the most to go in and out of your home. Hold the coin in your power hand, and empower it by saying three times:

> *I empower this coin with the power*
> *To attract money and prosperity*
> *I welcome wealth and happiness into my home*
> *In the name of the Lady and Lord, so be it!*

Next, place the coin under the center of the doormat. Sprinkle the fenugreek over the coin, and then place the doormat back down and leave it there to welcome wealth and happiness into your home.

July 7 ROMAN MONEY MAGIC

Today is a sacred day of the Roman Goddess Juno, the Queen of Heaven, whose temple contained the Roman Mint. She is also called Moneta, meaning money. Her counterpart is the Roman God Jupiter, whose expansive powers are perfect for expanding your bank account.

You will need a green candle, a blue candle, four dollar bills, eight pinches of flaxseed, and a small green pouch.

Do this spell at 8:00 A.M. Begin by drawing a magic circle around your home. Call in the elements. Put the candles next to each other on the altar, the green one on the left, and the blue one on the right. Next, light the green candle, dedicating it to Juno. Then light the blue candle, dedicating it to Jupiter. Take the dollar bills and put one just inside your front door, one just inside your back door, and two on your altar between the two candles. Each time you lay a dollar bill down, say:

> *Dear Juno and Jupiter grant me*
> *Plenty of money and prosperity*
> *Bring green cash, and bring it fast*
> *By the Lady and Lord, blessed be!*

Sit or stand comfortably in front of the lit candles on your altar, and merge with the flames for a few minutes. As you do, imagine plenty of money and cash in your bank account. Smile to yourself, knowing you have all the money you need to live a comfortable and happy life. Now retrieve the two dollar bills from the doors. Put them, plus the two dollar bills on the altar, into the pouch. Then add the pinches of flaxseeds. Hold the pouch between your palms, and say:

> *By the powers of Juno and Jupiter*
> *I charge this money pouch with divine power*
> *May it draw money and riches to me*
> *By the Lady and Lord, blessed be!*

Allow the candles to burn down safely on their own. When you are done, thank Juno and Jupiter, bid farewell to the elements, and close the circle. Put the money pouch in your desk drawer or at your workplace where you can see it every day for at least eight months to draw more green money to you.

July 8   FORTUNE COOKIE CHARM

You will need a positive fortune from a fortune cookie, sesame oil, and a wand.

Begin by putting a drop of oil on the fortune. Then tape the fortune to your refrigerator where you can easily see it. Each morning, tap the fortune eight times with your wand, and say:

> *Good fortune come my way*
> *Today is my lucky day!*

Read the fortune out loud several times during the day and evening for twenty-eight days (one moon cycle) to reinforce its fortune-drawing power.

July 9   RINGING IN THE GREEN

You will need jasmine scented oil, a sprig of clover, and a small bell.

Begin by drawing a magic circle. Draw a second circle of bright golden light over the first one, and call in the elements. Next, anoint yourself with the jasmine oil: Rub three drops on the insides of both of your wrists, three drops on your throat, and three drops on your third eye. Face the altar, and ring the bell nine times, in three series of three. Then say:

> *Magic rings, three times three*
> *I now ring in the magic green*
> *By the powers of earth, air, fire, and sea*
> *By the ancient powers of the blessed faeries*
> *May my days be filled with joy and prosperity.*

Now ring the bell seven times, and sit or recline comfortably. Hold the clover in your receiving hand, and breathe in to the count of three, hold your breath for three counts, and then breathe out for three counts. Do this three times. Then imagine inhaling and exhaling bright golden light. Do this for a couple of minutes. In your mind's eye, see yourself stepping into a magical faery ring of clover. As you step into the ring, you are instantly transported to Faeryland. You suddenly see and sense all sorts of generous starspun faeries gathering around you. Imagine their magical powers flowing from them into your entire being. Breathe in their magical energy, and allow the starspun faery power to fill you to the brim. Do this for at least fifteen minutes. When you are done, ring the bell once, thank the helpful and generous faeries for their presence in your circle, bid farewell to the elements, and close both circles of light.

July 10 STARLIGHT MONEY SPELL

You will need almond-scented oil and three almonds.

Just before dusk take the oil and almonds outdoors, and wait for the first star to appear in the night sky. While you wait, anoint yourself with the almond oil on the wrists and ankles. As the first star appears, gaze at it and say:

> *Starlight, star bright*
> *First star I see tonight*
> *I wish I may, I wish I might*
> *Have my prosperity wish tonight.*

Then state your wish three times out loud to the star. Each time you state your wish, eat one of the almonds. Next, on the ground in front of you, use a stick or stone to draw a five-pointed star. Drip three drops of almond oil into the center of the star and say:

> *Star light, star bright*
> *Earth star of divine delight*
> *I wish I may, I wish I might*
> *Have my prosperity wish tonight.*

Once again state your wish out loud three times. Take a bit of earth from the star you have drawn on the ground, and rub the soil briskly between your palms for a minute. As you do, imagine your wish already coming true. Step into the future, and enjoy the bliss of getting your wish. Do this for a few minutes. When you are done, clap your hands three times to bring you back to the present time and place.

July 11   CRYSTAL WEALTH STONE

You will need a tumbled clear quartz crystal, a green candle, a ballpoint pen, and a smudge stick.

Begin by drawing a magic circle and calling in the elements. Use the pen to write the letters *N* for north, *E* for east, *S* for south, and *W* for west on the candle. Next, inscribe a dollar sign on top of each of the four letters. Light the candle, dedicating it to a favorite goddess of wealth such as Anu (Celtic) or Juno (Roman). Then light the smudge stick with the candle flame, and thoroughly smudge the crystal in the smoke. Be sure to completely extinguish the smudge stick. Now hold the stone in your power hand, and merge with the

Goddess. Close your eyes, and take a few deep breaths to center yourself. Imagine breathing in bright, emerald-green light, and breathing out any residue tensions. Do this at least three times. Then imagine breathing bright green light into the crystal in your hand. Visualize money and cash filling the stone. Imagine it getting larger and larger, filling with money. Also imagine your bank account getting larger and larger just like the crystal, filling with money. Still holding the crystal, say:

> *Magical stone bring to me*
> *By earth, air, fire, and sea*
> *Bountiful wealth and prosperity*
> *By the Goddess, blessed be!*

Keep your Crystal Wealth Stone in your pocket, purse, or medicine pouch. You can recharge it as often as you like by holding it in your power hand and saying:

> *Magical stone bring to me*
> *By earth, air, fire, and sea*
> *Bountiful wealth and prosperity*
> *So be it! Blessed be!*

July 12   GOLDEN DREAMS CHARM

You will need a gold candle, a ballpoint pen, lavender-scented oil, a gold ring, and a smudge stick.

Make this charm at night, just before you go to sleep. Begin by drawing a magic circle around your bedroom, and calling in the elements. Next, inscribe the words *Golden Dreams* on the candle. Dress the candle with lavender-scented oil and then anoint yourself. Wipe the oil from your hands and light the candle, dedicating it to a favorite goddess of prosperity, such as Boann (Celtic) or Lakshmi (Hindu). Light the smudge stick with the candle, and smudge the ring and yourself. Now hold the ring in your power hand, and focus on the candle flame. Imagine a new, prosperous you in the flame. Say three times:

> *Golden dreams, come tonight*
> *Bring wealth and riches bright.*

Now put the ring on a finger of your receiving hand. Continue imagining the image of the new, prosperous you. Become one with the image. Allow the candle to safely burn down, or snuff it out. Keep the ring on. As you drift to sleep, repeat silently to yourself:

> *Golden dreams, come tonight*
> *Bring wealth and riches bright.*

In the morning, write down everything you recall from your dreams. Thank the prosperity goddess, bid farewell to the elements, and close the circle. Wear your gold ring day and night to bring wealth into your hands.

July 13   TALISMAN OF ABUNDANCE

This magical talisman can be used specifically to help draw more abundance to you.

You will need a green candle, a red candle, amber-scented oil, and a piece of malachite.

Begin by drawing a magic circle, and then draw another circle of green light on top of the first circle. Call in the elements. Dress the candles with the amber-scented oil. Put them next to each other on the altar with the green candle on the left and the red candle on the right. Then anoint the insides of your wrists, the insides of your ankles, and the back of your head (on the "soft" spot). Wipe the oil from your hands, light the green candle, and say:

I dedicate this candle to the goddess of abundance.

Next, light the red candle, and say:

I dedicate this candle to the god of abundance.

Now cover the malachite with amber-scented oil. Rub the stone between your hands until it gets warm. Then put it on the altar directly in front of you between the red and green candles. Merge with the candle flames, with the stone, with the goddess and god of abundance, and with oneness. Now fill your mind with a bright green emerald light, green being the color of growth and abundance. Imagine the bright green light turning into money, riches, joy, and plenty. Breathe this light into your being. Next, breathe the bright green light of abundance into the stone. Do this by imagining a laser beam of bright emerald light flowing from your third eye, or through your hands, into the stone. Keep imagining this for several minutes as you focus on the stone in front of you. Think of everything that you can think of that's green and abundant, and imagine putting it into the stone. Imagine your thought-energy being absorbed and locked into the atomic structure of the malachite. Next, imagine the area of influence of the Talisman of Abundance by seeing and sensing a bright emerald green field of energy being emitted by the stone, shooting out about fifty feet in all directions. When you are done, clap your hands three times. Bid farewell to the elements, thank Deity, and close the circle. Carry the talisman with you during the day, and enjoy the abundance it draws to you. Put it on your altar while you sleep.

July 14 APPLE ABUNDANCE POTION

You will need a green candle, a ceramic or glass pot, a cup of unfiltered apple juice, a quarter-cup of papaya nectar, one teaspoon of honey, a slice of lemon, four cloves, and a cinnamon stick.

Begin by putting all the ingredients into the pot and heating them slowly. Do not let them boil. As you stir the potion in a clockwise motion, chant:

Abundance come my way today.

Pour the potion into a cup, and let it cool. Then slowly sip the potion. As you do, gaze at the candle flame, and imagine all kinds of abundance filling you: an abundance of money, good luck, love, happiness, good health, and people who care about you.

July 15 BETTER BUSINESS MAGIC

This spell is designed to bring you better business and more financial rewards.

You will need a bowl, eight pinches of sweet basil, and eight pinches of uncooked rice.

Begin by putting the basil and rice in the bowl. Mix them together with the fingers of your power hand, and chant:

Bountiful fortune come my way
Bring me better business today.

When the basil and rice are thoroughly mixed together, hold the bowl upward with both hands, and merge with the divine. Say:

> *Dear Goddess and God, I pray you*
> *Assist me in this rite*
> *May bountiful fortune come my way*
> *And bring me better business today.*
> *By the Lady and Lord, so be it!*

Now sprinkle the mixture outside the entrance of your business place, under your desk, and around your working area. As you do, chant:

> *Bountiful fortune come my way*
> *Bring me better business today.*

July 16   PUMPKIN PROSPERITY PLACKET

A placket is a magical pocket.

You will need eight pumpkin seeds, eight pinches of dill, a dollar bill, a photo of yourself, a green felt-tip pen, two 8-inch by 4-inch pieces of green construction paper, a stapler, and scotch tape.

Begin by stapling the two squares of paper together along three sides, leaving one side open. Use the felt-tip pen to write your name on both the front and back of the placket. Now write your name on the front and back of the dollar bill. Slide the photo and dollar bill into the inside of the pocket, making sure they are face to face. Then add the pumpkin seeds and dill. Staple the top closed, and then use the scotch tape to tape all of the sides of the placket, starting at the top and moving sunwise (clockwise). Now hold the prosperity placket in your hands, and empower it by saying three times:

> *Placket of green, bring prosperity to me*
> *As I will, so shall it be. Blessed be!*

Tape the placket to the inside of your front door to bring more prosperity your way.

July 17   MILLION DOLLAR MAGNET

You will need a million dollar magnet (an image of a million dollar bill on a magnet), a green candle, and a smudge stick. (Note: You can find a million dollar magnet in gift shops, supermarkets, discount stores, the Internet, or you can make one from play money.)

Begin by lighting the candle, dedicating it to your favorite prosperity Goddess. Carefully light the smudge stick with the candle flame, also dedicating it to the same goddess of prosperity. Smudge the magnet with the smoke to purify it, and then extinguish the smudge stick completely. Next, hold the magnet in your power hand, gaze at the candle flame, merge with the goddess of prosperity, and say:

> *North, east, south, and west*
> *By the Goddess, I am divinely blessed*
> *With this magnet I attract riches*
> *From the north, east, south, and west*
> *By the Goddess, I am divinely blessed*
> *I draw prosperity and wealth to me*
> *From north, east, south, and west*
> *I am divinely blessed! Blessed be!*

Now continue to hold the magnet in your power hand as you gaze at the candle flame for a few minutes. As you do this, imagine actually having the million dollars on the magnet in your hand. Imagine the things you would do with it, how drawing wealth to you would change your life. Just allow yourself to dream about it for a few minutes. When you are done, put the magnet on your refrigerator at home or somewhere at work where you will frequently see it, such as your file cabinet. Charge your million dollar magnet once a day in the morning by holding it in your power hand and saying:

> *I draw prosperity and wealth*
> *Into my life each and every day.*

When you are done charging the magnet, put it back where you can see it.

July 18   FAERY DUST MAGIC

You will need a mortar and pestle, a pinch of dried ginger, a pinch of dried jasmine, a pinch of cinnamon spice, a pinch of allspice, a pinch of dried rosebuds, and a pinch of dried mint, and three almonds.

Gather the items together and go outdoors, where it's often easier to commune with the faeries. Find a quiet spot where you won't be disturbed for about fifteen minutes. Put the ingredients in the mortar and grind the herbs and nuts together into a fine powdery dust. As you do, imagine the magical powers of the faeries flowing into the powder and chant:

> *Faeries of earth, air, fire, and sea*
> *Bring abundance and prosperity to me.*

Sprinkle the faery dust outside your front door in the shape of a dollar sign. Also sprinkle a bit in your wallet, purse, in your safe, or your place of business.

July 19   SUNNY MONEY SPELL

You will need a gold candle, cinnamon oil, and fresh yellow flowers. Begin by drawing a magic circle and calling in the elements. Dress the candle with the cinnamon oil, and set it in its holder. Be careful to wash and wipe the cinnamon oil from your hands as it can be irritating to your skin and eyes. Next, lay the fresh flowers around the candle, in a clockwise circle. Light the candle, dedicating it to a favorite goddess of prosperity. Merge with the candle flame and say:

> *Golden candle of prosperity*
> *Draw gold and money to me*
> *As I will, so mote it be.*

Continue to merge with the flame, and imagine being surrounded by and filled with a brilliant, golden light for about fifteen minutes. As you do this, visualize inhaling and exhaling gold sunlight. This will add more sunny power to the spell. Bid farewell to the elements, thank the Goddess, and pull up the circle when you are done. Take the flowers outside and cast them gently into a running river, creek, or stream to get your sunny money flowing into your life.

July 20 CURRENCY FLOW SPELL

For this spell, you will need a bowl, eight pinches of ground ginger, eight pinches of rolled oats, eight pinches of rosemary, and eight maple leaves. Put all the ingredients in the bowl. Use the fingers of your power hand to mix them together. As you do, chant over and over:

> *Currency come to me and grow,*
> *Money come to me and flow.*
> *So be it! Make it so!*

Now take the bowl and contents and go to a flowing body of water such as a river, creek, stream, or ocean. Sprinkle the mixture into the water, and chant:

> *Currency come to me and grow,*
> *Money come to me and flow.*
> *So be it! Make it so!*

July 21 IDEAL JOB DREAM STONE

You will need a small, tumbled piece of clear crystal (you can use your Crystal Wealth Stone from July 11 if you like), a white candle, and soft music. Just before you go to sleep, set up an altar in your bedroom. Draw a magic circle, and call in the elements. Put the candle on the altar and light it, dedicating it to the goddess of abundance. Next, recline in bed and hold the stone in your power hand. Gaze at the candle's flame, and take a few deep, complete breaths to center yourself. With your mind's eye, see your ideal job, the best possible job for you and your abilities, something that you would enjoy doing so much that you would pay someone to be able to do it. Now speak aloud, and ask the Goddess for your ideal job. Be specific. Continue holding the crystal, and say:

> *Bright crystal of prosperity,*
> *Bring the ideal job to me.*
> *By the Goddess, blessed Be!*

Now continue holding the stone in your power hand. As you drift to sleep, repeat to yourself over and over:

> *As I dream, bring the ideal job to me.*

Safely allow the candle to burn down, or snuff it out before you go to sleep. In the morning, thank the Goddess, bid farewell to the elements, and close the circle. Make a job inquiry. Hold the crystal in your receiving hand when you make the call or contact. Continue making a job inquiry a day until you get your ideal job.

July 22   OAK TREE ABUNDANCE OFFERING

For this spell, you will need a living oak tree, four slices of bread, a cup of milk, and a cup of birdseed.

Go the oak tree, and walk clockwise around the base three times. As you do, chant:

> *Blessed be, abundant oak tree*
> *As you grow, so does my prosperity.*

Put the bread slices in the nooks of the branches for the birds and small animals. Then pour the milk on the roots of the oak. As you do, again chant:

> *Blessed be, abundant oak tree*
> *As you grow, so does my prosperity.*

Now scatter the birdseed around the base of the tree in a clockwise circle and chant:

> *Blessed be, abundant oak tree*
> *As you grow, so does my prosperity.*

July 23   PROSPERITY MIRROR

For this spell, you will need a small mirror and a grease pen or lipstick.

At dawn, just as the sun is coming up, take the mirror and pen outside. Use the pen to write in large numbers the exact amount of money you would want to manifest from your work in the next three months. Now hold the mirror so you can see your face and the dawning sun in the mirror. All becomes one in the reflection in the mirror—the sun, your image, and the amount of money you wrote on the glass. As you look at your reflection in the mirror, say:

> *Morning sun, so golden bright*
> *My prosperity grows in your dawning light*
> *As I will, so shall it be!*

Imagine your luck and prosperity growing with the dawning light. Delight in the morning sunlight and your newfound abundance.

July 24 PROSPERITY FOOT POWDER

For this spell, you will need a mortar and pestle, a pinch of nutmeg, a pinch of allspice, a pinch of dill, and a pinch of marjoram.

Use the mortar and pestle to grind the herbs together into a powder. As you grind the herbs, chant:

> *Sacred herbs of prosperity,*
> *Bring wealth my way every day.*

As you mix the ingredients together, imagine bringing more prosperity and wealth into each day. Do this for at least five minutes. Then sprinkle the powder inside your shoes before you go to work so you can walk your walk and talk your talk right into a bright prosperous day.

July 25 MONEY SWIFTING SPELL

You will need a black candle, a brown candle, a green candle, a large plate, a ballpoint pen, and sea salt. Draw a magic circle and call in the elements. Use the pen to inscribe the black candle with the word *Debts*. Then inscribe the brown candle with the words *Swiftly Shift*. Now inscribe the green candle with the words *Riches*. Set the candles in a row on the plate—black, brown, and green. Leave room between them so they don't melt each other when they are lit. Set the plate on your altar. Now pour a line of salt on the plate around the three candles in a clockwise circle. Light the candles in order, dedicating them all to a favorite goddess or god of abundance. Merge with the candle flames, and imagine that your debts are completely paid and you have plenty of money to do the things you want to. Do this for about five minutes, and then say:

> *Circle of salt, black, brown, and green*
> *Bring money and riches in a steady stream*
> *Bring it swiftly to me, with ease*
> *So be it! Blessed be!*

Continue to gaze at the candles, and imagine your finances swiftly shifting from debts to riches. Do this for at least fifteen minutes. Allow the candles to burn down safely on their own. When you are done, thank the goddess or god of abundance, bid farewell to the elements, and close the circle. Throw the candle remains and the salt in the trash. Wash the plate before using it again.

July 26   MOJO MONEY BAG

Make this gris-gris bag in the morning.

You will need a gold candle, sandalwood incense, paper and pen, a gold drawstring bag or pouch, eight pinches of echinacea, and a silver dollar.

Begin by drawing a magic circle and calling in the elements. Then light the candle and say:

> *My mind is free, my heart is free*
> *My body is free, my life is my own.*
> *On this day, and all days*
> *In this world, and all worlds*
> *At this time, and all times*
> *I stand at the crossroads*
> *I stand before the Goddess and God*
> *I stand beneath the morning sun*
> *May the Shining Ones protect and guide me*

Blessed be the sun! Blessed be sweet prosperity!
Blessed be! Blessed be! Blessed be!

Next, light the incense with the candle flame, dedicating it to a favorite goddess of prosperity. Pass the silver dollar through the incense smoke to clear it of any unwanted energies. With the pen, purposefully write down your most wanted prosperity wish in large letters on the paper. The wish needs to be something you feel very strongly about, something you really, truly desire with your entire being. Draw five suns around your writing, and then draw four clockwise circles around the suns and writing. Put the silver dollar in the middle of the paper, and fold the paper four times. Hold the folded paper and coin in your power hand, and stand so the morning sun is shining directly on you. Say three times:

Sunlight so beautiful and bright
Grant my wish in your golden light
As I will, so be it.

Say your prosperity wish out loud to the sun, and squeeze the folded paper and coin in your fist as hard as you can. Close your eyes tight, and wish so hard for your prosperity wish that it makes you a little light-headed. Next, put the folded paper with the silver dollar into the gold bag and add the echinacea. Hold it between your hands, and empower it by saying:

By the powers of the Goddess and God,
By the sacred light of the sun
I bind the solar power within this bag.
This spell is cast, and will hold fast.
As I will so be it! Blessed be!

When you are done, thank the Goddess, bid farewell to the elements, and release the circle. Put the bag on a windowsill in the sun to bring bright, sunny money to you every day.

July 27   POWER ANIMAL PROSPERITY

For this spell, you will need a green candle and a clear quartz crystal. You can use your Crystal Wealth Stone if you like (see July 11).

Begin by lighting the candle, dedicating it to the animals of earth. Next, hold your crystal in your receiving hand, and sit or recline comfortably. Take a few deep breaths to relax and center yourself. Close your eyes and imagine a magical garden in your mind's eye. In the garden there is a mysteriously shaped tree. Next to the tree is a small pool with fragrant blossoms surrounding it. You can smell the scent of the water and the flowers. You breathe in deeply several times, relaxing, and feeling more and more peaceful. You sit by the side of the pool and look at the flowers and their reflection upon the pool's glassy surface. As you look at the surface of the pool, you begin to see a soft shimmering light. From the center of the shimmering light, your power animal appears. You gaze at the animal's beauty for a few moments. Without fear, you touch the animal, making contact. As you do, all of the knowledge and legacy of the power animal immediately passes into you. Now ask the animal its name. If you have any trouble discovering your power animal's name, repeat your question and wait for a response. Repeat your power animal's name over and over again to yourself. Ask your power animal exactly how you can create more prosperity in your life. Listen carefully for its answer. The answer often comes in a telepathic manner. As you remain in contact with the animal in your mind's eye, imagine that its strength and power are merging with you and empowering you. Imagine becoming one with your power animal, integrating its knowledge and power into your own being. Do this for at least fifteen minutes.

When you are done, thank your power animal for its help. Clap your hands three times. Now bid farewell to the elements, and close the circle. In your Book of Shadows, write down your power animal's name and the answers you received.

July 28 BINDRUNE BOUNTY CHARM

Bindrunes are two or more (generally three) upright runes hooked together that exhibit a single, powerful runic force.

You will need a green candle, cedar incense, cedar-scented oil, paper and pen, a piece of pyrite, and a sixteen-inch piece of green ribbon.

Begin by drawing a magic circle and calling in the elements. Inscribe the candle with your initials. Then on top of your initials, inscribe the runes Fehu [ᚠ], Wunjo [ᚹ], and Othala [ᛟ], connecting them together into one symbol. Fehu represents mobile wealth such as money and consumer goods; Wunjo brings joy and pleasure; and Othala is the rune of reward and inheritance. Dress the candle with the cedar oil, and then wipe the oil from your hands. Light the candle, dedicating it to the Norns of Norse mythology: Urd (pronounced *urth*), Verdandi (*verthanthae*), and Skuld (*skulth*). Light the incense with the candle flame, also dedicating it to the Norns. Pass the paper, pen, ribbon, and pyrite through the incense smoke to empower them. Then use the pen to write your initials on the center of the paper in large letters. Once again, draw the runes Fehu [ᚠ], Wunjo [ᚹ], and Othala [ᛟ] on top of your initials. Bind the runes together into one larger symbol by hooking them together, and draw a clockwise circle around the whole thing. Rub the cedar-scented oil into the pyrite, and put the stone in the center of paper on top of the bindrunes and your initials. Drip eight drops of green wax on the pyrite, and fold the paper in half with the stone inside. Then fold it in half again, and once more, for a total of three times. Wind the ribbon around the charm eight times, and knot the end eight times. Hold the bindrune charm in your power hand, and imagine bountiful prosperity filling your life. Smile to yourself, knowing that you have all that you need, now and forevermore. Do this for a few minutes. Then while you are still holding the charm, empower it by chanting three times:

> *Bountiful prosperity come to me*
> *From here and there, near and far,*
> *By the power of the Norns,*
> *And the Earth, sun, moon, and stars*
> *Fu, Fa, Fi, Fe, Fo*
> *Wu, Wa, Wi, We, Wo*
> *Othul, Othal, Othil, Othel, Othol*
> *Hu, Ha, Hi, He, Ho*
> *Hu, Ha, Hi, He, Ho*
> *Hail prosperity! Blessed be!*

Allow the candle to burn down safely. When you are done, thank the Norns, bid farewell to the elements, and close the circle. Put your Bindrune Bounty Charm in the pocket of a green coat, sweater, pants, or shirt. Leave it there for at least eight months to draw the bountiful riches of the Norns to you.

July 29 SWEET ABUNDANCE POTION

For this spell, you will need one cup of papaya nectar, a quarter-cup of raspberry juice, four orange slices, and a half-cup of crushed ice.

Put all the ingredients except the orange slices into a blender and mix them until smooth. As the ingredients are mixing, chant:

Sweet abundance fill my life.

Now pour the potion in a glass, and before each sip, say:

Sweet abundance fill my life
As I will, so be it.

July 30 EMPLOYMENT MAGIC

Originally both a Roman moon and sun goddess, the powerful huntress Diana can be called upon to give you the lunar and solar strength to hunt down the best job possible.

You will need a white candle, pine-scented oil, eight cashews, and a glass of orange juice.

Draw a magic circle, and call in the elements. Light the candle, dedicating it to the Roman goddess Diana. Hold the juice in your hands, and chant her name nine times. Then toast Diana by holding the glass of juice up in your power hand, and saying:

Huntress Goddess so bright and wise
I toast to your ever-shining light
Please, Lady, by earth, air, fire, and sea

The best possible job, bring to me
In Diana's name, so mote it be!

Now drink the juice slowly. Next, hold the cashews in your power hand, and chant Diana's name nine times. Then eat each nut one at a time. Just before eating each nut, say,

Cashews of wealth and prosperity
Bring the best possible job to me.
In Diana's name, Blessed Be!

Now imagine yourself already having the best possible job. Go ahead and picture yourself exactly where you will be, and what your actions and feelings will be in your new job. See the images of your new job unfolding in a bright, colorful, and exciting light. Merge with Diana, and ask her to show you the pathway into the future. Follow that pathway, and stand where the action is; think the thoughts, and feel the feelings. Now amplify the intensity of your desire for the job, creating an even more compelling image in your mind's eye. *Really* want the job with your heart, body, and soul! Know that you have the abilities to carry out the actions needed to get the job. Make an effort to see each action clearly. Make a mental note of the steps you need to take for success. Now, allow yourself to savor the joy of getting and working at your new job for a few moments. Delight in seeing the new resources, abilities, and skills you now carry with you as part of your unfolding adventure. Come back to the present moment, knowing that you will be successful in securing the job of your dreams. Use the pen and paper to write down the actions you need to take to get the job. Put a drop of pine-scented oil on each of the four corners of the paper. When you are done, allow the candle to safely burn down, thank Diana, bid farewell to the elements, and close the circle. Put the paper somewhere prominent where you will see it every day. Read the steps out loud once a day, follow them, and you are sure to get the best job possible.

July 31 $4,000 MONEY POUCH

For this spell, you will need a smudge stick, a green felt-tip pen, four dollar bills, four pinches of cinnamon, four pinches of ground ginger, four oak leaves, four bay leaves, and a pouch.

Begin by lighting the smudge stick, dedicating it to a goddess and god of prosperity. Then smudge the items listed. Use the pen to write *$4,000* on both sides of each of the bay and oak leaves. After the ink dries, put the leaves into the pouch. Add the dollar bills, cinnamon, and ginger. Charge the pouch by holding it in your hands and saying:

> *I am discovering*
> *Four thousand ways*
> *To bring money today.*

Put the pouch in your top desk drawer, charging it each morning by holding it in your hands, and repeating,

> *I am discovering*
> *Four thousand ways*
> *To bring money today.*

Keep doing this until you receive $4,000. Afterward, open the pouch and pour the contents on the ground outside your front door to bring you even more money.

UGUST

August 1 LUGHNASSAD PICNIC MAGIC

Today is the feast of Lugh, and Lugh is a Celtic god of mastery and plenty. Plan a picnic feast with your beloved or your family to honor Lugh and his consort Rosemerta on this special sabbat. A beautiful sunny day with pleasant company in nature is one of the most enjoyable ways to spend your time. Be sure to bring plenty of good food and drink, especially water. Select a picnic spot that you have had good luck with and have enjoyed before, or carefully choose a spot that has been highly recommended by a reputable source. Be sure to bring cups, plates, silverware, and napkins—and don't forget a bottle opener and ice. Some picnic foods suitable for this sabbat are: whole grain bread, corn bread, and sourdough bread; berries, apples, grapes, oranges, and peaches; and bite-sized fresh vegetables.

To make Lughnassad cornbread, blend two eggs with two cups of buttermilk, and a quarter-cup of olive oil. Then add two and a half cups of cornmeal, a quarter-cup of honey, three tablespoons of vanilla, one teaspoon of baking soda, and salt to taste. Mix the batter until it is smooth. Stir it clockwise, and chant:

> *Lugh, divine Lord of light*
> *Bring me abundance bright!*

Pour the batter into a well-greased glass pan, and bake at 350°F for twenty-five to thirty minutes.

Take your time, and enjoy your picnic together. Wait until the sun sets before packing up and leaving your picnic spot. As the sun sets, chant:

> *Lugh, divine Lord of light*
> *Bring me abundance bright!!*

In honor of Lugh, return any food scraps and leftover beverages into the earth before you leave. Be sure to leave the area in its natural, beautiful, trash-free state.

August 2   CORNUCOPIA DREAMS

The cornucopia or horn of plenty overflows with flowers and fruit. It is a symbol of prosperity and abundance. Spin this spell just before you go to sleep.

You will need a horn of plenty, paper and pen, fresh flowers, fresh fruit (such as oranges and apples), and a white candle.

Begin by writing the words *My life overflows with abundance and prosperity* on the piece of paper in large letters. Then light the candle, dedicating it to a goddess of plenty such as the Celtic goddess Rosemerta or the Roman goddess Cornucopia. Merge with the candlelight, and for a few minutes, imagine your life overflowing with abundance and prosperity. Go ahead and unleash your imagination. Fold the paper four times and then carefully seal it with candle wax. Hold the sealed paper in your receiving hand and say:

As I sleep peacefully tonight
Dreams of prosperity so bright
Abundance and wealth flow to me
By the Goddess of plenty, blessed be!

Put the sealed paper into the horn of plenty and then add flowers and fruit. Place it next to your bed, on a bedside table or dresser. Allow the candle to burn down safely. As you drift to sleep, imagine your life overflowing abundance and prosperity. Repeat to yourself:

Dreams of overflowing prosperity.

For the best results, do this for eight nights in a row. Write down all that you recall from your dreams. Eat the fruit from the horn of plenty, and cast the spent flowers from the horn into a flowing body of water.

August 3   AUGUST PROSPERITY BATH

You will need a green candle, lemongrass oil, four orange slices, four chamomile tea bags, and a warm bath.

Begin by drawing a warm bath. Next, set the candle by the bathtub so you can see it. Rub the candle with the lemongrass oil, and wipe the oil from your hands. Light the candle, dedicating it to a goddess and god of prosperity and wealth. Now add eight drops of the lemongrass oil to the bathwater; add the tea bags and orange slices. Immerse yourself in the bathwater for a few minutes. Merge with the candlelight, and imagine being prosperous and happy every day of the year. As you relax in the bathwater, chant softly for a few minutes:

> *Divine fruits of prosperity*
> *Share your power with me.*

Soak for a few more minutes, and then get out of the tub and dry off. Compost the orange slices and tea bags. Snuff out the candle, and use it again when you repeat this prosperity bath. Now lay back for a few minutes, and imagine being prosperous and happy each and every day.

August 4   SUNSHINE WEALTH WATER

You will need a clear glass jar and sunshine.

At dawn, fill a clear glass jar with spring or well water. Hold the jar in your hands and say three times:

> *With bright sunshine and light*
> *Bring abundant wealth and good health.*

Now set the jar outside where it can soak up the rays of the sun. Move the jar around during the day, so it is in the sun at all times. Each time you move the jar, hold it with both hands and say:

> *With bright sunshine and light*
> *Bring abundant wealth and good health.*

Just before sunset, bring the jar indoors. Drink half of the Sunshine Wealth Water immediately to fill your body with bright sunshine wealth and good health. Use the other half to power prosperity spells, or sprinkle the water around your workplace; rub it on your desk or on your wallet, checkbook, or purse, to bring more bright and sunny abundant wealth and good health.

August 5   EGG PROSPERITY SPELL

In Finnish mythology, the daughter of nature, the goddess Luonnotar was all alone. Tired of being alone, she fell into the primal ocean where she floated in the sea and became fertile. A duck swam by the goddess and built her nest on the goddess's knee. The duck laid three eggs, and sat on them for three days. The goddess felt a burning pain on her knee, and moved it so quickly that the eggs and the duck fell into the sea. The eggs became the bountiful earth, animals, plants, sky, clouds, sun, and the starry heavens. The goddess then dug up springs and planted the first seeds of life so the earth would grow and flourish.

You will need a park pond with ducks, a piece of bread, a cup, and a packet of seeds.

Begin by taking the bread, cup, and seeds to the pond. Walk around the pond clockwise three times. As you walk, sing or chant softly:

> *My abundance is flowing*
> *Prosperity is growing*
> *By the daughter of nature, blessed be!*

As you walk around the pond the first time, look down on the ground and find an egg-shaped stone. Wash the stone and put it in your pocket. After you have walked around the pond once, break the bread into tiny bits, toss it to the ducks, and repeat:

My abundance is flowing
My prosperity is growing
By the daughter of nature, blessed be!

As you walk around the pond the second time, plant the seeds here and there, and water them with the pond water. With each seed you plant, repeat:

My abundance is flowing
My prosperity is growing
By the daughter of nature, blessed be!

After you walk around the pond the third and final time, hold the egg-shaped stone in your power hand, and imagine abundance and prosperity growing and flowing into your life. Say three times:

My abundance is flowing
My prosperity is growing
By the daughter of nature, blessed be!

Toss the stone into the pond. As you do this, state out loud in a firm and strong voice,

Abundance and prosperity flow to me and grow!

Now and again, revisit the pond. Walk around it three times and chant:

My abundance is flowing
My prosperity is growing
By the daughter of nature, blessed be!

August 6   LITTLE CAT TREASURE CHARM

Jewelry shaped like a cat, or with a cat fashioned into it, can be used for magical protection, good luck, prophecy, drawing riches to you, and granting your deepest wishes. The Little Cat in Irish and Roman folklore was the guardian of a magnificent treasure. It could turn into a flaming ball and burn any thief to ashes. The cat was also a powerful totem of many of the Gaelic tribes, for example the clan of the Catti, or cat people. In many countries, cats have been fierce guardians. For example, in Egypt cats guarded the temples and pyramids.

You will need a piece of jewelry that is cat shaped or has a cat on it, sandalwood incense, and a gold candle.

Do this spell after dark. Begin by lighting the candle, dedicating it to the Little Cat from Roman and Irish folklore. Next, light the incense with the candle, also dedicating it to the Little Cat. Pass the piece of jewelry through the incense smoke for a few minutes to clear it of any unwanted energies. Holding the cat jewelry in your power hand, empower it by saying,

Feline form, cat charm
Protect me from all harm
Beautiful and fierce guardian
Share your treasure with me
In the name of the Little Cat
So be it! Blessed be!

Gaze into the candlelight, still holding the cat in your power hand, and repeat:

Feline form, cat charm
Protect me from all harm
Beautiful and fierce guardian
Share your treasure with me
In the name of the Little Cat
So be it! Blessed be!

Wear the piece of cat jewelry for protection and to help you discover your very own treasure. Add to the power of the charm by holding it in your power hand once a month on the full moon and repeating:

Feline form, cat charm
Protect me from all harm
Beautiful and fierce guardian
Share your treasure with me
In the name of the Little Cat
So be it! Blessed be!

You can make Little Cat Treasure Charms for the cat lovers in your family, especially your children, and for a few lucky feline-loving friends.

August 7   LIGHTHOUSE PROSPERITY

The Lighthouse of Alexandria, also called the Pharos Lighthouse, was one of the Seven Wonders of the Ancient World, and was the last of the wonders to disappear. Dedicated to the savior gods and depicted on Roman coins, it was the tallest building on earth, and was adorned with a statue of Poseidon, the Greek god of the sea. The Pharos Lighthouse had a mysterious mirror. The reflection of the mirror could be seen more than thirty-five miles away, and was used to guide ships as well as to destroy enemy ships. You can use this spell to light your way and guide you to prosperity, as well as protect you from negativity.

You will need a lighthouse keychain or charm, a white candle, a small hand-held mirror, and a smudge stick.

First draw a magic circle, and call in the elements. Light the candle, dedicating it to Poseidon, the Greek god of the sea. Next, light the smudge stick with the candle flame, also dedicating it to Poseidon. Pass the lighthouse keychain or charm and the mirror through the smudge smoke. Completely extinguish the smudge stick. Hold the keychain or charm in your power hand and charge it by saying:

> *Poseidon, divine god of the sea*
> *Please guide me to prosperity*
> *Protect me from negativity*
> *In Poseidon's name, blessed be!*

Place the lighthouse keychain or charm on top of the mirror, and put them where the candlelight reflects off the mirror's surface. Gaze at the mirror's surface for at least fifteen minutes, all the while imagining being guided to fortune and prosperity, as well as being completely protected from all negativity. Allow the candle to burn out safely, and then bid farewell to the elements, thank Poseidon for his presence, and then pull up the circle. Put your keys on the keychain and use it daily. If you used a lighthouse charm instead of a keychain, carry the charm with you in your pocket, purse, briefcase, portfolio, or car.

August 8 WATCHTOWER WEALTH SPELL

Use this spell to enlist the power of the Watchtowers to guide abundance and wealth to your door.

You will need a bowl of earth, a feather, a flashlight, and a cup of water.

Begin by taking everything outside just before dawn or just before sunset. Do this somewhere private where you won't be disturbed. Next, draw a magic circle, and call in the elements. Face north and hold up the bowl of earth. Merge with the earth element and say:

> *Hail and welcome, mighty Watchtowers of the North,*
> *Divine powers of Earth, I pray you*
> *Guide wealth and abundance to my door.*

Set the bowl down and pick up the feather. Face east and wave the feather back and forth. Merge with the air element and say:

> *Hail and welcome, mighty Watchtowers of the East*
> *Divine powers of Air, I pray you*
> *Guide wealth and abundance to my door.*

Set the feather down and pick up the flashlight. Face south, turn on the flashlight, and wave it back and forth. Merge with the light, with the fire element, and say:

> *Hail and welcome, mighty Watchtowers of the South*
> *Divine powers of Fire, I pray you*
> *Guide wealth and abundance to my door.*

Set the flashlight down, and pick up the cup of water. Face west, hold up the cup of water. Merge with the water element and say:

Hail and welcome, mighty Watchtowers of the West,
Divine powers of Water, I pray you
Guide wealth and abundance to my door.

Now stand in the center of your circle with all of the elements and say:

Mighty Watchtowers of north, east, south, and west,
I pray you, bring wealth and abundance to my door
By the powers of earth, air, fire, and sea
As I will, so shall it be! Blessed be!

Next, gaze around you and imagine wealth and abundance coming into your life from all directions. Enjoy this prosperous future. Do this for at least fifteen minutes. Then thank the Watchtowers, bid farewell to the elements, and close the circle. Return the earth to the ground. Drink the water. Take the flashlight and feather and go back indoors when you are done.

August 9   RINGING IN THE GREEN

You will need citrus-scented oil, a stack of old magazines, scissors, a glue stick, a sheet of green posterboard, and a bell.

Anoint yourself with the citrus-scented oil. Go through the magazines and cut out pictures of things that make you think of wealth, riches, prosperity, happiness, joy, fulfillment, and things you like such as homes, cars, vacation spots, pets, gardens, gorgeous beaches, magical forests, mountaintops, musical instruments, video cameras, family groupings, children playing, masterpieces, and so forth. Cut out pictures of things that really attract you, images that draw your attention. Now trim and glue the pictures to the posterboard in a collage. Use the picture that you especially like in the center of the collage, and then fan out from there. When you are finished, anoint the four corners of the poster board with a drop of the citrus-scented oil, starting with the top-right corner and ending with the top left.

Put the collage in front of you, and look at the pictures. Ring the bell nine times, in three series of three, and say three times:

> *Three times three,*
> *I ring in the green*
> *Dear Goddess and God*
> *Please help draw to me*
> *These images of prosperity*
> *As I see it, so shall it be!*

Now imagine each of the images on your collage in front of you naturally manifesting itself in your life. Each time you focus on another picture, ring the bell three times. Then put the collage where you can easily see it. Take a few minutes each morning for the next three months to focus on the pictures. Each time you do this, ring the bell nine times in three series of three and imagine manifesting those images into your life. Say,

> *Three times three*
> *I ring in the green.*
> *I manifest prosperity.*

August 10   PILLAR OF WEALTH CANDLE SPELL

For this spell, you will need a green pillar candle, vanilla-scented oil, cinnamon oil (you can make this by mixing a pinch of ground cinnamon in a teaspoon of olive oil), and a ballpoint pen.

Use the pen to write your full name on the body of the candle. Then write the words, *Riches, Joy, Plenty*, on top of your name. Rub the candle with the vanilla and cinnamon oils. Next, hold the pillar candle in your hands until it feels warm. Put the candle on the altar, and wipe the oil from your hands. Light the candle, saying three times:

> *By the divine light of the Lady and Lord*
> *Pillar of Wealth bring me riches, joy, and plenty*
> *As I will, so shall it be! Blessed be!*

Focus on the candlelight, and imagine a life of riches, joy, and plenty. Unleash your imagination and have fun. Do this for at least thirty minutes. When you are done, snuff out the candle. Each night for the next eight nights, relight the candle, repeat the incantation three times, and once again imagine a life filled with riches, joy, and plenty. On the eighth night, allow the candle safely to burn down.

August 11   SOCK OF PLENTY

You will need cedar incense, a piece of jade, paper and pen, pine-scented oil, and a green sock. Begin by lighting the incense, dedicating it to the goddesses and gods of prosperity. Write down four ways in which you would like to be prosperous. For example, you might like to have a perfect job, a lovely home, a great family garden, and a fantastic lifestyle. Other options are family pets you would like, vacations, an electric car, a solar energy system for your home, an ideal car stereo, and so forth. Fold the paper four times. Hold it in your power hand and say:

> *Dear Goddesses and Gods of prosperity*
> *Please grant these four desires to me.*

Next, pass the jade through the incense smoke to clear it of any unwanted energies. Rub pine-scented oil on the piece of jade. Hold the stone in your power hand and say:

> *Dear Goddesses and Gods of prosperity*
> *Please fill this stone with your blessings.*

Then put four drops of the pine-scented oil on the folded paper. Next, open the sock and put four drops of oil into the opening. Put the folded paper into the sock, following with the jade. Firmly knot the sock, hold it in your power hand, and say:

> *Dear Goddesses and Gods of prosperity*
> *Please grant these four desires to me.*

Hold the sock in your hands, and imagine it as magical, filled to the brim with your four desires. Visualize plenty of money, checks, riches, and other kinds of abundance, coming from all kinds of sources such as the mail, your paycheck, from selling merchandise or real estate, saving your pennies, and so forth. Also visualize sharing your wealth with others and giving generously to worthy charities. When you are done, put the sock in your sock drawer for the next eight months to draw your four prosperous desires to you.

August 12   GOLDEN TREE MAGIC

You will need a fruit tree, a six-foot-long piece of gold ribbon, and a cup of
Sunshine Wealth Water (see August 4). Take the ribbon and water outside,
and find a fruit tree. Walk clockwise around the tree three times, sprinkling
the Sunshine Wealth Water around the tree and chant:

> *Beautiful and gracious tree*
> *May you live strong and free.*

Then tie the gold ribbon around the tree trunk in a large bow. Next,
place your hands on the tree and say:

> *Beautiful and gracious tree*
> *May you live strong and free*
> *Please empower and bless me*
> *And bring golden opportunities*
> *In summer, fall, winter, and spring*
> *As I will, so shall it be!*

Now lean your body against the tree and place both palms against the
bark. Imagine the abundant, fruitful power of the tree filling your body, mind,
and soul. Close your eyes, breathe in the color gold, and breathe out any tension you may be feeling. Continue to breathe in gold for several minutes.
When you are done, untie the ribbon. Retie the ribbon next to the main
entrance of your home or businessplace to encourage golden opportunities
throughout the year.

August 13 RAINING MONEY SPELL

Considered the most powerful of the goddesses of Asia, the Hindu goddess Lakshmi symbolizes all forms of wealth and prosperity of the world. She rose from the ocean covered with necklaces, bracelets, and pearls, crowned and golden, bearing a lotus.

You will need lotus-scented oil, a squirt bottle filled with water, and a cup of uncooked rice.

Begin by going outdoors. Draw a magic circle and call in the elements. Anoint yourself with the lotus-scented oil and say:

> *Lakshmi of the Lotus, great goddess of prosperity*
> *Divine and beautiful Mother, please come to me.*

Next, sprinkle the rice clockwise around your circle, clockwise. As you do this, say:

> *Ommmmmm, Ommmmmm, Ommmmmm*
> *Lakshmi of the Lotus, great goddess of prosperity*
> *May money, joy, and plenty now rain down on me*
> *By the lotus-gem Mother Goddess, blessed be!*

Now use the squirt bottle and squirt the rice that you have sprinkled around the circle. Start in the north quarter of the circle, and move clockwise all the way around the circle. As you do this say,

> *Ommmmmm, Ommmmmm, Ommmmmm*
> *Lakshmi of the Lotus, great goddess of prosperity*
> *May money, joy, and plenty now rain down on me*
> *By the lotus-gem Mother Goddess, blessed be!*

When you are done, thank the goddess Lakshmi, bid farewell to the elements, and close the circle. Use the heel of your power foot to blend the rice into the earth. Keep the squirt bottle full, and squirt it up in the air above you, at your front door, or in your car, in all those places you would like more money, joy, and plenty to rain down on you.

August 14   SWEET PROSPERITY POTION

You will need a bowl, a scoop of natural vanilla ice cream, a half-teaspoon of sweetened cocoa or chocolate soy-drink powder, a quarter-cup of crushed toasted almonds, and a cherry.

Put the ice cream in the bowl, and then sprinkle the cocoa over the top of the ice cream in a clockwise circle. As you do, say,

Sweet abundance and prosperity, now come to me.

Next, sprinkle the crushed almonds in a clockwise circle around the circle of cocoa and repeat:

Sweet abundance and prosperity, now come to me.

Now put the cherry in the middle of the circle of almonds, and repeat a third time:

Sweet abundance and prosperity, now come to me.

Then focus on drawing more sweet abundance and prosperity to you as you eat the tasty potion. Imagine just how sweet it is!

August 15 TURTLE WEALTH CHARM

The turtle has magical qualities of stability and security. It can be used to gain financial rewards and stability.

You will need a metal figurine of a turtle, a smudge stick, a plate of pebbles, and a cup of water.

Begin by lighting the smudge stick, dedicating it to a favorite goddess of abundance. Then pass the turtle through the smudge smoke for several minutes. Also pass the plate and pebbles through the purifying smoke. Hold the turtle between your hands and say three times:

> *With this charm, I am divinely blessed*
> *By abundance from north, east, south, and west.*

Place the turtle on the plate of pebbles in the north quadrant of your home to attract better career opportunities. Or, put the plate and turtle next to the entrance of your home, in a hidden spot, facing inside. When you have positioned the plate with the turtle, then pour the water into the plate. When the water evaporates from the plate, replenish it. Each time you do this, your abundance of joy, love, and prosperity are also replenished.

August 16 FAERY FORTUNE DUST

For this spell, you will need a bowl, a mortar and pestle or coffee grinder (one you won't be using for coffee), four pinches of dried lavender flowers, four pinches of dried ginger, four pinches of dried jasmine flowers, and four pinches of oak bark.

Begin by grinding all the ingredients into a fine powdery dust. As you grind the herbs, imagine being in a lush and enchanting garden filled with all kinds of helpful and generous faery beings. Do this for a few minutes. Then put the Faery Fortune Dust in the bowl. Hold the bowl up with both hands, and say three times in a forthright voice:

> *Please share your faery fortune with me*
> *In the name of the fae, blessed be!*

Now sprinkle tiny pinches of Faery Fortune Dust around the four corners of your home and businessplace (north, east, south, and west, in that order). Also sprinkle a bit of the magic dust in your pocket, purse, wallet, bankbook, and checkbook to bring you the fortune and magical riches of the faeries.

August 17   JUICY ABUNDANCE POTION

You will need a half-cup of unfiltered, organic apple juice, a half-cup of organic grape juice, a half-cup of papaya nectar, a bowl, and a tall, ice-filled glass. Stir the juices together clockwise in the bowl. As you stir, chant,

> *Divine abundance, come to me*

Now pour the potion into the glass over the ice. Before you take each sip, say:

> *Divine abundance, come to me.*

As you drink the potion, imagine an abundance of love, joy, and prosperity coming to you from all different sources, from near and far away, today and every day of your life.

August 18   BUDDHA EIGHT-DAY CANDLE SPELL

This simple candle spell is particularly powerful.

You will need a large, red candle in the shape of Buddha, a plate covered with aluminum foil, and a ballpoint pen.

Begin by writing your initials three times on the candle. Then place it on the plate, facing the candle toward the main door of your home. Light the candle and say:

> *I dedicate this candle to Buddha bright*
> *Help me discover joy in your light*
> *Bring abundance into my home today*
> *Dear Buddha, please light the way!*
> *Bring abundance and harmony into my home.*

Now allow the candle to burn for at least three hours. As it does, imagine all sorts of abundance flowing into your home from many different sources. Enjoy the visualization. After three hours, snuff out the candle. Relight it the next day, repeating the dedication when you do so. On the eighth day, allow the candle to safely burn down. (Note: You will need to work with the candle to keep it burning by fishing out the wick from the melted wax and relighting it if it extinguishes itself.)

August 19   GARDEN OF PROSPERITY

For this spell, you will need a photograph of yourself, or one of you and your family, a photograph or picture of your ideal garden, three green candles, and a drum.

Light the first candle, then light the second with the first, and the third with the second. As you light each one, say:

> *I dedicate this candle to earth, air, fire, and sea*
> *By the Lady and Lord of prosperity, blessed be!*

Next, place the pictures in front of the candles where you can easily see them. Imagine a soft green mist filling the candle flames. Say three times:

> *In the magical green mist I see*
> *A blessed garden of prosperity*
> *So be it, blessed be!*

Now imagine a beautiful garden of prosperity in the green mist of the candle flames. Let your imagination run wild. Fill your magical garden with extraordinary faery beings, with flowers of every color and vegetables of every kind, as well as fruiting trees, splendid old-growth trees, your power animals, and a clear, glassy pool and powerful waterfall. Enjoy the abundant beauty of the magical garden in the candle flames. Now pick up the drum and drum your garden into life. As you drum, chant:

> *Blessed garden of prosperity*
> *Come to life, blessed be!*

Do this for at least fifteen minutes. Allow the candles to safely burn down. Put the two images together, with the garden image placed behind the image of yourself (or of you and your family). Keep these images on your refrigerator. Pick up your drum, focus your attention on the two images, and drum your way to your garden of prosperity anytime you like to draw more abundance into your life. To manifest a live garden of prosperity, plant plenty of flowers, vegetables, and trees around your home during the year, and tend them with loving care.

August 20 SILVER MONEY CANDLE SPELL

For this spell, you will need a silver taper candle and a candleholder, a ball-point pen, four pinches of mint, four pinches of ground ginger, and four pinches of basil.

Use the pen to write your name on the candle. Next, write the words *Silver Riches and Money*, and *Blessed Be!* Hold the candle in your hands until it gets warm. As you do so, imagine plenty of silver money and riches coming to you. Then put the candle in its holder, and set it on the altar. Sprinkle the pinches of mint, ginger, and basil clockwise around the candle in three circles. Light the candle and say three times:

> *Silver riches and money*
> *Bright shining candlelight*
> *Bring me joy and prosperity*
> *As I will, so shall it be!*

Next, take a few minutes to imagine all of the gifts you have been given over the years, and how blessed you have been. Now imagine some of the future gifts of joy and prosperity you truly desire. Do this for at least fifteen minutes. Allow the candle to safely burn down.

August 21 LAUGHING BUDDHA MAGIC

You will need a statue or picture of the laughing Buddha. Place the statue or picture directly in front of you, and focus all of your attention on the laughing Buddha for a couple of minutes. Then say:

Laughing Buddha, generous god
Please grant me your divine gifts
As one becomes two becomes three
In Buddha's name, blessed be!

Continue to gaze at the laughing Buddha. Imagine your finances improving threefold. Do this for at least five minutes. Keep the statue or place the picture so that it faces the main door of your home or office, or position the laughing Buddha diagonally opposite to, and facing, the main door. This will bring you the divine gifts of Buddha: personal success, and financial gain.

August 22 TOOTH FAERY SPELL

This spell is dedicated to this day in August, the official Tooth Faery Day. You don't have to lose a tooth to benefit from the Tooth Faery.

You will need a white beeswax pillar candle and a candleholder, a bowl of cool water, a ballpoint pen, fresh flowers, and lavender-scented oil.

Begin by washing the candle in cool water and drying it. Use the pen to write your initials on the candle in large letters. Now write the words *Tooth Faery Gifts*, on top of your initials. Rub the candle with the oil and then anoint yourself. Put the candle in its holder on the altar, and place the fresh flowers around the candle in a clockwise circle. Wipe the oil from your hands, and light the candle, dedicating it to the helpful and generous faeries. Now gaze into the candlelight, and imagine all kinds of wonderful and magical gifts from the faeries showering down upon you. Say three times:

> *Bright fae of earth, air, fire, and sea*
> *Please shower your magical gifts upon me.*

Burn the candle for at least sixteen minutes a day for eight consecutive days. Each time you light the candle, turn your mind toward being showered with magical faery gifts, and repeat three times:

> *Bright fae of earth, air, fire, and sea*
> *Please shower your magical gifts upon me.*

On the eighth day, allow the candle to safely burn down. Take the candle remains outside and bury them under a flower bush as an offering to the helpful and generous fae.

August 23 HOLLYHOCK AND YARROW DOLLY

You can make this prosperity dolly with your children and other family members.

You will need eight large hollyhock stalks with dried seeds, eight yarrow flowers with stems, and eight sixteen-inch green ribbons.

Gather all the items together and go outside. Bundle the hollyhock stalks and yarrow together and tie them with the ribbons. As you tie each ribbon around the stalks and stems, say:

> *We are tying happiness and prosperity into our lives right now.*

When you are done, place the dolly in the yard where you can easily see it. Each day, take a few of the hollyhock seeds from the dried pods on the stalks and scatter them around the outside of your home in the spots where you want hollyhocks. Water the seeds with your children to encourage them to sprout and grow. As they grow, your happiness and wealth will also grow and bloom, year after prosperous year.

August 24   THE SECRET WEALTH OF PLANTS

In Feng Shui, the jade plant brings wealth and good luck.

You will need a living plant, preferably a jade plant.

Put the jade plant in the southeast corner of your home. The southeast is the direction of wealth and good luck. After you set the plant in place, focus your attention on its beauty, and say three times to the plant:

> *Beautiful plant, as you thrive and grow*
> *So too does my wealth and good luck grow.*

Tend and water the plant regularly. As it grows and thrives, so will your wealth and good luck.

August 25   STEPPING INTO THE GREEN

For this spell, you will need a pair of green socks and a lawn. Just before dawn, put the green socks on your feet, and go outside and walk around on green grass for at least five minutes. As your socks become damp with morning dew, chant softly:

> *I'm stepping into the green*
> *New prosperity now come to me.*

When you're done, take off the socks and knot them together. Put them in the morning sun to dry and wear them today to attract new prosperity. You can repeat this as often as you like.

August 26   RUNE FORTUNE COOKIES

You can make these Rune Fortune Cookies with your entire family.

You will need a recipe for oatmeal cookies and all the ingredients, a cup of toasted cashew pieces, and milk.

Mix the oatmeal cookie batter, and then shape large cookies. Flatten the cookies, and use the cashew pieces to make these three runes on the tops of the flattened uncooked cookies; Sowilo [𐍃], Fehu [ᚠ], and Jera [ᛃ]. Sowilo's energy helps strengthen your personal power and mental skills; Fehu's energy helps manifest more mobile wealth like money and goods; and Jera's energy brings rewards, fruitful harvests, and good luck.

When the cookies have finished baking, let them cool, and then eat them one at a time. Just before eating each rune cookie, chant the rune you are eating nine times. For example:

> *Sowilo, Sowilo, Sowilo*
> *Sowilo, Sowilo, Sowilo*
> *Sowilo, Sowilo, Sowilo!*

This empowers them with even more runic energy. Don't forget to drink your milk, too!

August 27   MUSIC MELODY SPELL

You will need some relaxing music with a melody that you love to hum to yourself, five green candles, five dollar bills, and patchouli oil.

Begin by turning on the music. Rub the scented oil on the candles, and then anoint yourself. Arrange the candles in a five-pointed-star shape on your altar. This represents the five elements of earth, air, fire, water, and spirit. Now place the five dollar bills in front of each of the candles. Anoint each of the dollars with a drop of oil. As you do, say:

> *Money attracts money*
> *Bring more money to me*
> *As I hum this melody*
> *So be it! Blessed be!*

Now wipe the oil from your hands and light the candles one at a time, starting with the candle at the top of the star and moving clockwise. Just before lighting each candle, say:

> *Money attracts money*
> *Bring more money to me*
> *As I hum this melody*
> *So be it! Blessed be!*

Sit back and gaze at the candles. As you do, hum the melody of the music you are listening to right now. Play the music over and over again, humming the melody and enjoying the dancing candle flames. Now imagine plenty of money coming to you as naturally as the melody of the music flows through your mind. Allow the candles to burn down safely. Each and every day, hum the money melody to attract money and prosperity.

August 28   GRIS-GRIS MONEY BAG

For this spell, you will need a green votive candle, a green drawstring bag, a piece of green tree moss, eight whole cloves, eight pinches of allspice, eight almonds, eight capsules of echinacea, a dollar bill, and a small quartz crystal.

Begin by lighting the candle. Put all the items in the bag one at a time. Fold the dollar bill four times, and put it in last. Close the bag, hold it in your power hand, and empower it by saying three times:

> *Magic money bag of green*
> *Bring cash and bring it fast*
> *Bring happiness and make it last*
> *So be it! Blessed be!*

Put the bag in front of the candle as the candle burns safely down. When you are done, put the bag in your desk drawer to bring you more money and happiness every day of the year.

August 29   THE CHECK'S IN THE MAIL SPELL

You will need a gold pillar candle and a candleholder, cinnamon oil, your checkbook, an outstanding bill, and a ballpoint pen.

Begin by using the pen to write on the candle the name of the company or person that you own money to right now. Then write down the amount you owe. Rub the candle with cinnamon oil and put it in its holder on the altar. Next, wipe the oil from your hands. Use the pen to write a check out for the amount you owe on the bill. Get the bill all ready to be mailed. Put the check in the envelope, seal it, and put a stamp on it. Put the sealed envelope under the candle on the altar. Light the candle and say:

> *This candle lights the way*
> *And brings money to pay*
> *This debt I owe today*
> *So be it! Blessed be!*

Next, gaze at the candle for several minutes while imagining the income and money coming into your life so you are easily able to pay your bill in a week. Visualize sending the envelope with the check in it in a week's time. Do this for fifteen minutes, and then snuff the candle out. Repeat this process every day for a week. On the seventh day, allow the candle to safely burn down. Within that time, you will most likely have secured the money to pay the bill and send the envelope.

August 30   DRAGON TREASURE SPELL

Dragons symbolize good luck, elemental power, great potency, wisdom, and wealth. Dragons guard magnificent treasures of precious gems and metals, secretly hidden in deep caverns and caves. Even today, some say dragons can still be found at sulfur springs, wells, lakes, ocean caves, and inside mountains. The dragon is synonymous with the Ouroboros or Earth Serpent, the never-ending, ever-beginning symbol of power and wisdom.

For this spell, you will need a silver candle, a gold candle, a ballpoint pen, a statue of a dragon, dragon's-blood oil, eight pinches of sweet basil, and some powerful music.

Begin by drawing a magic circle, and calling in the elements. Turn on some powerful music, a selection that really gets your blood flowing. Next, write your initials on the candle. Then write the words *Dragon Treasure* on top of your initials. Dress the candle with the dragon's-blood oil, and then anoint yourself with the oil. Put the candle on the altar and scatter the pinches of sweet basil clockwise in a circle around the candle. The sweet basil helps soothe the dragon energy. Next, light the candle, dedicating it to the helpful dragons. Say three times,

Great and mighty dragons, blessed be!

Rub the statue with the dragon's-blood oil. Hold the statue in your hands and say three times:

Great dragons of earth, air, fire, and sea
Share your dragon treasures with me
From north, east, south, and west
By the powers of the dragons, I am blessed!

Continue to hold the statue in your hands for a few minutes as you gaze at the candlelight. Imagine attracting your dragon's share of treasure in the next few months. When you are done, thank the powerful dragons, bid farewell to the elements, and close the circle. Put the statue by the candle as it burns down safely. Then place the dragon in the east part of your home or office to attract good luck and your dragon's share of treasure.

August 31 HONEY MONEY MAGIC

For this spell, you will need a green candle, a candleholder, and two teaspoons of honey.

Draw a magic circle and call in the elements. Coat the candle with one teaspoon of honey. Put the candle in the holder, and wash off your hands. Then light the candle and dedicate it to a favorite goddess of abundance. Gaze at the candle flame, and say three times:

> *Magic honey, divine and sweet*
> *Joy and good luck stick to me*
> *By the Goddess, blessed be!*

Warm both of your hands in the candle flame for a couple of minutes, being careful not to burn your skin. Then apply the other teaspoon of honey to your hands and rub them together for a few minutes. As you do this chant,

> *Money sticks to me like honey.*
> *By the Goddess, blessed be!*

When you are done, wash your hands. Then thank the Goddess, bid farewell to the elements, and close the circle. Allow the candle to burn down safely.

SEPTEMBER

September 1 SUN POWER SPELL

You will need a pot of living flowers and eight pinches of basil.

Just before sunrise, begin by drawing a magic circle. Outline the circle with the flowers. Sprinkle the basil clockwise around the outline of the flower circle. Then call in the elements. Face east, preferably somewhere you can see the rising sun, and hold up the pot of flowers. Say:

> *By the Lady and the Lord,*
> *May the prosperous power of the sun*
> *Help these flowers grow and thrive*
> *As well as bring abundance into my life*
> *As I will, so it is done!*

Now, imagine the bright energy of the sun filling the flowers, and filling your being to the brim with sunlight and radiant fortune. Do this for at least thirty minutes. When you are done, thank the Goddess and God, bid farewell to the elements, and close the circle. Then plant the flowers outdoors in a bright sunny spot and water them regularly. Or you can put the pot on your balcony or in a sunny window and care for it. As the plant grows and thrives, so will your fortune.

September 2 MAGIC MIST SPELL

You will need peppermint oil, thyme oil, rosemary oil, a half-cup of spring or well water, and a fine-mist spray bottle.

Fill the bottle with the water and add twenty drops of peppermint oil, ten drops of thyme oil, and ten drops of rosemary oil. Cap the bottle and shake it well. As you shake it, chant:

> *Magic mist, blessed be*
> *Bring me divine prosperity.*

Close your eyes and spray the mist over your head several times. Breathe in the aroma. Each time you spray the mist over your head, chant:

> *Magic mist, blessed be*
> *Bring me divine prosperity.*

Use the mist over the next three days for best results.

September 3 MAGIC COIN

You will need a smudge stick, a large feather or feather fan, a silver coin, and paper and pen.

Begin by drawing a magic circle and calling in the elements. Use the pen and paper to notate exactly the kind of abundance you want to draw to you in the next month. Next, light the smudge stick, and thoroughly smudge the coin in the purifying smoke. Then smudge yourself. Use the feather to "brush" the smoke over the coin and yourself. Extinguish the smudge when you are done. Hold the coin in your power hand, and read your notes aloud three times. Put the coin in the middle of the paper, and fold the paper and coin together three times. Hold the folded paper and coin in your power hand and say three times:

> *Magic coin of plenty*
> *Bring divine prosperity.*
> *So be it! Blessed be!*

Imagine drawing exactly the kind of abundance to you that you desire. Also imagine the many ways that abundance will flow to you from your efforts, ideas, and from magically being at the right place at the right time. When you are done, thank the elements and bid farewell to them, and close the circle. Put the folded paper and coin into your wallet or purse. From time to time, empower the magic coin by holding the folded paper and coin in your power hand and repeating:

> *Magic coin of plenty*
> *Bring divine prosperity.*
> *So be it! Blessed be!*

Then put the paper and coin back into your wallet or purse.

September 4   SCAVENGER WALK MAGIC

You will need a large green posterboard, a bag, glue, gold and silver glitter pens, and a family member or friend. (Note: You can do this solitary, but it's more fun with someone you like.)

Take a walk outside in your neighborhood or a nearby park, and collect small things like leaves, twigs, berries, flowers, stones, slips of paper, a penny, a candy wrapper, odd pieces of plastic, fabric, or metal. Collect whatever feels "right" from many different spots and put the items you find in the bag. Every time I take this scavenger walk, I always wind up collecting the most amazing things. When you have collected sixteen or more things, take your bag back indoors. Use the glitter pens to write on the posterboard all the kinds of prosperity and abundance you would like in your life. Then write down the names of some of your favorite goddesses and gods of prosperity and abundance on the poster board. Take out the items you collected on your scavenger hunt walk, and arrange them on the posterboard. Don't so much think about what you are doing, but rather "feel" the items on the board. Put them where they feel right. Then glue the items onto the board. When you are done, focus your attention on the work of art you have created, and bless it by saying:

> *Bless this poster of divine prosperity*
> *By the Goddesses and Gods, blessed be!*

Now hang the art someplace where you can easily see it for the next year to draw divine prosperity and abundance to you. You can repeat this work anytime you need to create more prosperity.

September 5   NUTS ABOUT SUCCESS SPELL

You will need four cashews, four pistachio nuts, four almonds, and a green candle.

Begin by lighting the candle, dedicating it to a favorite Goddess of prosperity such as Anu (Celtic) or Lakshmi (Hindu). Next, place the nuts around the candle in a clockwise circle. Focus your awareness on the candle flame,

WICCAN SPELL A DAY

and imagine actually experiencing the success and prosperity you have always desired and deserved. Continue doing this as you eat the nuts, one at a time, starting with the topmost nut, and eating clockwise. Before eating each nut, imagine delicious prosperity filling you, and say:

> *Blessed be, divine prosperity!*

When you are done, continue meditating on the candle flame, all the while imagining more delectable prosperity and abundance filling your life.

September 6   HAPPY TUNE MAGIC

You will need a stereo, CD player, or cassette player, a happy tune, and patchouli oil.

Begin by anointing yourself with the scented oil. Then turn on a happy tune. For example, you might play Laverne Baker's rendition of "Shake A Hand" or James Brown's "I Feel Good." Play the song at least three times. As you go through the day, hum and sing the happy tune again and again. Each time you sing or hum the tune, you attract more happiness and good fortune. You can repeat this as often as you like.

September 7   FRUITFUL HARVEST BATH

You can take this bath whenever you like. It's a magical way to start your day!

You will need a warm bath, a green votive candle, vanilla oil, a half-cup of apple juice, and four orange slices.

In the morning, fill the tub with warm water. Then add eight drops of vanilla oil, the juice, and the orange slices to the water. Dress the candle with the vanilla oil and wipe the oil from your hands. Light the candle, dedicating it to a favorite goddess or god of prosperity. Place the candle where you can easily see it. Get in the water and soak. Gaze into the candlelight, and as you do, imagine your dreams coming to fruition in the flame. Now close your eyes, and, in your mind's eye, move your awareness into the future, where you are joyful, successful, and fruitful. Soak in these uplifting images and thoughts for at least fifteen minutes. When you are done soaking, get out and dry off. Then anoint yourself with the vanilla oil. Snuff out the candle, and enjoy a fruitful and successful day.

September 8   HOME SWEET PROSPEROUS HOME

There are many folk tales and stories about a person becoming rich through a dream. One such tale is about a wealthy young man who loses everything, and has to earn his living by hard labor in Dublin. One night, an old wizard comes to him in a dream, and says, "Your fortune is in London, go there to seek it." So the young man sets out for London. He arrives after dark and takes shelter in a park. A gang of thieves rob him while he sleeps. In the morning, he sits under a large oak tree in the park, wondering what to do, when an old wizard in tattered rags walks up to him and asks, "Where do you come from?" The young man answers, "From Dublin." The old man asks, "What brought you here?" The young man tells him about his dream and the robbery. The old man laughs, and says, "You fool. A man has come to me three times in my dream and described a house in Dublin where a great treasure is supposedly buried beneath an old oak tree. He also told me to go there and dig it up, but you don't see me going off on some wild goose chase." The old man talks for a while, describing the details of his dream, the house, and the tree. Then he pulls a few coins out of his tattered coat pocket, and says, "This will help you return home, you young fool." The young man thanks him and takes the money. He also realizes that the man has just described his own house in Dublin and the oak tree next to it. When he returns home, he digs up the great treasure, and he is fortunate and lucky for the rest of his life.

You will need a tree in your yard, a trowel or small shovel, and a small quartz crystal.

Go outdoors with the trowel and crystal. Now dig a small hole for the crystal at the eastern base of the tree. If you don't have a tree or a yard, then use a living tree in a pot placed in the east quadrant of your living room. Hold the crystal in your power hand and say:

> *By the divine grace and generosity*
> *Of the Goddess and God*
> *Please bring fortune and good luck*
> *To my home sweet, prosperous home*
> *Please bring much joy and love*
> *To my home sweet, abundant home*
> *By the grace of the Goddess and God*
> *So be it! Home sweet home. Blessed be!*

Place the stone in the hole, and cover it over with soil. Place three small stones or sticks on top, and say three times,

> *So be it! Home sweet home. Blessed be!*

As you fall asleep for the next twenty-eight nights, repeat over and over to yourself:

Home sweet, prosperous home
Home sweet, abundant home
So dream it! So be it!

September 9 RIVER WEALTH SPELL

You will need a small piece of bloodstone and a cup of uncooked rice.

Begin by taking the stone and rice with you and going outdoors and locating a running river or stream. Sit or stand next to the water, and find three small stones on the ground nearby. Toss the stones into the water one at a time. Each time you toss in a stone, say:

River spirits, blessed be
As you flow, wealth flows to me
As you thrive, my fortune comes alive
By north, east, south, and west,
By the river spirits, I am blessed.

Then run your hands in the water for a few minutes. Touch, smell, and see the water. Look into the water, take a deep breath, and become one with the river for a few minutes. Toss the bloodstone into the water and repeat:

River spirits, blessed be
As you flow, wealth flows to me
As you thrive, my fortune comes alive

By north, east, south, and west,
By the river spirits, I am blessed.

Next, toss the rice into the water a few pinches at a time. After you finish tossing the rice into the water, say:

River spirits, blessed be
As you flow, wealth flows to me
As you thrive, my fortune comes alive
By north, east, south, and west,
By the river spirits, I am blessed.

When you are done, thank the river spirits and enjoy the river for as long as you like.

September 10   FLOWER FORTUNE CHARM

You will need four hollyhock stalks with seed pods, four goldenrod stalks, and a twenty-four-inch length of green ribbon.

Begin by going outdoors and tying the ribbon around the hollyhock and goldenrod stalks. After you are done, empower the charm by saying three times:

Magic charm of fortune and wealth
Bring abundance and good health
By the hollyhock and goldenrod fae
Please bring prosperity my way.

Put the charm in your front yard to encourage more abundance and prosperity. Within the next month, plant the dried seeds that are in the pods around your yard and water them regularly. As they thrive, so too does your fortune, wealth, and good health.

September 11   EARTH ABUNDANCE PRAYER

We will all remember this day with sadness and pain for the rest of our lives. Rather than dwelling on the negative events of this day, this hopeful prayer promotes peace, love, harmony, tolerance, abundance, and beauty.

You will need nine-inch pieces of ribbon in the colors of the rainbow.

Begin by holding the ribbons in your hands and tying them together. As you do this, merge with the Mother Goddess and Father God. Then hold the ribbons in your hands as if to pray, and say this prayer just as the sun rises, early in the morning. This Earth Abundance Prayer is especially powerful when you pray with your family and friends:

> *Dear Mother Goddess and Father God*
> *I pray you, help us know world peace*
> *I pray you, help us know divine love*
> *I pray you, help us learn tolerance*
> *I pray you, help us live in harmony*
> *I pray you, help us share our abundance*
> *I pray you, help us create beauty*
> *I pray you, dear Lady and Lord*
> *May all terror and pain be washed away*
> *Please help unite us all as One world*
> *In the name of the Goddess and God, blessed be!*

Now tie the ribbons to a healthy tree or bush outdoors. Each time you pass by or look at the ribbons, repeat the prayer to encourage peace, love, tolerance, harmony, abundance, and beauty, now and forevermore.

September 12   GOLDEN RICHES MAGIC

You will need eight King Alfred daffodil bulbs, bulb food, and a hand trowel.

Begin by going outdoors and finding a clear, sunny spot to plant the bulbs. Dig the holes for the bulbs with the trowel, and fill them with a little bulb food. Before putting each of the bulbs in the ground, hold them, one at a time, and empower them by saying:

> *Draw divine golden riches to me*
> *By the daffodil fae, blessed be!*

Then plant the bulbs and cover them over with soil. As you do this repeat:

> *Draw divine golden riches to me*
> *By the daffodil fae, blessed be!*

As the bulbs leaf, bud out, and bloom brightly golden by next spring, so too will your faery riches.

September 13   HOT POTATO POTION

You will need two tablespoons of extra-light olive oil, two yellow onions, two garlic cloves, four large russet potatoes, a bay leaf, a small sprig of thyme, a small bunch of fresh parsley, two pints of nonfat milk, a quarter-cup of chopped chives, a large ceramic pot, and a wooden spoon. Put the onions and garlic in the pot and bake them in the oven at 250°F for about an hour. Let them cool. Then put the oil in the pot and turn on the stove to medium heat. Finely chop the onions and garlic. As you do, chant:

> *Potion of prosperity,*
> *Fill me with plenty*
> *Blessed be!*

Then add them to the pot on the stove and sauté them until they are golden. As you cook, stir the ingredients clockwise with the wooden spoon, and chant:

> *Potion of prosperity*
> *Fill me with plenty*
> *Blessed be!*

Next, add the potatoes (chopped) and sauté them as well. As you chop and stir in the potatoes, chant:

> *Potion of prosperity*
> *Fill me with plenty*
> *Blessed be!*

Break the bay leaf four times and add it to the potion. As you stir it in, chant:

> *Potion of prosperity*
> *Fill me with plenty*
> *Blessed be!*

Next, add the thyme leaves, finely chopped (remove the stem and return it to the earth or put it in your compost bin). As you stir the chopped thyme into the potion, chant:

> *Potion of prosperity*
> *Fill me with plenty*
> *Blessed be!*

Then add the parsley, finely chopped. As you stir it in, chant:

> *Potion of prosperity*
> *Fill me with plenty*
> *Blessed be!*

Now add the milk. As you stir the potion clockwise with the wooden spoon, repeat the chant:

> *Potion of prosperity*
> *Fill me with plenty*
> *Blessed be!*

Simmer the potion for thirty to forty minutes, stirring occasionally to keep it from sticking to the bottom of the pot. Then use the spoon to find and remove the bay leaf pieces. (Note: You can let the mixture cool if you like and run it through a food processor and heat it back up if you prefer a smooth potion.) Serve the hot potato potion in bowls or mugs and garnish with the chopped chives. Before taking each spoonful of the potion, say:

> *Potion of prosperity*
> *Fill me with plenty*
> *Blessed be!*"

September 14   MONEY UNDER EVERY BUSH

For this spell, you will need a flowering bush, a dollar bill, a sixteen-inch length of flexible grapevine, eight pinches of marjoram, eight cloves, and eight almonds.

Begin by taking everything outdoors and selecting a flowering bush in your yard. Draw a magic circle around the bush, and then scatter the marjoram, cloves, and almonds clockwise around the inside of the circle. Next, call in the elements. Fold the dollar bill a total of eight times, and then hold it in your power hand and say:

> *May my wealth and fortune bloom as does this bush*
> *By the helpful faeries of earth, air, and sea, blessed be!*

Tie the folded dollar on the flowering bush with the length of grapevine. When you are done, thank the helpful faeries, bid farewell to the elements, and close the circle. Be sure to water and care for the bush so that it thrives. As the bush buds and blossoms, so will your wealth and fortune.

September 15   LOTS OF BREAD SPELL

Bread is a sacred symbol of life.

You will need poppy- or sesame-seed bread, your favorite vegetable or cheese spread, and a knife.

Begin by spreading your favorite vegetable or cheese spread onto slices of the bread. Before eating each slice, hold it in your hands and say:

> *Sacred symbol of abundance*
> *Empower me. Blessed be!*

When you are done eating, put a small piece of bread at your front door, at your back door, and in your pocket, to draw more abundance to you.

September 16   MONEY MIST SPELL

You will need lemon oil, vanilla oil, neroli oil, a half-cup of spring or well water, and a fine-mist spray bottle.

Fill the bottle with the water, and then add forty drops of lemon oil, twenty drops of vanilla oil, and ten drops of neroli oil. Cap the bottle and shake it well. As you shake it, chant:

> *Money shower over me*
> *So be it! Blessed be!*

Then spray the mist over your head several times with your eyes closed. Breathe in the aroma to uplift your spirits. Each time you spray the mist over your head, chant:

> *Money shower over me*
> *So be it! Blessed be!*

Use the mist in the next few days for best results.

September 17   PECAN MONEY CAKE

You will need a pecan cake, a green candle, a ballpoint pen, cinnamon oil, and a knife. Use the pen to write a dollar sign eight times on the candle. Write your initials on top of the dollar signs. Then dress the candle with cinnamon oil. Thoroughly wash and wipe the oil from your hands. Light the candle, dedicating it to a favorite goddess or god of wealth and prosperity. Use the knife to inscribe the cake with eight dollar signs. Cut the cake into eight sections, each with a dollar sign. Before eating the pecan cake, say:

> *Delicious abundance fill me*
> *With fortune and prosperity*
> *So be it! Blessed be!*

September 18   PROSPERITY AND PEACE AFFIRMATION

You will need a small piece of tumbled amethyst, lavender-scented oil, and neroli oil.

Begin by anointing the amethyst with the neroli and lavender oil, and then anoint yourself with both oils. Hold the amethyst in your receiving hand. Take a deep and complete breath to center yourself, and then merge with the goddesses and gods of prosperity and peace. Next, say this affirmation aloud:

> *I am at peace with myself and my world, and I am empowered*
> *by divine prosperity and abundance, today and every day.*
> *Blessed be the Goddess and God!*

Repeat this affirmation at least eight times throughout the day on this international day of peace. Continue saying the affirmation for the next twenty-eight days (a moon cycle) for best results.

September 19   WEAVING RICHES SPELL

You will need a green candle, pine oil, and sixteen-inch lengths of green, white, and gold ribbon.

Begin by taking a few deep breaths and centering yourself. Then rub the oil on the candle. Put the candle in its holder on the altar. Anoint the ribbons with the oil as well as your wrists and ankles. Wipe any remaining oil from your hands. Light the candle, dedicating it to your favorite goddess of prosperity and wealth. Hold the ribbons in your hands, and slowly knot them together in the center. As you tie the knot, say:

> *One, two, three*
> *Weaving prosperity*
> *Drawing riches to me*
> *So be it! Blessed be!*

Now braid the two remaining lengths together, and knot them at the ends. With each knot you tie, repeat:

> *One, two, three*
> *Weaving prosperity*
> *Drawing riches to me*
> *So be it! Blessed be!*

Now knot the ribbons five more times. With each knot you tie, say:

> *One, two, three*
> *Weaving prosperity*
> *Drawing riches to me*
> *So be it! Blessed be!*

Hold the ribbons in your hands and gaze at the candlelight. As you do this, imagine weaving material and spiritual riches into your life just as you have been weaving and tying the ribbons together. Use the touch of your fingers and power of your thoughts to empower your desire. Now merge with the ribbons and with your desire, with Goddess and God, and with Oneness. Do this for at least fifteen minutes. When you are done, allow the candle to safely burn down. Tie the woven and knotted ribbon to your front door, mailbox, or front gate to weave more riches into your life.

September 20   SAGE SUN SPELL

You will need a gold candle, a ballpoint pen, cedar oil, and a bunch of fresh sage.

Just before sunrise, draw a magic circle and call in the elements. Next, scatter half of the fresh sage clockwise along the inside of the circle. Then use the pen to write the Sowilo "S" Rune [ᛋ] on the candle body eight times to invoke the powers of the sun. Next, write your initials on top of the eight runes. Dress the candle with the cedar oil and put it in its holder on the altar. Wipe the oil from your hands, and sprinkle the remaining sage clockwise around the base of the candle. Light the candle, and dedicate it to a favorite goddess or god of the sun such as Bridget (Celtic) or Apollo (Greek). Merge with the goddess or god for a few minutes as you gaze at the candle flame. As you do this, direct your awareness toward empowering thoughts, actions, people, and events that will shed some light on you and bring your more bright prosperity and fortune. Do this for at least thirty minutes. When you are done, thank the Goddess and God, bid farewell to the elements, and pull up the circle. Allow the candle to safely burn down. Return the sage to the earth.

September 21   HELLITH'S EVE CASTLE MEDITATION

You will need some relaxing music, a clear quartz crystal point, golden-colored fresh flowers, a sage smudge stick, and a feather.

After dark, draw a magic circle and call in the elements. Turn on some relaxing music and put the flowers on your altar in a vase filled with water. Next, light the smudge stick and use the feather to fan the smoke. Thoroughly smudge the crystal and yourself with the purifying smoke and then extinguish the smudge. Hold the stone in your power hand and take several deep breaths to center your awareness. Merge and become one with the stone. As you continue to breathe slowly and easily, gaze at the flowers on the altar and also become one with them. Just let your mind diffuse like a cloud, moving into the stone and flowers naturally and effortlessly. Use your deep breathing to facilitate this. As you continue to gaze at the flowers, imagine a doorway in the golden petals, a doorway to a beautiful, magical castle made of crystal and gold. Imagine stepping through that doorway into the magical castle. As you do, allow your senses to come alive as you see, touch, smell, hear, taste, and intuit the interior of the radiant and shining castle. Now imagine entering a room filled with golden sunlight shining on you from every direction. Bathe in the golden light, allowing it to fill you to the brim with is powerful energy. Inhale and exhale the golden light. See and sense the golden light within and without you. As you do this, imagine your life filled with gold and riches, with plenty of money and prosperity. Enjoy this image and the joyful sensations that accompany it for at least fifteen minutes.

When you are done, bid farewell to the elements, and close the circle. Return the flowers and water to the earth after the flowers fade. Keep the crystal point on your altar to draw magical riches to you. You can repeat this mediation as often as you like.

September 22 GREAT DAY TREASURE PICNIC

Picnics can be a great source of uplifting fun and creative adventure.

You will need a picnic lunch, a paper bag, and a hand trowel.

Begin by going on a picnic in nature on this autumn sabbat, either alone or with family and friends. Take the bag and trowel with you. When you are done eating, take a short walk and collect a few things from nature that you like, things that make you feel good, and put them in the bag. Dig a small hole in the ground beneath a tree, deposit the contents of the bag into the hole, and cover the hole over. Stand on top of the covered hole, face north, and say:

> *Earthly treasures of the north,*
> *I pray you on this Great Day*
> *Come and share your riches with me.*

Face east and say:

> *Windy treasures of the east,*
> *I pray you on this Great Day*
> *Come and share your riches with me.*

Face south and say:

> *Bright treasures of the south,*
> *I pray you on this Great Day*
> *Come and share your riches with me.*

Face west and say:

> *Watery treasures of the west,*
> *I pray you on this Great Day*
> *Come and share your riches with me.*

Now put three small stones on top of the covered hole, finish your picnic, and depart the area, leaving it clean of debris and as undisturbed as possible.

September 23   ABUNDANCE AND HARMONY AFFIRMATION

You will need lavender-scented oil, a white index card, and a green gel pen.

Begin by anointing yourself with the lavender oil on the wrist, ankles, neck, and back of the head. Then use the gel pen to write the following affirmation on the index card:

> *Each and every day with the help of the Goddess and God,*
> *I bring more divine abundance and harmony my way.*

After you have written the affirmation on the card, read it out loud three times. Carry the card with you and, during the day, read the affirmation aloud at least five more times. For the next twenty-eight days, anoint yourself with the lavender oil, and read the affirmation aloud at least eight times a day for the most powerful results.

September 24   FOLLOW YOUR HEART MAGIC

Today you will be giving someone a gift. It doesn't have to be anything big, just a small token of appreciation and caring. For example, pay for the car behind you at the toll booth, buy a friend lunch, or send your parents or grandparents a humorous, uplifting card. The idea is that you will discover that the more you give from your heart, the more you receive from life. Just before you give the gift, say:

Giving, caring, fortunate sharing
Blessed be, sweet generosity!

September 25   SWEET APPLE POTION

This potion is fun to make and share with your family.

You will need a food processor, four apples, a quarter-cup of spring or well water, one tablespoon of lemon juice, a pinch of cinnamon, and two tablespoons of honey.

Begin by coring, peeling, and cubing the apples. As you do this, chant:

> *Sweet fruit of abundance and prosperity*
> *Fill my life with blessed opportunities.*

Next, add the apples to the food processor and process. As you do, chant:

> *Sweet fruit of abundance and prosperity*
> *Fill my life with blessed opportunities.*

Now add the water, lemon juice, cinnamon, and honey. Blend the ingredients until smooth, all the while chanting,

> *Sweet fruit of abundance and prosperity*
> *Fill my life with blessed opportunities.*

Serve the potion in bowls. Before taking each bite of the Sweet Apple Potion, repeat,

> *Sweet fruit of abundance and prosperity*
> *Fill my life with blessed opportunities.*

September 26   CHALICE OF GOOD FORTUNE

You will need a silver or gold-colored chalice, eight pine nuts, eight eight-inch sprigs of pine, eight eight-inch sprigs of cedar, citrus scented oil, and eight green ribbons.

Begin by putting the pine and cedar sprigs into the chalice. As you do this, say:

Divine good fortune come to me, blessed be!

Then add sixteen drops of citrus-scented oil. As you do, repeat:

Divine good fortune come to me, blessed be!

Next, add the pine nuts. As you do, once again say:

Divine good fortune come to me, blessed be!

Tie four of the ribbons into bows and add them to the chalice contents. Then tie the remaining four ribbons onto the chalice stem. As you tie each ribbon, repeat:

Divine good fortune come to me, blessed be!

Now hold the chalice in your hands, and repeat:

Divine good fortune come to me, blessed be!

Keep the chalice on your kitchen table for a month. After that time, go outside and pour the contents, except the ribbons, into the ground. Tie the ribbons on your front door knocker or on your mailbox to bring you divine good fortune every day.

September 27   ROSE PROSPERITY WISH

You will need a white rose and a prosperity wish.

Begin by thinking about a single yes-or-no question regarding your prosperity wish. Turn your mind completely to your question for a few minutes. Now hold the rose in your hands, and begin taking the petals off, one at a time. As you take the first petal off, say "yes." As you take off the second petal, say "no," with the third petal, say "yes," and so on until you take off the last petal. Make a note of the answer, "yes" or "no," as you take off that last petal. This is your answer to your question. You can repeat this work a total of three times for more clarification.

September 28   VIDEO SUCCESS SPELL

You will need a favorite uplifting video with a happy ending. Put on the video and watch it. Then face north, merge with the powers of earth, and say:

> *By the powers of earth*
> *By the Goddess and God*
> *Success and happy endings*
> *Fill my each and every day!*

Now face east, merge with the powers of air, and say:

> *By the powers of air*
> *By the Goddess and God*
> *Success and happy endings*
> *Fill my each and every day!*

Face south, merge with the powers of light, and say:

> *By the powers of fire*
> *By the Goddess and God*
> *Success and happy endings*
> *Fill my each and every day!*

Next, face west and merge with the powers of water. Say:

> *By the powers of water*
> *By the Goddess and God*
> *Success and happy endings*
> *Fill my each and every day!*

Now move to the center of your sacred space, and say:

> *By the powers of spirit*
> *By the powers of Oneness*
> *Success and happy endings*
> *Fill my each and every day!*

September 29   WEALTH RUNE CHARM

You will need a green pillar candle, patchouli oil, and a ballpoint pen.

Begin by drawing a magic circle and calling in the elements. Use the pen to write the Fehu [ᚠ], Igwaz [◇], and Laguz [ᚱ] runes on the candle. Then write your initials on top of the three runes. Fehu is the rune of mobile wealth, plenty, and prosperity. Igwaz is the rune of peace and plenty, and Laguz is the rune of magical power and growth. Now dress the candle with the patchouli oil, and also anoint yourself with the oil. Wipe the oil from your hands. Next, light the candle, dedicating it to the Norse goddess Freya and the Norse god Frey. Turn your awareness to the candlelight, and imagine the three runes in your mind's eye. Imagine breathing the rune symbol into your being, and imagine breathing the symbol out. Chant the runes:

> *Fehu, Igwaz, Laguz*
> *Fehu, Igwaz, Laguz*
> *Fehu, Igwaz, Laguz!*

Do this for thirty minutes or longer. When you are done, allow the candle to burn for at least an hour, and then snuff it out. Relight the candle every day for eight days and allow it to burn for at least an hour each day. On the eighth day, safely allow the candle to burn down.

September 30 FAERY FORTUNE POWDER

You will need eight tablespoons of corn starch, along with orange oil, vanilla oil, and sandalwood oil. Begin by pouring the corn starch into a glass jar. As you do, chant:

> *Fortunate fae, blessed be*
> *Please grant me prosperity!*

Now add sixteen drops of the orange oil, mix it in, and repeat the chant:

> *Fortunate fae, blessed be*
> *Please grant me prosperity!*

Mix in sixteen drops of vanilla oil, and chant:

> *Fortunate fae, blessed be*
> *Please grant me prosperity!*

Next, add eight drops of the sandalwood oil, mixing it well as you repeat the chant:

> *Fortunate fae, blessed be*
> *Please grant me prosperity!*

Cap the powder potion and allow it to sit for twenty-four hours. Before using it, mix it again. As you do, repeat the chant:

> *Fortunate fae, blessed be*
> *Please grant me prosperity!*

Sprinkle the powder inside your shoes, wallet, and purse. Lightly dust yourself with the powder, and sprinkle it inside your car, office, and home to draw the fortunate gifts of the faeries to you, today and every day of the year.

CTOBER

October 1 HEALTHY LIVING BLESSING

For this spell, you will need a serving of your favorite vegetable or fruit, and a clean plate.

First, wash the vegetable or fruit well. Next, sit comfortably, with the vegetable or fruit on the plate in front of you. Rub your hands briskly together several times until they feel hot and tingly. Then immediately place your hands, palms down, about an inch above the food. Take a deep breath and merge with the divine, with oneness. As you do, imagine you are a conduit for divine energy. Actually imagine divine energy flowing from the palms of your hands into the food in front of you. Now say this empowering blessing as you hold your hands over the food:

> *Dear God and Goddess*
> *Please bless and empower this food*
> *With your divine love and light*
> *I ask this in the Lord and Lady's name*
> *So be it. Blessed be.*

Next, eat the vegetable or fruit slowly, savoring its divine flavor. Imagine each bite you take empowering you, giving you plenty of energy to face the challenges and enjoy the pleasures of your day.

October 2   HABITAT MAGIC

Today is World Habitat Day, and this spell is in honor of this day.

You will need a picture of a favorite animal out in nature, a white beeswax candle, your checkbook, and a favorite nature charity. Begin by lighting the candle, dedicating it to the spirit-energy of the animal in the picture. Next, place the picture next to the candle so you can easily see it. Turn your awareness to the picture, and merge with it. Use deep, rhythmic breathing, breathing in to the count of three, stilling your breath for three counts, and breathing out to the count of three. Do this several times. As you relax, turn your mind toward the positive survival of this animal in the future. In your mind's eye, see the animal's habitat improving and thriving. Imagine Earth's animals and plants all flourishing together in harmony. Do this for fifteen minutes or so, and then write a check out to your favorite nature charity. Seal the envelope with a few drops of candle wax. As you do this, say three times:

> *May the Earth's animals and plants that are alive*
> *Grow, flourish, and thrive, forever and a day.*

Allow the candle to burn down safely, and then bury the candle remains in the earth. As you do this, repeat three times:

> *May the Earth's animals and plants that are alive*
> *Grow, flourish, and thrive, forever and a day.*

October 3   CHILDREN'S PRAYER POWER

For this spell, you will need a beeswax candle and a picture of your child or children, or a picture of a child you know. Begin by lighting the candle, dedicating it to the child or children in the picture. Place the picture next to the candle so that the faces in the picture are illuminated by the candlelight. Turn your mind to the picture and say:

> *Dear Lord and Lady,*
> *Please hear my prayer*
> *I ask that you bless, guide, and inspire*
> *This divine child of light*
> *And protect her* [or him] *from all harm*
> *Thank you my eternal friends*
> *So be it! Blessed be!*

Note: Simply change the prayer to the plural (*this* to *these* and *child* to *children*) when there is more than one child in the picture. Repeat this prayer as often as you like. Allow the candle to burn down safely.

October 4   TOOT YOUR FLUTE SPELL

You will need a small toy flute or whistle.

Today, start the day by blowing your toy flute three times and then say:

> *I greet the day with hope and joy*
> *I'm tooting my flute today, hooray!*

Carry the flute with you, and toot it whenever you feel the need to bring a little more hope and joyful energy into your day. Enjoy this process and have fun. For example, go ahead and toot your flute at the breakfast table, at the fast-food window, in your office before a sales meeting, just before a big test at school, or in your car while waiting in traffic. Use your flute-tooting to transform today into a magically musical one filled with renewed hope and joy!

October 5   SUN POWER MEDITATION

You will need a quartz crystal, a bowl of cool water, and a gold candle.

Begin by rinsing the stone and candle in cool water for at least a minute. Then light the candle, dedicating it to the sun. Sit back or recline comfortably, holding the crystal in your receiving hand and focusing your attention on the lit candle. Take a deep breath, and exhale into the stone any tension or stress you may be feeling. Do this three more times. Now imagine the candle flame as a bright sun. Imagine this bright sun filling the crystal with sunlight and warmth, clearing it of any unwanted energies. You may feel the stone grow warm in your hand. This is natural. Now imagine the sun shining above you, warming and relaxing you. Feel the bright, warm sunlight fill you completely. Inhale and exhale the color gold. Do this for several minutes until you feel that you are overflowing with golden sunlight. When you are done, thank the sun and allow the candle to burn down safely.

October 6   CREATIVITY AFFIRMATION

The divine resides in all things. Our universal companions include animals, plants, the elements of wind, water, fire, and earth, the stars, the planets, and the many unknown life forms we have yet to encounter. This affirmation focuses on bringing divine inspiration and creativity into your life.

You will need a sheet of paper, a green gel pen, and a red gel pen.

Write the following affirmation on the sheet of paper twenty-one times with the green gel pen, and 21 times with the red gel pen:

Each and every day, I am inspired by the divine unity of the Mother Goddess and Father God, and my creative powers are awakened anew.

Tape the paper in a conspicuous place in your home; for example, on your computer monitor or on your bulletin board. For the next twenty-eight days, repeat the affirmation aloud (like you mean it!) at least nine times a day to awaken your creative abilities.

October 7   MORNING RENEWAL SPELL

You will need a nine-inch length of white ribbon.

Begin by taking the ribbon outside early in the morning when the dew is still on the grass and leaves. Rub your fingers in the dew and apply the dew to your face, neck, and hands. Be thorough, making sure to cover your skin several times. As you rub the dew on your skin, chant:

Morning dew renew me, blessed be!

Now cover the ribbon with the dew. Go back indoors and tie the ribbon to the inside doorknob of your bedroom door. Each time you open your bedroom door, say:

My energy is renewed, blessed be!

You can repeat this spell whenever you like to bring more renewing energy to you.

October 8   SELF-EMPOWERMENT SPELL

For this spell, you will need a white taper candle, patchouli oil, and a ball-point pen.

Begin by drawing a magic circle and calling in the elements. Next, use the ballpoint pen to write on the candle the one thing you want in your life that you feel would be the most empowering to you. Keep it simple. Now dress the candle with the patchouli oil, and place it in its holder on the altar. Anoint your wrists and ankles, and wipe any remaining oil from your hands. Light the candle and say what you have written on the candle body aloud three times. Then focus your awareness on the candle. Imagine the empowering thing coming into your life in the candle flame. Close your eyes, and imagine being empowered now. Gently bring your mind back to being empowered whenever you find you have strayed from your focus. Do this for at least twenty minutes. When you are done, bid farewell to the elements and close the circle. Safely allow the candle to burn down.

October 9   FRIENDSHIP MIST MAGIC

Do this spell with a partner (your spouse, children, or a good friend).

You will need a misting bottle, a half-cup of spring or well water, vanilla essential oil, chamomile essential oil, and peppermint essential oil.

Put the water in the bottle and add twenty drops of vanilla oil, twenty drops of chamomile oil, and ten drops of peppermint oil. Cap the bottle and shake it, chanting:

> *Friendship mist, blessed be*
> *Bring delight and joy to me!*

Now hold the bottle between your hands and empower the potion by repeating,

> *Friendship mist, blessed be*
> *Bring delight and joy to me!*

Then have your partner hold the bottle in her or his hands and repeat:

> *Friendship mist, blessed be*
> *Bring delight and joy to me!*

Now mist each other. Have your partner close her or his eyes before you spray the mist high above his or her head. Breathe in the empowering fragrance of the Friendship Mist. Do this for several minutes and have fun until you use all the mist up.

October 10   SAY A LITTLE PRAYER

You will need a small piece of tumbled quartz crystal and a bowl of cool water.

Rinse the stone in the water for at least a minute. Carry it with you all day and night. Each time you see someone, people you know as well as strangers, who could use a little divine help, hold the crystal in your power hand, and direct this prayer toward the person needing help:

> *Dear Goddess and God*
> *Please help this person in need*
> *Shed your divine light upon them*
> *I ask this in the Lady and Lord's name*
> *Blessed be!*

You can carry the stone as long as you like, saying the simple prayer as needed. Through time, the crystal becomes a prayer stone. Just holding it will empower you with divine love and grace.

October 11 MIND GARDEN MAGIC

For this spell, you will need rose- and lavender-scented oils and soft music.

Begin by turning on the music. Anoint yourself with the oils. Next, sit or recline comfortably. Take several deep breaths and center your mind. Now close your eyes, and imagine a magical garden. In the garden is a thatched cottage, with white, thornless, climbing roses framing its windows and doorway. In the garden itself is a brass sundial, a stone birdbath, and a bubbling fountain in the shape of a butterfly. There is also a stone path hidden by masses of colorful flowers. You follow the path, walking through a wooden archway that is covered with fragrant yellow roses. As you pass through the archway, you notice the profusion of lavender bushes all around you. They fill the space between the roses, and the garden is redolent with their magical fragrance. Breathe in the fragrance. Continue doing this for at least fifteen minutes. You can repeat this meditation whenever you need a short and welcome break from the stresses of the day.

October 12 HOW SWEET IT IS CANDLE MAGIC

You will need a cup of fresh, fragrant red rose petals, a white candle in its holder, a bowl of cool water, and cinnamon oil.

Begin by washing the candle in cool water and drying it. Dress the candle with the cinnamon oil, and put the candle in its holder. Next, light the candle, dedicating it to a favorite goddess and god. Gaze at the candle for at least fifteen minutes, turning your mind toward the things in your life you would like to sweeten up—your love life, your relationship with your children, your bank account, your backyard or front porch, your garden, your business, your town, your state, your country, the world, and so forth. Have fun with the process, thinking about a sweet and bright future. Imagine having something to look forward to doing, something to look forward to experiencing. Now snuff the candle. Take the rose petals outside and, starting at your front door, scatter them all the way around your home in a clockwise circle. As you do this, chant:

> *Blessed be, how sweet it is.*

For the next week, relight the candle, and turn your mind toward a sweet and bright future for at least fifteen minutes each day. On the seventh day, allow the candle to burn down safely.

October 13 HAPPY HAIR DAY SPELL

You will need warm olive oil, lavender essential oil, a cotton towel, and your favorite shampoo.

Begin by mixing several drops of lavender oil into the warm olive oil. As you do, chant:

> *Happy hair day, bring joy and play*
> *Keep all unwanted energies away.*

Now apply the oil to your hair, working it down to the ends of your hair. Also rub the oil into your scalp. While you do this, chant:

> *Happy hair day, bring joy and play*
> *Keep all unwanted energies away.*

Soak the towel in hot water, wring it out, and wrap it around your hair. When the towel cools, repeat the process. Do this for about forty-five minutes. All during this process, imagine having a very happy, joyful, and playful happy hair day each and every day of the year. When you are done, shampoo your hair. As you shampoo and rinse your hair, chant:

> *Happy hair day, bring joy and play*
> *Keep all unwanted energies away.*

Dry and style your hair. As you do, repeat the chant:

> *Happy hair day, bring joy and play*
> *Keep all unwanted energies away.*

October 14   WOLF POWER MAGIC

You will need a picture of a wolf, a green candle, and a ballpoint pen.

Draw a magic circle of light and call in the elements. Use the pen to write the words *Wolf Power* on the candle body three times. Then write your initials on top of the words. Light the candle, dedicating it to the universal wolf spirit, to the "greenfire" in the core of the eyes of the wolf. Place the wolf picture so that the candlelight illuminates it. Gaze at the picture and merge with it. Merge with the universal wolf spirit. Become one with the keen powers and strengths of the wolf. See with a wolf's eyes. Hear as a wolf hears. Smell what a wolf smells. Taste food and water as a wolf does. Touch your world with the paws, nose, head, and body of the wolf. Experience your world as a wolf would experience it. Do this for at least fifteen minutes. When you are done, thank the wolf spirit, bid farewell to the elements, and close the circle. Put the picture of the wolf somewhere you will frequently see it to empower you with wolf power each and every day.

October 15   FINDING YOUR ROOTS MEDITATION

For this meditation, you will need a bowl of clean soil and a piece of hematite.

Sit or recline comfortably, holding the hematite in your receiving hand, keeping the bowl of earth within reach of your other hand. Take a deep and complete breath in, and as you exhale, just let go of any tension you may be feeling. Do this several times, relaxing more and more with each breath. Now gently mix the soil in the bowl with the fingers of your power hand. Sift it with your fingers, feeling its texture and earthy energy. After a minute or so, close your eyes and imagine walking barefoot in the soft green grass of a magical meadow. Enjoy the sensations of the experience, the feelings of groundedness and connection with the Earth. Get your senses involved, and imagine the feel of the grass on your feet, its smell, and its green, lush expanse. Now in your mind's eye, shapeshift into your favorite kind of tree. Imagine that your have roots that plunge into the earth from the bottoms of your feet. Now allow your awareness to move up through your legs, hips, pelvis, stomach, shoulders, neck, and head, and imagine tree branches sprouting from your head, reaching toward the blue sky. Allow your mind to expand like your branches expand upward. Now take a deep breath in, and imagine breathing in the power of the earth from your roots, your feet, all the way up through the trunk of your body, up through your arms and head. Imagine this earth energy flowing through your head, and then exhale this energy out of your branches that stretch upward with majesty and natural beauty and grace. Repeat this process a total of three times to ground yourself and empower yourself with the divine spirit the three worlds: the underworld, surface world, and sky world. When you are done, take a deep breath and come back to the present moment, feeling relaxed, refreshed, and completely grounded, yet energized. Slowly open your eyes and stretch your body like a cat.

October 16   PROTECTION BOTTLE SPELL

You will need a blue glass bottle, thirteen pins, thirteen small nails, thirteen white tacks, and water. Add the pins to the bottle and say:

> *Bottle of power, bottle of magic*
> *Protect me from evil and harm*
> *By the Lady, blessed be!*

Add the nails to the bottle. Hold the bottle in your hands and repeat:

> *Bottle of power, bottle of magic*
> *Protect me from evil and harm*
> *By the Lady, blessed be!*

Add the tacks to the bottle, hold it in your hands, and say:

> *Bottle of power, bottle of magic*
> *Protect me from evil and harm*
> *By the Lady, blessed be!*

Now pour the water into the bottle to the top, and cap it. Shake the bottle gently and, holding it between your hands, repeat once more:

Bottle of power, bottle of magic
Protect me from evil and harm
By the Lady, blessed be!

Put the bottle in your kitchen window for best results. The sharp objects within the bottle confuse and ward away evil and negative energies.

October 17   POWER BOWL CHARM

This simple spell can be used to bring more good times into your life.

You will need a golden-colored or brass bowl, nine pinches of crushed sage, nine pinches of thyme, nine pinches of flaxseed, and nine nine-inch-long green ribbons.

Add the pinches of sage to the bowl one at a time. As you do, chant:

Bowl of helpful divine power
Each and every hour
Bring delight and blessings bright
Each day and every night.

Next, add the pinches of thyme and repeat:

Bowl of helpful divine power
Each and every hour
Bring delight and blessings bright
Each day and every night.

Now add the pinches of flaxseed and chant:

> *Bowl of helpful divine power*
> *Each and every hour*
> *Bring delight and blessings bright*
> *Each day and every night.*

Tie the ribbons into small bows. As you tie each one, repeat:

> *Bring delight and blessings bright*
> *Each day and every night.*

Now add the ribbons to the bowl. Hold it up to the Goddess and God, and say:

> *Dear Goddess and God*
> *Please bless this bowl of power*
> *With your divine love and light*
> *Each day and every night*
> *So be it! Blessed be!*

Now keep the bowl on your dining room table or on your desk or bureau for twenty-eight days. After that time, return the organic contents of the bowl to the earth by scattering the herbs and seeds outside clockwise around your home. Put the ribbons on your altar to draw more delight and blessings to you.

October 18   GODDESS WHITE STONE

For this spell, you will need a white stone, a bowl of cool water, and vanilla oil.

Rinse the white stone in cool water for at least a minute. Next, rub the stone with vanilla oil. Anoint yourself with the oil. Hold the stone in your power hand for several minutes, and imagine putting love, joy, happiness, and compassion into the stone. Flood the stone with these positive images and sensations. Use your breath as a carrier wave for your thought energy. Breathe in, and as you breathe out, imagine planting the images and feelings of love, joy, happiness, and compassion into the stone itself. Imagine these things streaming into the stone. Go to the ocean or to a flowing river, stream, or creek. Hold the stone in your power hand, and say:

> *Dear Goddess, thank you for your divine blessings*
> *This white stone is a simple offering to you from me*
> *By the Lady, thank you, all-mother, blessed be!*

Now toss the stone into the water as an offering.

October 19   AMBER MAGIC

Amber resin can be used for attracting nature energies to you.

You will need amber resin and a piece of jewelry.

Begin by drawing a magic circle and calling in the elements. Then warm small bits of amber in your fingers and then rub them on your third eye, behind your ears, and on the insides of your wrists and ankles. Rub small bits on the piece of jewelry as well. With each bit of amber you rub on yourself or the jewelry, repeat:

> *Fragrant amber of nature*
> *Share your divine powers with me.*
> *By the Goddess and God, blessed be!*

Wear the jewelry to attract nature energies, such as helpful faeries, to you. When the amber fragrance fades, rub more amber resin on the jewelry and repeat:

> *Fragrant amber of nature*
> *Share your divine powers with me.*
> *By the Goddess and God, blessed be!*

October 20   PET COMPANION POWER

You will need your cat or dog, nine pinches of valerian, and a candle the same color as your cat or dog.

Begin by scattering the valerian in a clockwise circle around the candle; then light it. Call your cat or dog to you and begin petting it slowly and softly. As you do this, say,

> *My eyes are your eyes*
> *Your eyes are my eyes*
> *My ears are your ears*
> *Your ears are my ears*
> *My insights are your insights*
> *Your insights are my insights*
> *Blessed be* [say your pet companion's name]!

Now sit quietly and open your mind to new insights. Just let your imagination run wild and have fun. See and sense the world from your pet companion's vantage point. Do this for several minutes. When you are done, jot down any valuable insights you gain that can help empower your life.

October 21   PERSONAL HARMONY PLACKET

To make this placket, you will need three pinches of dried lavender flowers, three pinches of dried rose buds, 3 pinches of dried rosemary, two six-inch by six-inch pieces of green construction paper, a stapler, scotch tape, and a gold gel pen.

Begin by anointing yourself with the lavender oil. Next, staple and tape the two paper squares together on three sides, leaving the fourth open. Use the pen to write the word *Harmony* three times on both sides of the placket. Now put the lavender flowers, rose buds, and rosemary into the placket. Anoint the four corners of the placket with the lavender oil, saying:

> *Pocket of harmony, blessed be!*

Now hold the placket in between your palms, and charge it with divine power by saying three times:

> *I charge this harmony placket with divine power.*

Put the placket next to your bed for the next twenty-eight nights for best results. You can reuse the placket by returning its contents to the earth, and then refilling it with fresh ingredients and recharging it.

October 22   TRANSFORMATION SPELL

Associated with fire and the sun, frankincense is traditionally used for protection, divine rapport, transformation, and consecration. It aids in merging and meditation.

You will need frankincense and an incense burner.

Begin by lighting the incense. Sit back and focus on the one thing you would most like to transform in your life. Do this for a few minutes. In your mind's eye, step into the future for a few minutes, and imagine that the transformation has already happened. Be there, enjoying all the benefits and happiness of the transformation in your life. Allow the incense to safely burn down. You can repeat this spell as often as you like. If you prefer, you can use frankincense-scented oil and a diffuser instead of incense.

October 23   FIRELIGHT SPELL

You will need a fireplace, wood stove, campfire, or a beeswax candle. As you build your fire or light the candle, focus your awareness on the helpful aspects of fire, particularly warmth and light. Take a few deep breaths to center yourself, and then merge with the fire element as you gaze at the flame. Say three times:

> *May this fire warm the hearts of those who are afraid*
> *May this fire light the way for me and all bright souls.*

Allow the fire or candle to safely burn down. Take the ashes or candle remains outdoors and return them to the earth. As you do, chant:

> *By the Lady and Lord, blessed be!*

October 24   TEA MAGIC BATH

This bath is a tonic for your body and mind, ridding you of any unwanted energies, and purifying your personal energy field. This helps you connect with your higher self and oneness.

You will need three blessed thistle tea bags, three chamomile tea bags, neroli oil, and a warm bath. (You can purchase these items at most health food stores or Wiccan shops).

Draw the bath, and add the blessed thistle and chamomile, plus nine drops of the neroli oil. Immerse yourself in the bath, and take a deep breath, filling your senses with the aroma of the bath water. Imagine all of your past worries and problems flowing out of your mind, body, and spirit. Turn your mind to the now and to the future. Chant the words:

> *Magic waters refresh and empower me*
> *By the Lady and Lord, blessed be.*

Soak for about ten minutes, then dry off with a soft towel. Anoint yourself with the neroli oil, and then go to bed. As you go to sleep, repeat to yourself:

> *Magical dreams empower me. When I wake up I will*
> *remember my dreams.*

When you wake up, make a note of everything you recall from your dreams.

October 25   ELF LEAF DREAM SPELL

Use this spell to uplift you and bring solutions to any problems you may have via your dreams.

You will need nine rosemary (also called elf leaf) sprigs and a nine-inch length of green ribbon. You can grow the rosemary yourself or purchase fresh rosemary at most grocery stores.

Tie the rosemary sprigs together with the ribbon. Knot the ribbon nine times. Each time you tie a knot, say:

Magical elf sprig of green
Bring solutions in my dreams
Uplift and empower me
By the fae, blessed be!

Now place the tied sprigs under your bed to promote uplifting dreams and to discover solutions in your dreams. As you drift to sleep, repeat over and over:

Bring solutions in my dreams
And I will remember, blessed be!

In the morning, write down what you recall of your dreams. Repeat this process for nine nights in a row, and note any valuable insights. Use them to solve your day-to-day challenges. Return the rosemary sprigs to the earth after that time.

October 26   GOLDEN CORD VISUALIZATION

You will need a piece of pyrite (small pyrite cubes are ideal).

Begin by sitting in a chair with your feet on the ground, your hands resting on your lap, and your spine as straight as possible. Be sure to loosen any constricting clothing, belts, shoes, or jewelry. Hold the pyrite in your power hand. Take a deep breath in, and breathe out all the stress you may be feeling. Do this several times. Just let go of all your tensions and worries for a few minutes as you take this journey. Now close your eyes, and imagine that there is a golden cord that extends from your head down your spine, down through the chair and floor, and deep down into the earth itself. Imagine the golden cord extending to the very center of the earth where it is attached to the core of Mother Earth. This cord can be used for grounding your energies and centering yourself, and for ridding yourself of any unwanted energies. Now imagine any stress or worries dropping off of you and into the golden cord until they reach the Earth's core and transform into positive energy. Continue doing this for at least fifteen minutes. When you are done, take a deep breath in and out. Slowly open your eyes, stretch your muscles, and come back to the present time and place. You can repeat this visualization anytime you need to ground and center your awareness and energies.

October 27   HOME PICNIC MAGIC

You will need a dinner for two, three, or four (depending upon the size of your family or the number of friends you include) from your favorite take-out food restaurant. Bring the food home and set the stage for a tasty picnic in front of the television watching a special sports event, concert, or favorite inspiring movie. Use your best dishes, glasses, and cutlery. Use cloth napkins, too. Make a toast by lifting your glasses together, and saying:

> *There's no place like home*
> *There's no place like home*
> *There's no place like home*
> *Blessed be this home*
> *And all those who are present.*

Enjoy your picnic together, savoring the quality time and delicious food you are sharing.

October 28 PIN BALL POWER CHARM

You will need a styrofoam ball and 123 colored pins. Begin by inserting a pin into the ball. As you do, say:

> *One, two, three,*
> *May the Goddess and God*
> *Bless and empower me.*

Now move clockwise around the ball and insert another pin. As you do, say:

> *One, two, three,*
> *May the Goddess and God*
> *Bless and empower me.*

Continue inserting pins into the ball. With each pin you insert, repeat:

> *One, two, three,*
> *May the Goddess and God*
> *Bless and empower me.*

Once your have inserted all of the pins, put the Pin Ball charm on your desk, bureau, or entertainment center. Each day, hold the ball in your power hand and repeat:

> *One, two, three,*
> *May the Goddess and God*
> *Bless and empower me.*

This is a charm you can do with friends and family, too.

October 29 SAVING FACE SPELL

You will need a small cup or bowl, an egg, a tablespoon of milk, and tablespoon of honey. Mix the items together well. As you do this, chant:

> *Saving face, by the grace of the Goddess*
> *Every day my wisdom and patience grow and flow.*

Now apply the potion to your face and neck. Leave the potion on for fifteen minutes. All the while, repeat:

> *Saving face, by the grace of the Goddess*
> *Every day my wisdom and patience grow and flow.*

Then wash the potion off with warm water. Finish with a cold-water rinse. You can repeat this spell as often as you like. To add power to it, use a specific goddess and chant her name as you leave the potion on for fifteen minutes.

October 30 MEDICINE BAG MAGIC

You will need a medicine bag (a small pouch on a cord that is worn like a necklace), a stone, a feather, an acorn, a seashell, and sandalwood oil. Collect the items (except the oil) in nature if possible—at the river, ocean, mountains, in the park, or on a walk down a country road. Anoint the items with the sandalwood oil. As you do, chant:

> *Blessed be the elements of earth, air, fire, and sea!*

Put the stone in the bag and say:

> *Blessed be the earth element.*

Next, put the feather into the bag and say:

> *Blessed be the air element.*

Now add the acorn and say

> *Blessed be the fire element.*

Then add the seashell, and say:

> *Blessed be the water element.*

Hold the bag in your hands and empower it by saying:

> *Blessed be this medicine bag*
> *By the elements of earth, air, fire, and sea*
> *Shower me with divine energy*
> *So be it! Blessed be!*

Wear the bag to bring more divine and helpful elemental energy into your life.

October 31   SAMHAIN DUMB SUPPER

This Samhain custom is a feast for the spirits of your ancestors, for the Goddess and God, and for the spirits within the land. On Samhain, the veil between worlds is thinnest, and the doorway to the Otherworld is open for a time.

You will need a plate filled with food, a chalice filled with juice or water, a carved pumpkin with a candle, and a sprig of greenery.

Gather the plate, chalice, pumpkin, candle (and matches or lighter), and sprig together and go outside in your backyard or on your balcony. Arrange the items in a pleasing manner, and then light the candle in the pumpkin, dedicating it to your ancestors and spirits within the land. Say three times:

> *I make this offering to the Goddess and God*
> *May they bless, guide, and protect me, now and forevermore.*

Allow the candle to safely burn down during the night. The following morning, the food, drink, and the pumpkin can be returned to the earth as an offering to the Goddess and God. As you do so, repeat:

> *I make this offering to the Goddess and God*
> *May they bless, guide, and protect me, now and forevermore.*

$\mathcal{N}$OVEMBER

November 1   PENNY POWER

You will need nine pennies. Begin by taking a short walk. Go anywhere you want to go, and as you do, drop the nine pennies here and there, for example, in stores, on walkways, and in parking lots, for someone else to find. Just before you drop a penny, hold it in your power hand and say quietly:

> *Lucky penny bring fortune and joy*
> *To the person who finds you*
> *So be it! Blessed be!*

November 2   FAERY SINGING SPELL

You will need a small bell, a white candle, and rose oil. Do this spell after sunset.

Begin by drawing a magic circle and calling in the elements. Next, dress the candle and anoint yourself with the rose oil. Wipe any remaining oil from your hands, and light the candle, dedicating it to the helpful faeries and nature beings. Now hold the bell in your power hand, ring it three times, and say:

> *Every time the bell rings, my spirit sings*
> *Helpful faeries of magic and dream*
> *Please grant me your favors on this eve*
> *By the helpful fae, blessed be!*

Now ring the bell three more times, and repeat:

> *Every time the bell rings, my spirit sings*
> *Helpful faeries of magic and dream*
> *Please grant me your favors on this eve*
> *By the helpful fae, blessed be!*

Ring the bell three more times, and repeat once more:

> *Every time the bell rings, my spirit sings*
> *Helpful faeries of magic and dream*
> *Please grant me your favors on this eve*
> *By the helpful fae, blessed be!*

Turn your mind to the candlelight, and imagine the helpful faeries granting you magical favors as you sleep and dream. Do this for at least fifteen minutes. Allow the candle to safely burn down. Leave the circle up overnight as you sleep. As you drift to sleep, repeat to yourself:

> *Helpful faeries of magic and dream, my spirit sings.*

In the morning, thank the faeries, bid farewell to the elements, and close the circle.

November 3   ROSE MAGIC

You will need a rose, rose oil, and a flashlight. Spin this spell after sunset.

Begin by anointing yourself with the rose oil. Rub a few drops on your wrists, ankles, and third eye. Next, take the rose and flashlight outdoors where you won't be disturbed. Draw a magic circle of bright green light, and call in the elements. Hold the rose in your hand, and illuminate it with the flashlight three times by turning the flashlight on and then off. Each time, before turning the flashlight off, repeat:

> *By the ancient powers of the rose faeries*
> *Please fill my life with positive magic*
> *One times two times three, blessed be!*

Now breathe in for three heartbeats, still your breath for three heartbeats, and then exhale for three heartbeats. As you do this, smell the rose you are holding. Do this three times, and then begin to imagine the rose faeries all around you, helping you each and every day of the year. You can feel their magical powers empowering you. When you are done, thank the rose faeries, bid farewell to the elements, and close the circle. When the rose is spent, return it to the Earth as an offering to the rose faeries.

November 4   LIVING ROOM MAGIC

You will need a blanket, picnic basket filled with food and drinks, your favorite music, a travel video, your family, and a white votive candle for each person present. Begin by moving your furniture so you have ample room to picnic in. Then draw a magic circle around the room and call in the elements. Next, spread out the blanket on the floor (add a few cushions for comfort), and put the filled picnic basket on the floor next to the blanket. Next, turn on some enjoyable picnic music, something upbeat and joyful; or if you prefer a quieter picnic, select a CD or tape of nature sounds such as birds or the ocean. Now put on a travel video, for example of the world's most beautiful beaches or the castles of Europe, and turn the sound all the way down. Sit in a circle on the picnic blanket, with the votive candles in the center. The oldest person present lights the candles, one at a time. As each candle is lit, everyone says:

May magical light fill our lives.

When you are done lighting the candles, join hands, and say three times:

May magical light fill our bodies, minds, and souls.

Put the candles where they can safely burn down, and enjoy your picnic together. When you are done, bid farewell to the elements and close the circle.

November 5 FLOWER CANDLE SPELL

You will need a three-inch green pillar candle, rose oil, lavender-scented oil, and jasmine oil.

First draw a magic circle and call in the elements. Next, anoint the candle with the rose oil, and then anoint yourself with a couple of drops. Then anoint the candle with lavender oil, and anoint yourself with a couple of drops as well. Dress the candle with the jasmine oil, and anoint yourself with a couple of drops. Wipe any remaining oil from your hands, and then light the candle. As you do, say:

Flower faeries, please bring to me
Happiness, joy, and divine blessings.

Now gaze into the candlelight, and imagine being in a magical flower garden, surrounded by helpful flower faeries. The fragrant and colorful faeries give you magical gifts and bring joy and happiness to your very soul. Enjoy your adventure in the magical flower garden for a while, and then turn your mind to the candlelight. Say:

Thank you for your divine gifts blessed fae, blessed be!

When you are done, thank the flower faeries, bid farewell to the elements, and close the circle. Snuff out the candle. Relight it every night for three nights, and allow it to safely burn for at least thirty minutes. One the third night, allow the candle to safely burn down.

November 6   RELAXATION POTION

You will need a ceramic teapot, three cups of boiling water, two chamomile tea bags, one mint tea bag, a half-teaspoon of fresh lavender (or a quarter-teaspoon of dried lavender), and a half a vanilla bean cut into one-inch lengths.

Put all the ingredients, one at a time, in the ceramic teapot. As you do, chant:

Bless this potion with harmony and peace
By the Lady, blessed be!

Allow the potion to steep for at least twenty minutes. Strain the tea into a glass or ceramic pitcher, and then serve chilled over ice, garnished with a sprig of mint and a slice of lemon. Before taking each sip, say:

I am blessed with harmony and peace!

November 7   NOVEMBER AFFIRMATION BATH

You will need a white candle, neroli oil, vanilla oil, sandalwood oil, and a warm bath.

Begin by filling the tub with warm (but not hot) water. Then add three drops of each of the oils, saying:

Each and every day, I am filled with divine joy and purpose.

Next, light the candle, dedicating it to a favorite goddess or god. Place it somewhere you can see it from the tub. Immerse yourself in the bathwater for at least ten minutes. As you do, keep repeating aloud to yourself:

Each and every day, I am filled with divine joy and purpose.

When you are done, dry off with a soft towel, and anoint your wrists with a drop or two of the oils. As you do, say:

Each and every day, I am filled with divine joy and purpose.

Allow the candle to safely burn down.

November 8   APPLE PIE MAGIC

Today, give the all-American gift of apple pie to someone you like, for example your family, a friend, neighbor, the mail person, your boss, or your acupuncturist.

You will need a delicious apple pie.

Bless the pie by putting your hands palms down above it, but without actually touching the pie. Take a breath in and out to center yourself, and say:

Bless this food with the divine joy of the Goddess and God.

Give the pie as a gift to sweeten the day.

November 9   POSITIVE THOUGHT STONE

You will need a small white stone (one that you found in nature), and a bowl of cool water.

Rinse the stone in the water for a minute or two. Carry it with you as you move through your day, and notice the beautiful and positive people, animals, nature, and events that fill the day. See the divine in everyone and everything. Each time you notice the many aspects of beauty and majesty around you, hold the stone in your receiving hand and imagine breathing them into the stone. At the end of the day, put the stone next to your bed to inspire positively beautiful dreams.

November 10   OAK SEED CHARM

You will need three acorns, a small brown pouch, sandalwood oil, and a brown candle.

Begin by drawing a magic circle and calling in the elements. Next, dress the candle with the sandalwood oil, and then rub the oil on the acorns. Anoint your wrists with the oil. Now wipe any remaining oil from your hands, light the candle, and say three times:

Divine Lady and Lord, I pray you
Share your natural wisdom with me.

Hold each of the acorns in your power hand, one at a time, and charge them with magical energy by merging with the divine, with oneness, and saying:

> *Magic oak seed, divine indeed*
> *Share your natural wisdom with me.*

Put the acorns in the pouch. Add a few drops of candle wax, and three drops of the sandalwood oil. Hold the pouch in your power hand and say:

> *Magic charm of seeds*
> *Empower me, blessed be!*

When you are done, thank deity, bid farewell to the elements, and close the circle. Put the pouch somewhere close to your front door, or better yet, carry it with you to draw natural wisdom and knowledge directly to you.

November 11   CALLING DREAM SPELL

You will need a white tealight, a picture of yourself as a baby, and a recent picture of yourself.

Begin by drawing a magic circle and calling in the elements just before you go to sleep. Next, place your baby picture to the left of the candle and your recent photo to the right of the candle. Light the candle, dedicating it to your favorite goddess. Then turn your mind toward the candlelight and pictures for a few minutes, moving from one photo to the other, and back again. Take a deep breath in and out, and now say:

> *Do be, do be, do be, do be, do be*
> *As I dream, show my calling to me*

Do be, do be, do be, do be, do be,
As I will, so shall it be!

As you drift to sleep, repeat to yourself:

As I dream, show my calling to me
And I will remember when I wake up.

In the morning, write down what you recall from your dreams. Thank deity, bid farewell to the elements, and close the circle. Repeat this spell until you get a clear idea of your calling. After you do, pursue it with all your heart.

November 12   MORNING MAGIC MIST

You will need a misting bottle, a half-cup of spring or well water, lemongrass essential oil, rosemary essential oil, and lavender essential oil.

Make this magic mist first thing in the morning. Put the water in the bottle and add nine drops of lemongrass oil, ten drops of rosemary oil, and twenty drops of lavender oil. Cap the bottle and shake it, chanting:

Morning mist refresh me
Renew me, blessed be!

Now hold the bottle in your hands, and empower the magic mist by saying:

Morning mist refresh me
Renew me, blessed be!

Spray the mist above your head, close your eyes, and breathe it in. Each time you spray the mist, say:

Morning mist refresh me
Renew me, blessed be!

November 13   COMPLIMENTARY MAGIC

Today, I encourage you to pay someone a compliment as a way to empower her or him and also empower yourself. Mark Twain once said that he could live two months on a good compliment.

You will need sandalwood-scented oil.

Begin by anointing yourself with the sandalwood oil and say three times:

> *Kind thoughts create compassion*
> *Kind compliments create confidence.*

Go about your day, and pay close attention to the positive words, efforts, and actions of others, and pay someone a genuine compliment. Notice how both you and the person you complimented feel brighter and a little more cheerful as a result of the positive exchange. The more you genuinely compliment someone, the better you will feel about yourself and life as a whole.

November 14   SWEET DAY POTION

You will need one cup of mango juice, a half-cup of unfiltered apple juice, and a half-cup of papaya nectar. Mix the juices together, stirring clockwise, in a large glass or ceramic pitcher. As you mix them, focus on sweetening your day, making it bright and filled with success, and chant:

Sweet juices brighten today
So be it! So shall it be!

Pour the potion over ice and sip it slowly. Before taking each sip, say:

Sweet juices brighten today
So be it! So shall it be!

November 15 LAVENDER SLEEP MAGIC

This basic sleep empowerment spell uses the magical qualities of lavender to bring you a good night's sleep each and every night.

You will need lavender essential oil.

Begin by sprinkling your pillowcases with a few drops of lavender essential oil just before you go to bed. Anoint your wrists, ankles, third eye, and the back of your head with a couple of drops of the oil. As you drift to sleep, repeat to yourself over and over again:

I am sleeping peacefully and comfortably.

November 16 MIND TRAVEL MEDITATION

You will need a picture or video of another country, preferably somewhere you have never traveled to before. You can do this mediation whenever you need a few minutes away from it all.

Begin by putting the picture where you can easily see it, or by turning on the video with the sound turned down completely. Look at the picture or video and study it. Imagine stepping into the picture or video for a few minutes and taking a mini-vacation there. Take a deep breath in and out, and in your mind's eye, see and sense yourself there in the picture, having fun and enjoying your mind-travel adventure. Do this for about five minutes, and then take another deep breath in and out, and come back to the present time and place. You can repeat this mediation as often as you like, with different pictures, and for shorter or longer durations.

November 17 FLUSH THE PAST SPELL

You will need a small piece of paper and a pen.

Begin by writing on the pieces of paper the one thing in the past you would like to bury once and for all. Hold the paper in your power hand and say three times:

I let go of the past, right now, once and for all!

Tear the paper into tiny, tiny bits. As you do this, imagine ridding yourself of this problem or memory once and for all and chant:

I let go of the past, right now, once and for all!

Now flush the bits of paper down the toilet. As you do, say:

The past is washed away, once and for all!

Wash your hands thoroughly when you are done.

November 18 JUICY FRUIT SUCCESS POTION

You will need a half-cup of raspberry juice, a half-cup of unfiltered apple juice, a quarter-teaspoon of pure vanilla extract, ice, and a slice of lemon.

Begin by mixing the juices clockwise in a large glass. As you stir, chant:

Sweet success come to me
By the Lady, blessed be!

Now add the ice and lemon, once again stirring the mixture in clockwise circles, and chant:

Sweet success come to me
By the Lady, blessed be!

Now slowly sip the potion. Before taking each sip, say:

Sweet success come to me
By the Lady, blessed be!

November 19   DANCING IN THE DARK

Music acts as a magical salve for anger, frustration, worry, and stress. You always feel better after listening to music you enjoy and dancing around the room a little. Besides, listening and dancing to music can help you focus your mind on your personal goals as well as create a more conducive state of mind for merging with oneness.

You will need your favorite music, a green candle, and a red candle. Music has a dramatic influence when it moves you emotionally, so select music you love for this spell.

Perform this spell after dark. Begin by moving the furniture out of the way, giving you room to dance. Next, draw a magic circle around the room and call in the elements. Turn on the music. Now light the candles, one at a time, dedicating the green one to the Goddess and the red one to the God, and dim the lights, giving the room a magical candlelit atmosphere. Now get into the swing of the music and dance around the room free-form for a few minutes. As you do, chant:

> *Divine music fill me*
> *Ayea! Blessed be!*

When you are done, turn off the music, thank deity, bid farewell to the elements, and close the circle. Allow the candles to safely burn down. You can repeat this spell as often as you like.

November 20   ANIMAL EMPOWERMENT

You will need a quartz crystal, amber resin, and a green candle.

Perform this spell after sunset.

Begin by drawing a magic circle and calling in the elements. Next, rub bits of amber resin in your fingers, and then rub the heated resin on the candle and on the insides of your wrists and ankles. Wipe any remaining amber off your fingers, and light the candle, dedicating it to the animals of earth. Now hold the crystal in your power hand, and say three times:

> *Welcome helpful totems and power animals*
> *I invite you into this magic circle tonight.*

Sit or recline comfortably, holding the crystal in your receiving hand. Take a deep breath in and out, and close your eyes. Imagine being in a favorite place in nature. Now imagine a magical, shimmering light in front of you, and from the center of the shimmering light, an animal appears. Make a mental note of the animal. Study the animal for a few moments. Then ask the animal its name. Repeat the animal's name over and over again to yourself. Now take another deep breath and imagine merging with the strength, wisdom, and power of the animal. As you do this, you feel yourself being energized and empowered. Do this for a few minutes.

Now breathe in and out deeply and completely, three times, feeling more and more refreshed and peacefully aware with each breath you take. Thank the animal for sharing her or his power. Now take another deep breath, and wiggle your toes and fingers, and then slowly open your eyes. Stretch your body and come back to the present time and place.

When you are done, say a simple prayer for the animals of the earth, bid farewell to the elements, and close the circle. Allow the candle safely to burn down.

November 21   ASTROLOGY POWER CANDLE SPELL

You will need a candle in the color that corresponds to your zodiac sign (see below), a ballpoint pen, a bowl of cool water, and sandalwood oil. The traditional zodiac candle colors used in magic are: red/Aries, green/Taurus, yellow/Gemini, silver/Cancer, orange/Leo, blue/Virgo, rose/Libra, red/Scorpio, purple/Sagittarius, brown/Capricorn, all colors/Aquarius, turquoise/Pisces.

Rinse the candle in cool water and dry it. Draw a magic circle and call in the elements. Use the pen to write your complete name on the candle. Dress the candle in sandalwood oil, and then anoint yourself with the oil. Wipe any remaining oil from your hands, light the candle, and say three times:

> *I respectfully ask the helpful powers*
> *Of the zodiac and Oneness*
> *To empower me with universal energy.*

Now gaze into the candlelight. Imagine being filled with the powers of the universe. Have fun with this. Allow your imagination to roam through the multitude of stars, suns, moons, planets, and solar systems. Breathe in the stellar, solar, lunar, and planetary energy, slowly and completely. Do this for at least twenty minutes.

When you are done, bid farewell to the elements and close the circle. Allow the candle to safely burn down.

November 22   VIOLET SLEEP SPELL

You will need a pot of violets that are blooming, a violet or purple candle, and a ballpoint pen.

Begin by writing the words *Restful Sleep* on the candle. Next, light the candle, dedicating it to a goddess associated with flowers such as Io (Greek), Rosemerta (Celtic), or Venus (Roman). Holding the pot of violets in your hands, empower them by saying three times:

> *Divine violet faeries*
> *Please bring me restful sleep*
> *Blessed fae, so be it!*

Put the flowers in a place of honor in your bedroom where they will get plenty of indirect light to encourage restful sleep and sweet dreams. Be sure to water and fertilize them regularly.

November 23   SPRINKLE, SPRINKLE, LITTLE STAR

For this potion, you will need three pinches of dried rosemary, three pinches of dried thyme, two pinches of dried sage, one pinch of dried lavender flowers, and a coffee grinder (used only for grinding herbs, not coffee), or a mortar and pestle.

Before putting each of the herbs into the grinder or mortar, hold each one in your hands and focus your awareness on them, sending your magical goal into them, for example, personal empowerment, success, happiness, prosperity, good health, and so forth. Grind all of the herbs into a fine powder. As you do this, turn your mind to your goal and chant:

> *Great Goddess and God, bless this powder*
> *With your divine and shining power.*

Put the powder in a bowl and run your fingers through it, charging it more and more as you chant:

> *Great Goddess and God, bless this powder*
> *With your divine and shining power.*

When you are done charging the potion, sprinkle it in star shapes here and there, in your home, office, in the garden, in your car, anywhere you want to release its divine and shining power. As you do this, turn your mind toward your magical goal.

November 24   THANKFUL MAGIC

You will need a green spiral notebook and pen.

Every morning for a month, write down at least ten people and things you are thankful for in the notebook. Each time you make an entry, say:

Dear Goddess and God, thank you.

Whenever you are feeling down, just grab your notebook and read your entries. At the end of the month, send a thank-you card to someone special, letting them know that you really are thankful that she or he is in your life. Before sending the card, turn your mind to the recipient, and say:

Thank you for being in my life.

Over the days, months, and years, continue making entries in your thankful notebook. You can use your notebook to help you better understand the good things in your life, and better express affection to those you care about and love. It's a great pick-me-up when life is getting you down.

November 25   SWEEPING SUCCESS SPELL

For this spell, you will need a broom.

Face your altar with the broom in your hands. Take a deep breath, and imagine sweeping away any unwanted energy out of the room. Sweep the area around the altar, moving clockwise, and sweeping from the middle outward. Now take another deep breath, and imagine sweeping in success and reward into the room and to you. Sweep the area again, moving clockwise, but this time sweep from the outside to the center. As you do this, turn your mind toward sweeping extraordinary success to you, and say with each sweep you make:

Today and every day, I am sweeping success and reward into my life.

November 26   NATURAL POWER MAGIC

You will need a bowl of earth, a feather, a white votive candle, and a cup of water.

Draw a magic circle and call in the elements. Next, light the candle, dedicating it to your favorite goddess or god. Face north and hold up the bowl of earth. Sprinkle three pinches of earth in front of you. Merge with the earth element and say:

> *Powers of earth, blessed be*
> *Please share your natural powers with me.*

Now put the bowl down on the altar, and pick up the feather. Face east and merge with the powers of air. Hold the feather up, wave it three times, and say:

> *Powers of air, blessed be*
> *Please share your natural powers with me.*

Next, put the feather on the altar, and carefully pick up the candle. Face south, merge with the fire element, and say:

> *Powers of fire, blessed be*
> *Please share your natural powers with me.*

Then carefully put the candle on the altar, and pick up the cup of water. Face west, sprinkle the water in front of you three times, and say:

> *Powers of water, blessed be*
> *Please share your natural powers with me.*

Now put the cup of water on the altar. Face the altar, hold your arms up, and say:

Helpful powers of earth, air, light, and sea
Please share your natural powers with me
By the Lady and Lord, blessed be!

When you are done, thank deity, bid farewell to the elements, and close the circle. Return the water and soil to the earth. Allow the candle to safely burn down.

November 27   IDEAL JOB CHARM

You will need four quarters, sandalwood incense, and patchouli oil.

Begin by lighting the incense, dedicating it to your favorite goddess and god. Rub the patchouli oil on the four quarters, chanting:

One plus one plus one plus one equals four
North, east, south, and west, please open the door
And help me get the ideal job, dear Lady and Lord.

Hold the quarters in your power hand and imagine the ideal job, the best job possible. Make it something you would really enjoy doing. Now say exactly what kind of job you want aloud, and then take a deep breath in, still your breath, and imagine your ideal job. As you pulse your breath out through your nose, imagine planting the energetic image of your ideal job into the four quarters in your hand. Your breath is the carrier wave for your thoughts. Repeat this process a total of three times. Then put the coins in your pocket or wallet, and make a job inquiry. Continue to make a job inquiry every day until you get your ideal job.

November 28   SINGING SPIRIT MEDITATION

You will need a white candle, beautiful music, and amber oil. Your music selection needs to be one that makes your spirit sing.

Dress the candle with the oil, and then anoint yourself. Put on the music, and take a few deep breaths to center your thoughts. Now light the candle, dedicating it to a goddess or god of music. Then sit or recline comfortably and listen to the music. Take another deep breath in and out, close your eyes, and in your mind's eye, see yourself walking in nature. As you walk, you see the wonder and beauty of life in everything around you. Breathe in the sacredness of nature that shines in everything you see. Breathe in the living energy all around you. In your appreciation for nature, as you breathe in you realize that it's important to live every moment of your life to its fullest. You understand that giving joy to others fills your spirit with happiness and gladness. You realize that it's the people that you love in your life that give your life meaning, that give life natural beauty and joy.

Now take another deep and complete breath in and out, and move back to the present time and place, wiggling your toes and moving your fingers. Slowly open your eyes, and come back to the room, stretching your body. Allow the candle to burn down safely.

November 29   DREAM OIL SPELL

Make this mixture just before you go to sleep.

You will need two teaspoons of olive oil, lavender-scented oil, clary sage oil, vanilla oil, and a small cup.

Put the olive oil in the cup. Add four drops of the lavender oil, and say:

Divine dream oil empower me with blessed dreams.

Add two drops of clary sage oil, and repeat:

Divine dream oil empower me with blessed dreams.

Then add two drops of vanilla oil, and say:

Divine dream oil empower me with blessed dreams.

Next, mix the oil with the fingers of your power hand and chant several times:

Divine dream oil empower me with blessed dreams.

Rub the oil into the front and back of your neck. As you do, chant:

Divine dream oil empower me with blessed dreams.

As you drift to sleep, repeat to yourself:

Blessed dreams, so be it!

November 30   FRIENDSHIP RENEWAL TEA

You will need a ceramic teapot, two cups of boiling water, two chamomile tea bags, two teaspoons of honey, and two slices of lemon.

Put all the ingredients into the teapot. With each ingredient you add, say:

Blessed be, friendship renewal tea.

Now allow the mixture to steep for at least ten minutes before pouring it into cups and drinking it with a friend. Before taking each sip, repeat together:

We are renewing our friendship, so be it!

$\mathcal{D}$ECEMBER

December 1   HOLIDAY POWER DRESSING

Today, dress in green to honor the faeries for the holidays and to bring their blessings and magical gifts to you. One of the most powerful of faery nations, the Daoine Sidhe of Ireland, usually dress in green.

You will need a green outfit and cedarwood oil.

Before getting dressed, anoint yourself with a few drops of the oil on the bottoms of your feet, your ankles, wrists, and the top of your head. As you rub in the oil, say:

> *Helpful winged fae of air*
> *Helpful salamander fae of fire*
> *Helpful flowing fae of water*
> *Helpful nature fae of earth*
> *Please bless and enrich me*
> *Blessed spirits, so be it!*

Now don your green clothes. Once you have finished dressing, look at yourself in the mirror and repeat:

> *Helpful winged fae of air*
> *Helpful salamander fae of fire*

Helpful flowing fae of water
Helpful nature fae of earth
Please bless and enrich me
Blessed spirits, so be it!"

December 2   HAPPINESS POWDER

You will need a coffee grinder or mortar and pestle, three pinches of dried red clover, three pinches of dried marjoram, and three pinches of dried catnip. Grind all of the herbs together into a fine powder. As you do, turn your mind toward experiencing more happiness and chant:

Happy days are here again
I am filled with cheer again!

Sprinkle the happiness powder in every room of your home to bring happy and joyful vibes into your home for the holidays. As you sprinkle the powder, repeat the chant:

Happy days are here again
I am filled with cheer again!

December 3   HOLIDAY CARD SPELL

Use this spell to send out divine holiday blessings to your family and friends.

You will need holiday cards, a pen, pine, cedar, or bayberry oil, and stamps.

Draw a magic circle around the area in which you will be working on your cards. Call in the elements. Fill out your holiday cards and address them. Before you put each card in its envelope, rub a bit of scented oil on its edge. As you do this, turn your mind toward the person you are sending the card to, and say:

May the holidays bring you joy, love, and prosperity, blessed be!

Repeat the process with all the cards. Then hold the holiday cards in your hands, one at a time, and focus on the recipient again for a minute or so; then affix the stamp to the card. As you put the stamp on, say:

May the Goddess and God bless you and your family!

When you are done, thank deity, bid farewell to the elements, and close the circle. Then mail the cards.

December 4   DIVINE WISHES POTPOURRI CHARM

You will need a large wooden or ceramic bowl, pine boughs, cedar boughs, three pinecones, three cinnamon sticks, three small handfuls of whole cloves, vanilla oil, bayberry oil, and red, white, and green velvet ribbon.

Begin by lining the bowl with the pine and cedar boughs. As you do, say:

Wishes divine, wishes bright
Bring to me my heart's delight!

Next, add the pinecones and repeat:

Wishes divine, wishes bright
Bring to me my heart's delight!

Now add the cinnamon sticks and repeat:

> *Wishes divine, wishes bright*
> *Bring to me my heart's delight!*

Gently toss in the whole cloves and say:

> *Wishes divine, wishes bright*
> *Bring to me my heart's delight!*

Then add thirty-three drops of vanilla oil. As you do, repeat:

> *Wishes divine, wishes bright*
> *Bring to me my heart's delight!*

Next, add thirty-three drops of the bayberry oil and say:

> *Wishes divine, wishes bright*
> *Bring to me my heart's delight!*

Now tie three red bows, three white bows, and three green bows with the velvet ribbon. Place the bows decoratively on top of the potpourri in honor of the God, Goddess, and Oneness. Put the potpourri charm in your living room during the holidays. Return the bowl contents, minus the bows, to the earth after that time. Save the bows to use again.

December 5 HOT STUFF POTION

This potion improves your circulation, helps ease shivering, and warms your body on those cold winter days and nights.

You will need one cup of boiling water, a quarter-teaspoon of ground ginger, and one teaspoon of honey.

First rub your hands briskly together several times to charge them up. Then stir the ginger and honey clockwise into the cup of boiling water, and chant:

May the Goddess and God bless this potion with divine
healing warmth and goodness.

Allow the potion to cool enough to sip. Before you take each sip, say:

I am filled with divine healing warmth and goodness.

December 6   DECEMBER DE-STRESS BATH

You will need a hot bath, a white beeswax candle, one tablespoon of honey, one tablespoon of pure vanilla extract, and neroli oil.

Take this bath in the evening, just before you go to sleep. Draw a hot bath. As you add the honey, vanilla, and several drops of neroli oil, chant:

Bath of happiness, bath of glee
Fill me with joy and harmony.

Next, light the candle, dedicating it to a favorite goddess or god, and place it where you can see the candlelight when you bathe. Immerse yourself in the bathwater, and breathe in the sweet scent of the vanilla and neroli oil. Gaze at the candle, and take a deep breath in and out. Now imagine breathing in the bright light of the candle flame, and breathing out all your stress and worries. Repeat three times:

I am filled with joy and harmony.

For a few minutes, just let go of all your responsibilities, chores, things you have to do, things on your holiday list—let it all go for a while, as you breathe in bright light, and breathe out tension and stress. Continue doing this for several minutes, until the bath water cools down. Then get out of the tub, dry off, and anoint yourself with the neroli oil. As you do, repeat:

I am filled with joy and harmony.

Snuff the candle and use it again when you do this spell or another one that is similar. Or, if you prefer, allow the candle safely to burn down. As you drift to sleep, repeat:

My dreams are filled with joy and harmony.

December 7   HOLIDAY MAGIC MIST

You will need a misting bottle, a half-cup of spring or well water, cedarwood essential oil, orange essential oil, and vanilla essential oil.

Add the water to the bottle. Next, add twenty-seven drops of cedarwood oil, nine drops of orange oil, and twenty-seven drops of vanilla oil. Cap the bottle and shake it. As you shake it, chant:

Holiday Magic Mist empower me, blessed be!

Hold the bottle in your hands and repeat three times:

Holiday Magic Mist empower me, blessed be!

Now spray the mist above your head, close your eyes, and breathe in the refreshing vapors. Each time you spray the mist, say:

Holiday Magic Mist empower me, blessed be!

December 8   DREAM PROTECTION SPELL

For this spell, you will need frankincense incense. (Note: Frankincense also comes in other forms besides incense.)

Spin this spell just before you go to sleep. Begin by lighting the frankincense, dedicating it to Oneness. Now with the light still on, stare at either your hands or feet for at least ten minutes. Turn your mind completely toward your hands or feet, so that they leave an indelible impression on your mind. Now say a resounding "NO" as you focus on your hands or feet. Do this nine times. Now make sure the incense has burned down safely, or snuff it out, and then go to sleep. As you drift to sleep, repeat to yourself,

As I dream I will see my hands [or feet]*, and remember.*

Anytime when you are dreaming and you want to end the dream, simply look down at your hands or feet in the dream, and say a resounding "NO," and you will immediately wake up. This spell really works and it also starts you on the magnificent adventure called lucid dreaming. After all, if you can find your hands or feet when you are dreaming, then you can deliberately see or find other things in your dreams as well. This means you can control the direction of your dreams. Practice this spell until finding your hands or feet in your dreams becomes a snap!

December 9   POINSETTIA CHARM

You will need a living poinsettia and a green and red holiday basket to place it in.

Begin by putting the poinsettia in the basket. Make sure the basket has a plastic lining or use a bowl or saucer between the pot and basket to catch any water. Now hold the basket with the poinsettia in your hands. Take a deep breath in and out, and merge with the divine and Oneness. Now say three times:

> *Beautiful poinsettia faeries*
> *Grant me your bright blessings.*

Put the poinsettia in a prominent place until the plant is spent. Each day, place your hands over the plant and say:

> *Beautiful poinsettia faeries*
> *Grant me your bright blessings.*

(Note: You can plant the poinsettia in your yard after the holidays if you live in a temperate climate.)

December 10 CONE OF GRACE SPELL

You will need three beeswax candles, pine oil, a large pinecone, twenty-two small clear quartz crystals, a bowl of cool water, and glue.

Begin by drawing a sacred circle and calling in the elements. Next, light the three candles, dedicating them to the three Graces, who are the three Roman goddesses who represent abundance (Thaleia), splendor and radiance (Aglaia), and joy and happiness (Eurphrosyne). Next, rinse the stones in the cool water for at least a minute. Dry them, and glue the stones onto the pinecone in a decorative fashion. Before gluing each stone onto the pinecone, hold it in your power hand. Take a deep breath in and out, and charge the crystal with divine grace by merging with the divine and saying:

> *May the Graces bless this stone*
> *With abundance, splendor, and joy.*

Position the pinecone in such a way that the candlelight illuminates the crystals. Turn your mind toward the glimmering crystal-covered pinecone, and imagine that each glistening crystal on it is a doorway to abundance, splendor, and radiance, as well as joy and happiness. Now in your mind's eye, imagine stepping through these doorways, one at a time. Each time you step through another crystal doorway, you are more and more empowered with the magic of the Graces. Do this for at least thirty minutes. When you are done, thank deity, release the elements, and close the circle.

December 11   MAGICAL MORNING POTION

You will need a cup of hot cocoa (or a café latte) and a spoon.

Do this spell in the morning after you eat breakfast to fill your day with holiday blessings. Begin by stirring your cocoa or coffee in clockwise circles with the spoon. As you do, chant:

> *Magical morning, magical day*
> *May holiday blessings come my way!*

Now slowly sip the Magical Morning Potion. Before each sip, say:

> *Magical morning, magical day*
> *May holiday blessings come my way!*

December 12   HOLIDAY JOY MEDITATION

You will need a red candle, a green candle, and some instrumental holiday music. Celtic music is ideal.

This meditation is best done at dawn. Begin by turning on the music, and then lighting the candles, dedicating the green candle to the Goddess and the red candle to the God. Now sit back or recline and gaze at the candlelight. Take a few deep breaths in and out to relax and center yourself. Now shift your body around a little to get even more comfortable.

In your mind's eye, imagine standing in front of the most beautiful Yule tree you have ever seen. Breathe in its splendor and beauty. As you do, think about the things you are thankful for in your life, your many blessings. Imagine sharing your love and light with others, sharing good times and cultivating happy memories. Now fill your mind completely with positive and loving thoughts, all the while imagining the beautiful Yule tree in your mind's eye. Be glad for the divine privilege of life. Know that you are divinely blessed, guided, and protected, today and every day.

Now take another deep breath in, and breathe in the harmony and peacefulness of your positive and loving thoughts and images. Take another deep breath, and breathe in the divine beauty of the magnificent Yule tree. Continue doing this for several minutes. Then start to come back to the present time and place by moving your hands and feet and slowly opening your eyes. Stretch your muscles and clap your hands together three times. Allow the candles to burn down safely.

December 13 FLOATING SWEET POTION

You can make this spell with your children.

You will need one cup of Hanson's Root Beer, three scoops of Breyer's Vanilla Ice Cream, a tall glass, and a spoon.

Begin by putting the ice cream in the glass. As you do, chant:

> *By the sun, moon, and stars above*
> *Bless the holidays with divine love.*

Now slowly pour the root beer over the ice cream. As you do, repeat:

> *By the sun, moon, and stars above*
> *Bless the holidays with divine love.*

Next, stir the potion clockwise and chant:

> *By the sun, moon, and stars above*
> *Bless the holidays with divine love.*

As you spoon and drink your way through the Floating Sweet Potion, imagine the holidays being blessed with laughter and love.

December 14 KISSING SPELL

Sacred to the goddess of love, mistletoe symbolically bestows life, which is one of the reasons people kiss beneath it.

You will need a green candle, three sprigs of mistletoe, an eighteen-inch length of green ribbon, an eighteen-inch length of red ribbon, an eighteen-inch length of gold ribbon, and bayberry oil.

Begin by drawing a magic circle and calling in the elements. Dress the candle with the bayberry oil. Wipe any remaining oil from your hands, and light the candle. As you do, say:

> *Kiss, kiss, kiss me*
> *By the Lady, blessed be.*

Now braid the three ribbons together and knot the end of the braid. Tie the ribbon around the sprigs of mistletoe, and knot the ribbon securely. As you knot the ribbon, say:

> *Kiss, kiss, kiss me*
> *By the Lady, blessed be.*

Now anoint the mistletoe and ribbon with several drops of the oil, hold it in your hands, and say,

> *Kiss, kiss, kiss me*
> *By the Lady, blessed be.*

Next, tie the mistletoe over your kitchen door or archway. When you are done, thank deity, bid farewell to the elements, and pull up the circle. Over the holidays, when someone you loves comes into the kitchen, be sure to give them a kiss. When you do, say:

> *Kiss, kiss, kiss me*
> *By the Lady, blessed be.*

(Caution: Be careful that small children or pets do not chew or swallow fallen mistletoe stems, leaves, or berries.)

December 15 ANGEL LIGHT SENDING

You will need an angel tree ornament and a bell.

Begin by holding the ornament gently in your hands and focus your awareness on someone you love: your spouse, your child, a family member, or friend. Turn your mind toward the person, and think positive thoughts about him or her. Now imagine a flock of angels in front of you. The angels can be faerylike with wings, bright white balls of light, or large and powerful beings—imagine them in whatever way suits you and your beliefs. Now take a deep and complete breath in and out, and imagine sending the angels directly to the person you were focusing on. Ask them to go and shower that person with divine love and light. Imagine them doing just that. Do this for a few minutes. When you are done, thank the angels and put the angel ornament on your faery tree. During the holidays, send the angel light to everyone you love and care about. You can also send angel light to those who have passed on.

December 16 SILVER AND GOLD FAERY TREE

You will need some classical or soft instrumental music, a small tree in your yard or in a pot, silver and gold ribbon, and a package of silver-colored bells.

Turn on the music, and then begin decorating the tree. With every ribbon and bell you tie onto the tree, say:

> *Magic faery tree, please share your beauty*
> *May the holidays be enchanting and happy,*
> *Filled with joy and divine blessings.*

When you are done decorating the tree, hold your hands above the top of it, palms toward the tree, and say:

Magic faery tree, please share your beauty
May the holidays be enchanting and happy,
Filled with joy and divine blessings.

December 17 GIFT OF PRAYER MAGIC

You will need a holiday gift or gifts, a white candle, and cedarwood oil.

Begin by anointing the candle with the cedarwood oil. Wipe the oil from your hands, and then light the candle, dedicating it to the divine. Take a few deep breaths to center yourself, and then wrap the holiday gifts. As you do, chant:

Blessed be this gift of light
May it bring joy and delight.

When you are done wrapping the gifts, anoint them with a drop of the cedarwood oil. Hold each package in your hands, or place your hands on them, merge with the divine, and say this simple holiday prayer:

Dear Goddess and God
Please bless, guide, and protect
[Say the gift recipient's name]
I ask this in the Lady and Lord's name
Blessed be!

Now give the gift to the person it is for.

December 18   HOLIDAY SONG CREATIVITY

You will need a CD of uplifting holiday music, a green pillar candle, and a ballpoint pen.

Do this magical work just after sunset. Begin by turning on the music. Next, take a deep and complete breath to center yourself. With the pen, write your full name on the candle. Then, write the words *Divine Creativity* on top of your name. Light the candle, dedicating it to music and song. Now sit or stand comfortably and gaze into the candlelight. Imagine your creative abilities increasing and expanding more and more. Use your breath to get a clear image of your expanded and increased creativity, both personally and professionally. Continue doing this for at least fifteen minutes. When you are done, allow the candle to burn for a couple of hours and then snuff it out.

Every evening, turn on the uplifting music and relight the candle. Gaze at its light for a few minutes, and in your mind's eye, imagine your creative abilities increasing and expanding. Allow it to burn for a couple of hours each evening until it is completely burned down.

December 19   STOCKING CHARM

You will need a large Yule stocking, nine walnuts, three apples, three mandarin oranges, and three bananas. (You can add candy if you like.)

Begin by putting the fruit and nuts (and candy) into the Yule stocking. Then hold the stocking in your hands and merge with the divine. Say three times:

> *Stocking charm of nature's bounty*
> *Share your magic power with me.*

Hang the stocking where you can see it every day. On Yule, eat the goodies inside the stocking. As you do, say:

> *Stocking charm of nature's bounty*
> *Share your magic power with me.*

December 20 THE MAGIC CAP SPELL

You will need a round or conical green cap and patchouli oil.

Anoint yourself with the oil. As you do, smile and say:

> *Putting on the green*
> *Magic abounds around me*
> *Blessed be!*

Then put on the green cap before you go out today. As you put it on, smile brightly and repeat:

> *Putting on the green*
> *Magic abounds around me*
> *Blessed be!*

During the day, make an effort to be aware of the magic in everyone and everything. Notice the light and beauty around you, in the people you interact with, in your pet companions, and in the shopkeeper's face if you purchase a holiday gift or groceries.

December 21   YULE LOG MAGIC

The Yule log brings warmth and light on this Yule Eve, and represents the birth of a new solar year on the Winter Solstice. Burning the Yule Log is one of the oldest magical rituals. You can make and burn this Yule Log with your family and friends.

You will need a beeswax candle, an oak, cedar, or birch log, a fireplace or woodstove, cedar, holly, and pine branches, and green, red, and white ribbon.

Begin by drawing a magic circle around the room and fireplace or woodstove, and then call in the elements. Next, light the candle, dedicating it to the Mother Goddess and Father God. Tie the cedar, holly, and pine branches around the log with the green, red, and white ribbon. As you do this, say:

> *Blessed Yule Log of plenty,*
> *Bring us good luck and good health*
> *And divine prosperity, blessed be!*

Now drip some of the wax from the candle on the log. As you do, repeat:

> *Blessed Yule Log of plenty,*
> *Bring us good luck and good health*
> *And divine prosperity, blessed be!*

Before putting the log into the fire, place your hands over the Yule log and say this prayer:

> *Dear Goddess and God*
> *On this Eve of Yule, I pray you*
> *Please grant us the gifts*
> *Of good health and good luck*

And divine prosperity.
May the divine spirit shine brightly
With each new year and every day
In the Lady and Lord's name, blessed be!

Enjoy the warmth and light of the Yule fire. Before you go to sleep, thank the Goddess and God, bid farewell to the elements, and close the circle.

Tomorrow morning, take some of the ashes from your fireplace or woodstove, and scatter them clockwise around the outside of your home, including your front and back doors, to bring you and your family good luck, good health, and prosperity. Offer the remains of the beeswax candle to the earth.

December 22   YULE SPICE CAKE

You will need two ceramic mixing bowls, a mixer, a wooden spoon, one and a half cups of flour, two teaspoons of baking powder, one teaspoon of baking soda, a half-cup of butter or margarine, a half-cup of confectioners sugar, a half-cup of light brown sugar, two teaspoons of pure vanilla extract, five tablespoons of whipping cream, one large egg (beaten), a half-teaspoon of cinnamon, a quarter-teaspoon of nutmeg, a half-teaspoon of ground ginger, a half-cup of pecan pieces, and a half-cup of golden raisins.

First roast the pecan pieces, and preheat the oven to 325°F. Then blend the flour, baking powder, and baking soda in the ceramic bowl. As you stir the dry mixture in clockwise circles, chant:

Spicy and delicious Yule cake, blessed be
Sweeten the new year with divine opportunities.

Now set the flour mixture aside, and put the softened butter in the second bowl. Add the confectioners sugar, brown sugar, and vanilla to the softened butter and blend it together well with the mixer. As you do, chant:

> *Spicy and delicious Yule cake, blessed be*
> *Sweeten the new year with divine opportunities.*

Add the cinnamon, nutmeg, and ground ginger to the butter mixture, blend together, and repeat:

> *Spicy and delicious Yule cake, blessed be*
> *Sweeten the new year with divine opportunities.*

Now add the butter mixture to the flour mixture, and stir in the whipping cream and the egg. Next, add the raisins and roasted pecans. Stir the mixture clockwise, and chant:

> *Spicy and delicious Yule cake, blessed be*
> *Sweeten the new year with divine opportunities.*

Pour the cake batter into a greased and floured bunt cake pan or a greased and floured 2-pound loaf pan, or you can use decorative holiday cupcake muffin cups. As you pour, chant:

> *Spicy and delicious Yule cake, blessed be*
> *Sweeten the new year with divine opportunities.*

Bake the cake at 325°F for forty to forty-five minutes (bake cupcakes about eighteen to twenty-two minutes). Whip the rest of the whipping cream up with your mixer on high. Add one teaspoon of pure vanilla extract and five teaspoons confectioner's sugar as you blend the whipping cream. Top the

Yule cake or cupcakes with the whipping cream, and enjoy a delicious and magical Yule celebration.

December 23   LIVE LONG AND PROSPER CIDER

You will need a ceramic pot, two cups of apple cider, two teaspoons of honey, one cinnamon stick, one orange slice, and three whole cloves.

Begin by putting the cider, honey, and cinnamon stick into a ceramic pot. As you do, say:

> *By the divine powers of the Goddess and God*
> *May I live long and prosper. So be it!*

Now push the cloves into the orange slice, and put the slice into the mixture. As you do, say:

> *By the divine powers of the Goddess and God*
> *May I live long and prosper. So be it!*

Simmer but do not boil the potion. Pour it into a mug. As you are sipping the brew, imagine yourself living a long and prosperous life. Allow your mind to flow into the future, and see the images there. Then move those images into the potion by taking a deep and complete breath, and say:

> *By the divine powers of the Goddess and God*
> *May I live long and prosper. So be it!*

December 24   AWAKENING MEDITATION

Begin by taking a walk during the day in nature; in the woods, a nearby park, or in your garden or backyard. Pick up a small stone you find along the way. Hold the stone in your receiving hand, and take a deep breath in and out to center yourself. Become totally aware of your surroundings. Use each of your senses to experience all of the things around you—the smells in the air, the feel of the earth under your feet, the sights and colors around you, and the sounds you hear. Even taste the air as you breathe in and out.

Now merge with everything around you in nature, one specific thing at a time. For example, if there is a large cedar tree in front of you, say:

> *I am the cedar tree*
> *The cedar tree is me*
> *We are one.*

As you become each thing, try to be aware of all the qualities that make up that thing (for instance, as the cedar tree, feel your bark, boughs, needles, and roots). Do this for a few minutes before moving onto the next thing in nature that you see around you. Merge with at least nine things in your natural surroundings to begin awakening your natural wisdom. Keep the stone on your altar and use it every time you practice this meditation.

December 25   A DIVINE GIFT

A gift is about the momentary bond that is established between the person giving and the person receiving. In a divine sense, it is the relationship between each of us and the divine giver of life. Christmas is a day of recognizing that divine gift by giving something in return.

You will need a white candle and pine oil.

As you rub some of the pine oil into the candle, envision what gift you would like to give to the divine in return for the gift of your life. It can be anything from a universal feeling of peace on earth to your personal expressions of love. Let it be something you feel from your heart. Wipe the oil from your hands, light the candle, and say:

> *Dear Goddess and God,*
> *Please accept this gift from me,*
> *As heartfelt thanks for your gift of life,*
> *And giving me the chance to be*
> *Thank you Lady and Lord, blessed be.*

Looking into the flame of the candle, imagine giving your gift to the divine. Sense your gift being accepted and the divine saying thank you with a burst of light that energizes every part of you.

December 26   ELVES AND GNOMES MAGIC

The magical elves and gnomes love nature and are often drawn to the part of your garden that is a bit wild and unkempt. This small area will make your magical friends feel welcome.

You will need a shiny wind chime.

Begin taking a few deep breaths in and out to center yourself. Hold the wind chime in your hands and say:

> *Helpful elves and gnomes, I offer you this gift*
> *And respectfully ask you to come into my garden*

Be with me here now, those of you who are my friends
Please bestow your beneficial gifts upon me.

Hang the wind chime in your garden. The magical elves and gnomes also like bits of leftover food, milk, beer, juice, and honey. Offer these to the earth to entice more magical beings to your garden. Also plant bulbs and perennials that will come up and flower next spring, and the faeries will grant you divine favors and gifts year after year.

December 27   GUIDING DREAMS POTION

You will need a ceramic pot, three cups of boiling water, lavender oil, cedar oil, amber oil, and nine crushed bay leaves. *Do not drink this potion.* Instead, you will inhale its vapors. Pour the boiling water into the pot. Add nine drops each of the three oils, add the crushed bay leaves, and say:

Divine potion of dreams,
Let my sleep be sound and sweet
So be it! Blessed dreams!

Cover the pot for five minutes. Take the covered pot into your bedroom and put it on a sturdy surface. Remove the cover and carefully inhale the steam for a few minutes. Be very careful not to burn yourself. Leave the cover off so the aroma fills your bedroom. Now go to bed. As you drift to sleep, repeat to yourself:

Blessed dreams, blessed be.

December 28 BLESSING FOR THE GODDESS

You will need a few pictures, figurines, or objects that represent the Goddess and creation to you. This is a simple prayer of thanks to the Goddess for what she has given you and what she is about to give you. The time after the winter solstice is one of reflection and thanks. Keep this in mind as you say the following blessing:

> *Goddess of Creation,*
> *Mother of All*
> *Thank you for your guiding light*
> *Every day and every night*
> *Whenever I call you*
> *I am surrounded by your divine light*
> *Thank you Mother Goddess, and bless you.*

Survey the pictures, figurines, or objects you have gathered together, and think about how the Goddess has influenced and helped move your life forward.

December 29 PERSONAL POWER RITUAL

Your will need a blue candle, a green candle, and a gold candle. These candles represent your past, present, and future, respectively. Begin by drawing a magic circle and calling in the elements. Invite the divine energies into your circle by saying:

Ancient shining and powerful Ones,
Come, I pray you,
Bring the light of the sun,
Into everything I do
And illuminate my path
So that my efforts are true.

Light the blue candle and envision all the negativity in your life burning up and becoming part of the past. Next, light the green candle and envision the patterns of the present being planted and growing healthy and strong. Now light the gold candle and see the patterns of your present turn into gold, representing the future fruition of your efforts. When you are done, thank deity, bid farewell to the elements, and close the circle. Allow the candles to burn down safely.

December 30   FLOWER POTION MAGIC

Make and drink this magic potion before going out today.

You will need a cup of boiling water, a teaspoon of honey, and a bag of jasmine tea.

Hold the jasmine tea bag in your hands, and say three times:

Devas of jasmine, let your glamour shine within me,
So that I may know your magical powers from now to eternity.

Put the tea bag into the cup of boiling water. Let the tea potion steep for about five minutes, and slowly sip it while filling your imagination with images of divine beauty and love.

December 31 NEW YEAR'S EVE SCRYING

Scrying is an ancient divination technique that often uses a crystal, but in this case you are using a holiday snow globe as the medium for perceiving what the coming year has in store for you.

You will need a snow globe (preferably made of glass and containing lots of snow) and a desire to view the future.

Start by placing the globe on a contrasting colored surface so that the globe and the images in it are easily viewed. Pick the globe up and say,

I empower this globe as a divine oracle.

Next, think about a question regarding your future. Turn your mind completely toward your question. Then shake the globe vigorously several times, churning up the contents, while saying:

Send the wisdom of the fates,
Through the waters of time,
So I may know what waits,
In the next year, what I will find?

Now put the globe back down on the surface, and begin moving your awareness into the water, snow, and images in the globe. Continue to ask the question about your future as you meld and become one with the water, snow, and images in the globe. Perceive yourself in the coming year, doing the things that are now only dreams waiting to be actualized and brought into creation. The end of one year is the beginning of another; such is the nature of time. New Year's Eve is a powerful time for reflection and also a time to renew your dreams, hopes, and aspirations, and send them like beacons of divine light forward into the coming year.

$\mathscr{A}$PPENDIX

Helpful Goddesses and Gods

Adonis (Greek)   God of beauty, love, romance, sexuality, abundance, empowerment, healing, fertility, and plants.

Angus Og (Celtic)   God of love, youth, romance, beauty, dreaming, empowerment, healing, protection, and divination.

Annapurna (Hindu)   Mother Goddess of prosperity, abundance, wealth, fortune, empowerment, and giver of plenty.

Aphrodite (Greek)   Goddess of love, romance, passion, lovers, fertility, feminine beauty, flowers, and empowerment.

Apollo (Greek)   God of the sun, enrichment, magical power, creative arts, inspiration, wisdom, healing, protection, and divination.

Balder (Norse)   God of innocence, beauty, love, devotion, loyalty, and rebirth.

Bast (Egyptian)   Cat goddess of enrichment, love, healing, music, fertility, abundance, cunning, pleasure, dancing, protection, and empowerment.

Belenus (Celtic)   God of the sun, love, enrichment, abundance, magical power, protection, and healing light.

Bran (Celtic)   God of musicians, poets, singers, prophecy, divination, empowerment, protection, and abundance.

Bridget (Celtic)   Goddess of the sun, fertility, hearth, home, healing, inspiration, medicine, protection, abundance, enrichment, and empowerment.

Buddha (Buddhist)   God of wisdom, knowledge, spiritual love, healing, abundance, dreaming, meditation, and empowerment.

Clio (Greek)   The muse of history, writing, archives, ancestry, inspiration, enrichment, and lore.

Concordia (Roman)   Goddess of harmony, calm, relaxation, agreements, tranquility, empowerment, and peace.

Coventina (Celtic)   Goddess of the sacred well, fertility, childbirth, healing, protection, renewal, empowerment, abundance, and new beginnings.

Cupid (Roman)   God of love, romance, and passion.

Dagda (Celtic)   God of wisdom, knowledge, abundance, wealth, love, pleasure, sexuality, celebrations and parties, protection, leadership, and empowerment.

Danu/Anu (Celtic)   Mother Goddess of ancestry, healing, abundance, love, wisdom, creativity, protection, enrichment, empowerment, and prosperity.

Demeter (Greek)   Mother Goddess of abundance, fertility, prosperity, rebirth, renewal, creativity, plants, protection, matrimony, and empowerment.

Edain (Celtic)   Goddess of grace, love, romance, beauty, shapeshifting, transmigration, magical power, enrichment, and empowerment.

Flora (Roman)   Goddess of flowers, plants, the Spring season, love, fertility, sexuality, abundance, growth, creativity, and empowerment.

Fortuna (Roman)   Goddess of fortune, abundance, enrichment, wealth, prosperity, love, good luck, and sexuality.

Frey (Norse)   God of abundance, wealth, enrichment, fertility, joy, peace, happiness, protection, and empowerment.

Freya (Norse)   Goddess of beauty, love, romance, passion, sexuality, fertility, enrichment, empowerment, and protection.

Frigga (Norse)   Mother Goddess of enrichment, abundance, creative arts, protection, healing, magical power, sustenance, and empowerment.

Gaea (Greek)   Mother Goddess of the seasons, abundance, fertility, love, healing, empowerment, and enrichment.

Graces (Roman)   Three goddesses named Thaleia (abundance), Aglaia (splendor and radiance), and Eurphrosyne (joy and happiness).

Gwydion (Celtic)   God of creativity, love, romance, eloquence, shapeshifting, knowledge, abundance, enrichment, prosperity, dreaming, magical power, protection, and healing.

Hathor (Egyptian)   Mother Goddess of creativity, love, romance, beauty, abundance, prosperity, wealth, magical power, healing, protection, and empowerment.

Hera (Greek)   Goddess of love, fertility, sexuality, matrimony, childbirth, motherhood, abundance, and empowerment.

Hermes (Greek)   God of communication, creative arts, business, travel, messages, inspiration, protection, enrichment, and magical power.

Inanna (Sumerian)   Mother Goddess of civilization, love, romance, passion, rebirth, abundance, prosperity, enrichment, creativity, healing, protection, and empowerment.

Isis (Egyptian)   Mother Goddess of love, femininity, beauty, healing, abundance, prosperity, enrichment, and empowerment.

Juno (Roman)   Mother Goddess of love, romance, passion, fertility, matrimony, home, abundance, enrichment, and prosperity.

Jupiter (Roman)   Father God of magical power, enrichment, abundance, travel, communication, protection, and wisdom.

Kernunnos/Cernunnos (Celtic)   God of nature, love, passion, sexuality, virility, prosperity, abundance, enrichment, and empowerment.

Kerridwen/Cerridwyn (Celtic)   Goddess of knowledge, wisdom, inspiration, shapeshifting, enrichment, and empowerment.

Krishna (Hindu)   God of love, enrichment, delight, happiness, and bliss.

Kuan Yin (Asian)   Goddess of love, beauty, healing, protection, compassion, abundance, enrichment, and kindness.

Lakshmi (Hindu)   Goddess of beauty, abundance, wealth, good luck, prosperity, fortune, enrichment, and empowerment.

Lugh (Celtic)   God of the sun, champions, creative arts, creativity, inspiration, protection, love, romance, sexuality, beauty, strength, empowerment, abundance, prosperity, wealth, and enrichment.

Manannan Mac Llyr (Celtic)   God of empowerment, shapeshifting, love, romance, creativity, beauty, travel, prosperity, abundance, and wealth.

Math, Son of Mathonwy (Celtic)   God of the seasons, wisdom, knowledge, shapeshifting, magical power, enchantment, enrichment, prosperity, abundance, intuition, renewal, rebirth, and empowerment.

Maya (Hindu)   Goddess of creativity, enrichment, and empowerment.

Mercury (Roman)   God of creativity, communication, creative arts, inspiration, messages, enrichment, and empowerment.

Merlin (Celtic)   God of nature, magical power, shapeshifting, healing, enrichment, wisdom, love, empowerment, and knowledge.

Nanna (Norse)   Goddess of love, romance, fertility, abundance, enrichment, prosperity, and wealth.

Nodens (Celtic)   God of dreaming, sleep, and empowerment.

Norns (Norse)   Three sisters, Urd, Verdandi, and Sculd, who determine each person's fate.

Odin (Norse)   Father God of protection, ancestry, lore, love, passion, beauty, wisdom, knowledge, healing, abundance, enrichment, magical power, wealth, creativity, and inspiration.

Ogma (Celtic)   God of invention, writing, literature, empowerment, eloquence, knowledge, enrichment, and creativity.

Rhiannon (Celtic)   Mother Goddess of abundance, prosperity, wealth, enrichment, creativity, strength, nobility, and travel.

Robur (Celtic)   Forest god of nature, the seasons, enrichment, strength, renewal, and empowerment.

Rosemerta (Celtic)   Goddess of love, romance, fertility, matrimony, abundance, prosperity, enrichment, beauty, flowers, and empowerment.

Sadv (Celtic)   Goddess of the forests, nature, deer, magical power, creativity, and ancestry.

Saga (Norse)   Goddess of writing, literature, poetry, history, memory, knowledge, and empowerment.

Shakti (Hindu)   Mother Goddess of love, romance, sexuality, fertility, femininity, enrichment, abundance, and magical power.

Shiva (Hindu)   God of creation, love, sexuality, magical power, enrichment, masculinity, and empowerment.

Taliesin (Celtic)   God of creativity, creative arts, inspiration, writing, music, poetry, enrichment, and empowerment.

Thor (Norse)   Thunder god of incredible protection, magical power, enrichment, inspiration, and personal strength.

Triana (Celtic)   Triple goddess; Sun-Ana, Earth-Ana, and Moon-Ana, of wisdom, knowledge, healing, protection, protocol, empowerment, abundance, prosperity, enrichment, love, and beauty.

Tyr (Norse)   God of justice, protection, strength, courage, astronomy, divination, and empowerment.

Zeus (Greek)   God of love, romance, passion, fertility, matrimony, enrichment, abundance, prosperity, wealth, healing, protection, knowledge, wisdom, empowerment, and hospitality.

$\mathcal{B}$IBLIOGRAPHY

Baumgartner, Anne. *A Comprehensive Dictionary of the Gods*. New York: University Books, 1984.

Bluestone, Sarvananda. *How to Read Signs and Omens In Everyday Life*. Rochester, Vt.: Destiny Books, 2002.

Borgman, Peggy Wynne. *Four Seasons of Inner and Outer Beauty*. New York: Broadway Books, 2000.

Bowes, Susan. *Notions and Potions*. New York: Sterling Publishing Co., 1997.

Buckland, Raymond. *Wicca For Life*. New York: Kensington Publishing Co., 2001.

Canfield, Jack et al. *The Power of Focus*. Deerfield Beach, Fla.: Health Communications, Inc., 2000.

Coffey, Lisa Marie. *Getting There With Grace*. Boston, Mass.: Journey Editions, 2001.

Creasy, Rosalind. *The Edible Herb Garden*. Boston: Periplus Editions, 1999.

Crosse, Joanna. *Encyclopedia of Mind, Body, Spirit, and Earth*. Boston, Mass.: Element, 1998.

Cunningham, Scott. *The Complete Book of Incense, Oils, and Brews*. St. Paul, Minn.: Llewellyn Publications, 1989.

———. *Encyclopedia of Magical Herbs*. St. Paul, Minn.: Llewellyn Publications, 1985,

———. *Living Wicca*. St. Paul, Minn.: Llewellyn Publications, 1993.

Currot, Phyllis. *WitchCrafting*. New York: Broadway Books, 2001.

Diamond, Denise. *Living With Flowers*. New York: William Morrow, 1982.

Drew, A. J. *Wicca For Men*. New York: Citadel Press, 1998.

———. *Wicca Spell Crafting For Men*. Franklin Lakes, N.J.: New Page Books, 2001.

Farrar, Janet and Stewart. *The Witches' Way*. London: Robert Hale, 1984.

———. *A Witches' Bible Compleat*. New York: Magical Childe, 1984.

Gannon, Linda. *Creating Fairy Garden Fragrances*. Pownal, Vt.: Storey Books, 1998.

Gimbutas, Marija. *The Language of the Goddess*. San Francisco: Harper & Row, 1989.

Gray, Deborah. *The Good Witch's Guide to Wicked Ways*. Boston, Mass.: Journey Editions, 2001.

Griffin, Sally. *Wicca Wisdom Keepers*. Boston, Mass.: Red Wheel/Weiser, 2002.

Grimal, Pierre (Editor). *Larousse World Mythology*. London: Paul Hamlyn, 1965.

Grimassi, Raven. *The Wiccan Mysteries*. St. Paul, Minn.: Llewellyn Publications, 1997.

Hay, Louise. *You Can Heal Your Life*. Carson, Calif.: Hay House, 1984.

Kemp, Gillian. *The Good Spell Book*. Boston, Mass.: Little, Brown, and Co., 1998.

Kluger, Marilyn. *The Wild Flavor*. Los Angeles: Jeremy P. Tarcher Inc., 1984.

Knight, Sirona. *A Witch Like Me*. Franklin Lakes, N.J.: New Page Books, 2001.

———. *Celtic Traditions*. New York: Citadel Press, 2000.

———. *Dream Magic: Night Spells and Rituals for Love, Prosperity, and Personal Power*. San Francisco: HarperSanFrancisco, 2000.

———. *Exploring Celtic Druidism*. Franklin Lakes, N.J.: New Page Books, 2001.

———. *Faery Magick*. Franklin Lakes, N.J.: New Page Books, 2002.

———. *Greenfire: Making Love with the Goddess*. St. Paul, Minn.: Llewellyn Publications, 1995.

———. *Goddess Bless!* Boston, Mass.: Red Wheel, 2002.

———. *The Little Giant Encyclopedia of Runes*. New York: Sterling Publishing Co., 2000.

———. *Love, Sex, and Magick*. New York: Citadel Press, 1999.

———. *Moonflower: Erotic Dreaming with the Goddess*. St. Paul, Minn.: Llewellyn Publications, 1996.

———. *The Pocket Guide to Celtic Spirituality*. Freedom, Calif.: Crossing Press, 1998.

———. *The Pocket Guide to Crystals and Gemstones*. Freedom, Calif.: Crossing Press, 1998.

———. et al. *The Shapeshifter Tarot*. St. Paul, Minn.: Llewellyn Publications, 1998.

———. *The Wiccan Spell Kit*. New York: Citadel Press, 2001.

——— and Patricia Telesco. *The Wiccan Web*. New York: Citadel Press, 2001.

———. *The Witch and Wizard Training Guide*. New York: Citadel Press, 2001.

Leach, Maria, Ed. *Standard Dictionary of Folklore, Mythology, and Legend*. New York: Funk & Wagnalls, 1950.

Long, Jim. *Making Herbal Dream Pillows*. Pownal, Vt.: Storey Books, 1998.

Melville, Francis. *Love Potions and Charms*. Hauppauge, N.Y.: Barron's, 2001.

Metcalfe, Joannah. *Pure Scents for Romance*. New York: Sterling Publishing, Inc., 1999.

Monaghan, Patricia. *The Book of Goddesses and Heroines*. St Paul, Minn.: Llewellyn Publications, 1990.

Morrison, Dorothy. *Everyday Magic*. St Paul, Minn.: Llewellyn Publications, 1998.

———. *Yule*. St. Paul, Minn.: Llewellyn Publications, 2000.

Nahmad, Claire. *Cat Spells*. London: Parkgate Books, 1998.

Oman, Maggie (Editor). *Prayers For Healing*. Berkeley, Calif.: Conari Press, 1997.

Rector-Page, Linda. *Healthy Healing*. Sonoma, Calif.: Healthy Healing Publications, 1992.

Sabrina, Lady. *The Witch's Master Grimoire*. Franklin Lakes, N.J.: New Page Books, 2001.

———. *Exploring Wicca*. Franklin Lakes, N.J.: New Page Books, 2000.

Schiller, David and Carol. *Aromatherapy Basics*. New York: Sterling Publishing Co., 1998.

Skafte, Dianne. *Listening To The Oracle*. San Francisco: HarperSanFrancisco, 1997.

Starhawk. *The Spiral Dance*. San Francisco: HarperSanFrancisco, 1979.

Stepanich, Kisma. *Faery Wicca, Book One*. St. Paul, Minn.: Llewellyn Publications, 1994.

———. *Faery Wicca, Book Two*. St. Paul, Minn.: Llewellyn Publications, 1995.

Stewart, R. J. *Celtic Gods, Celtic Goddesses*. New York: Sterling Publishing Co., 1990.

Telesco, Patricia. *Exploring Candle Magick*. Franklin Lakes, NJ: New Page Books, 2000.

———. *FutureTelling*. Freedom, Calif.: Crossing Press, 1998.

———. *Money Magick*. Franklin Lakes, N.J.: New Page Books, 2001.

———. *Spinning Spells, Weaving Wonders*. Freedom, Calif.: Crossing Press, 1996.

Thorsson, Edred. *Futhark: A Handbook of Rune Magic*. York Beach, Me.: Samuel Weiser, 1984.

Tuitean, Paul, and Estelle Daniels. *Pocket Guide to Wicca*. Freedom, Calif.: Crossing Press, 1998.

Valiente, Doreen. *Witchcraft for Tomorrow*. New York: St. Martin's, 1978.

Weinstein, Marion. *Earth Magic*. New York: Earth Magic Productions, 1998.

Williams, David, and Kate West. *Born In Albion*. Cheshire, England: Pagan Media, Ltd., 1996.

Worwood, Valerie. *The Complete Book of Essential Oils and Aromatherapy*. New York: New World Library, 1995.